344.4101

A Guide to the Employmen

Enfield Libraries

ENFIELD CENTRAL LIBRARY
Cecil Road, Enfield, Middx
EN2 6TW
(0181-379 8391)

**FOR REFERENCE ONLY
NOT TO BE REMOVED
FROM THE LIBRARY**

Please remember that this item will attract overdue charges if not returned by the latest date stamped above. You may renew it in person, by telephone or by post quoting the barcode number and your library card number.

ENFIELD
Leisure Services
working for people

30126 01489735 6

Previous titles in the series

A Guide to the Criminal Justice and Public Order Act 1994
A Guide to the Finance Act 1994
A Guide to the Police and Magistrates' Courts Act 1994
A Guide to the Sunday Trading Act 1994
A Guide to the Trade Marks Act 1994
A Guide to the Finance Act 1995
A Guide to the Pensions Act 1995
A Guide to the Criminal Procedure and Investigations Act 1996
A Guide to the Family Law Act 1996
A Guide to the Finance Act 1996
A Guide to the Housing Act 1996
A Guide to the Crime (Sentences) Act 1997
A Guide to the Finance Act 1997
A Guide to the Finance (No 2) Act 1997
A Guide to the Police Act 1997
A Guide to the Crime and Disorder Act 1998
A Guide to the Finance Act 1998
A Guide to the Data Protection Act 1998
A Guide to the Competition Act 1998
A Guide to the Finance Act 1999

A Guide to the Employment Relations Act 1999

Nicholas Randall, LLB, of the Middle Temple, Barrister
Ian Smith, MA, LLB, of Gray's Inn, Barrister
Clifford Chance Professor of Employment Law, University of East Anglia

both of Devereux Chambers, Devereux Court, London

Butterworths
London, Edinburgh, Dublin
1999

United Kingdom	Butterworths a Division of Reed Elsevier (UK) Ltd, Halsbury House, 35 Chancery Lane, LONDON WC2A 1EL and 4 Hill Street, EDINBURGH EH2 3JZ
Australia	Butterworths, a Division of Reed International Books Australia Pty Ltd, CHATSWOOD, New South Wales
Canada	Butterworths Canada Ltd, MARKHAM, Ontario
Hong Kong	Butterworths Asia (Hong Kong), HONG KONG
India	Butterworths India, NEW DELHI
Ireland	Butterworth (Ireland) Ltd, DUBLIN
Malaysia	Malayan Law Journal Sdn Bhd, KUALA LUMPUR
New Zealand	Butterworths of New Zealand Ltd, WELLINGTON
Singapore	Butterworths Asia, SINGAPORE
South Africa	Butterworths Publishers (Pty) Ltd, DURBAN
USA	Lexis Law Publishing, CHARLOTTESVILLE, Virginia

© Reed Elsevier (UK) Ltd 1999

All rights reserved. No part of this publication may be reproduced in any material form (including photocopying or storing it in any medium by electronic means and whether or not transiently or incidentally to some other use of this publication) without the written permission of the copyright owner except in accordance with the provisions of the Copyright, Designs and Patents Act 1988 or under the terms of a licence issued by the Copyright Licensing Agency Ltd, 90 Tottenham Court Road, London, England W1P 0LP. Applications for the copyright owner's written permission to reproduce any part of this publication should be addressed to the publisher.

Warning: The doing of an unauthorised act in relation to a copyright work may result in both a civil claim for damages and criminal prosecution.

Any Crown copyright material is reproduced with the permission of the Controller of Her Majesty's Stationery Office.

Nicholas Randall and Ian Smith have asserted their rights under the Copyright, Designs and Patents Act 1988 to be identified as the authors of this work.

A CIP Catalogue record for this book is available from the British Library.

ISBN 0 406 92942 4

Printed and bound in Great Britain by Hobbs the Printers Ltd

Visit us at our website: http//www.butterworths.co.uk

Preface

It has not been an easy task to write this book. Our legislators have shown scant regard for the interests of authors of legal textbooks. The original Bill as presented in the House of Commons was substantially amended throughout its progress through Parliament with more than 100 amendments being introduced in the House of Lords alone. Although many of these amendments were technical in nature there were also several changes to the substantive elements of the original Bill. The passage of the Bill, therefore, has not been easy to follow.

The difficulties associated with regular and late amendments have also been accentuated by the decision of the government to deal with certain substantial matters by the creation of wide powers to introduce regulations at a later date. This has meant that in some areas it has proved impossible to provide anything other than guidance as to what may be included in the regulations.

To enable readers to update their knowledge of the subject, the secondary legislation will be included on a web site at the following address—

http://www.butterworths.co.uk/content/products/publications

The necessary password is—

harvey

This site will contain the text of the secondary legislation made under the 1999 Act as and when it is enacted.

In view of the fact that the Employment Relations Act 1999 represents the first major industrial relations legislation of the new Labour government it was probably predictable that much of the debate in the House of Commons was crudely ideological in character and our aim as authors has been to avoid reference to this material as far as possible. We have instead attempted to concentrate upon the elements which have given some thoughtful insights into the legislation. Fortunately the quality of debate in the House of Lords was of a high standard and the draft legislation was probed with considerable skill from both sides of the ideological fence.

We hope that this guide will provide assistance to all who need to gain a speedy grasp of the essential elements of the Act. We owe a considerable debt, as ever, to the diligent staff at Butterworths who have provided us with their support and encouragement. Any errors and omissions (now actionable in the industrial relations field, at least: see Ch 4!) which remain are, of course, our responsibility.

Nicholas Randall
Professor Ian Smith

Devereux Chambers
Devereux Court
London WC2R 3JJ

September 1999

Contents

	Page
Preface	v
Table of Statutes	ix
Table of EC Legislation	xiii
Table of Cases	xv
1 Introduction	1
2 Recognition	4
3 Industrial action	11
4 Victimisation	15
5 Unfair dismissal	20
6 Maternity rights, parental leave and time off for dependants	27
7 Disciplinary matters	39
8 Part-time worker protection and extension of employment status	43
9 Reforms to statutory bodies	52
10 Miscellaneous provisions	59
Appendix 1	
Employment Relations Act 1999 (with annotations)	61
Index	173

Table of Statutes

	PARA
Data Protection Act 1998	4.15
Disability Discrimination Act 1995	
s 68	8.16
Employment Act 1980	2.2
Employment Act 1988	9.7
Employment Act 1990	5.17; 9.8
Employment Agencies Act 1973	10.2
Employment Protection Act 1975	2.7; 5.17; 6.1; 6.3; 9.1
s 1(2)	9.4
11–16	2.2
Employment Relations Act 1999	
s 3	4.13; 5.27
5	2.31
6	2.30; 5.27
10	
(1)(b)	7.6
(2)	7.8
(3)	7.7
(4), (5)	7.10
(6), (7)	7.11
11	7.6
(2)(b)	7.13
12	5.27; 7.6; 7.14
13 (4), (5)	7.6
14	7.6
15	7.6; 7.15; 10.4
17	5.27
(1)	4.10
(4)	4.10
18	5.12
19(1)–(5)	8.10
20(1)	8.11
(3), (4)	8.11
21	8.11
22	8.18; 10.5
23 (1), (2)	8.17
(4), (5)	8.17
24	9.2
25	9.3
26	9.5
27	9.6
28	9.7; 9.8
30	9.5; 10.8

	PARA
Employment Relations Act 1999—*contd*	
s 32	5.15
(3)	5.15
33 (1), (2)	5.8
34	5.9
(4)	5.6
35	5.9
37	5.7
38	10.7
39	10.5
40	10.6
42	8.17
Sch 1	1.6; 2.1; 2.11; 5.27
Sch 2	
para 2(2)	4.4
Sch 3	
para 5	3.10
6 (2)	3.9
(3)	3.8
8	3.11
9	3.4
10	3.7
Sch 4	
Pt I	6.4; 6.17
Pt II	6.23
Pt III	6.25
para 42	6.2
Sch 5	5.22; 5.26
para 3	5.23; 5.25
Sch 6	9.9
paras 2–5	9.11
6	9.9
7	9.11
8	9.12
9–11	9.11
12	9.12
13	9.9
15–18	9.11
19	9.13
22	9.14
23	9.14
Sch 7	10.2
Sch 8	10.4
Employment Rights Act 1996	8.17
s 8	6.23
Pt II (ss 13–14)	8.15
s 43A–L	8.15
47C	6.25
48	6.25

Table of statutes

	PARA		PARA
Employment Rights Act 1996—*contd*		School Standards and Framework Act 1998	
s 57A	6.24; 6.25	Sch 16, 17	10.6
(1)	6.23	Sex Discrimination Act 1975	
(2)–(6)	6.23	s 82	8.15; 8.16
57B (2)	6.23	Social Security Act 1989	
Pt VIII Ch I (ss 71–75)	6.4	Sch 5 para 5	6.4
s 71(1), (2)	6.4	Tax Credits Act 1999	5.12
(4)–(7)	6.4	Trade Union and Labour	
72(1)–(5)	6.5	Relations Act 1974	5.4
73(1)–(7)	6.6	Trade Union and Labour Relations	
74(7)	6.7	(Consolidation)	
75	6.7	Act 1992	3.1; 3.9; 9.11
Pt VIII Ch II (ss 76–80)	6.17	Ch VIIA	9.13
s 77	6.17	s 15	9.8
78, 79	6.18	16	9.8
80(2)–(4)	6.18	31	9.9
96	6.25	45D	9.12
99	6.25	56A	9.12
100	5.7	62	9.8
103A	5.7	70B	2.31
105(3)	5.7	72A	9.10
(6A)	5.7	108A–C	9.13
111(2)	6.18	108A(1)–(2)	9.13
124(1)	5.6	(3)	9.13
196	5.15	(5)–(7)	9.13
197	5.12	(8)–(10)	9.13
(1), (3)	5.10	(12)	9.13
Pt XIV Ch II (ss 220–223)	7.13	(14)–(15)	9.13
s 230(1), (2)	8.14	108B(2)–(8)	9.13
(3)	8.15	108C	9.13
236	6.2	109–114	9.7
Equal Pay Act 1970	8.2	109(2)	9.8
European Communities		146	4.2; 4.4; 4.11
Act 1972	8.10	(3)	4.3
s 2(2)	8.17	148(3)	4.5; 4.6; 4.7, 4.9
Health and Safety at		(3)–(5)	4.2
Work etc Act 1974	6.5	181–185	9.1
Industrial Relations		209	9.4
Act 1971	2.2; 5.4; 5.6; 5.17; 8.16	210–212	9.4
		226	3.4
National Minimum		226A	3.2; 3.5
Wage Act 1998	1.2; 1.4; 5.12; 8.1; 8.15	227(1)	3.11
s 44A	8.18	228	3.10
Public Interest Disclosure Act 1998		(4)	3.10
s 1	8.15	228A	3.10
Race Relations Act 1976		229	3.8
s 78	8.15		

	PARA
Trade Union and Labour Relations (Consolidation) Act 1992—*contd*	
s 230(2)	3.11
(2A)	3.11
232A	3.11
232B	3.4; 3.11
234	3.7
234	3.2; 3.5
235A	9.7
235B	9.7
235C	9.7
237	5.17
238	5.17
238A	5.23
(3)–(5)	5.23
(6)	5.24
256	9.14
256A–B	9.14
260(1)–(3A)	9.2
263(1), (4)	9.3
263A (1)–(2)	9.3
(5)–(6)	9.3
266–271	9.7
296	8.15
Sch A1	2.1; 2.11
Pt I	2.13; 2.14; 2.23
para 1	2.15
3 (3), (4)	2.15
4	2.16; 2.23
5	2.16; 2.23
6	2.16; 2.23
7	2.23
(2)	2.16
8, 9	2.23
11–13	2.16
14(4), (5)	2.17
19(3)(a)	2.18
(4)	2.18
22(1)	2.19

	PARA
Trade Union and Labour Relations (Consolidation) Act 1992—*contd*	
Sch A1—*contd*	
Pt I—*contd*	
para 22, (2)	2.19; 2.28
(3), (4)	2.19
para 23	2.19
29(3)	2.21
30(3)	2.21
31(3)–(5)	2.21
32	2.22
33–42	2.22
43–50	2.22
51	2.22
52	2.23
55(1), (3), (5)	2.24
(6)	2.23
58	2.25
59–62	2.25
63(1)–(3)	2.25
(5)	2.25
Pt III	2.26
Pt IV	2.27
Pt V	2.28
Pt VI	2.29
Pt VII	2.29
Pt VIII	2.30
para 161	2.30
Trade Union Reform and Employment Rights Act 1993	4.5
s 13	4.2
22	9.7
43(1)	9.4
Sch 8	9.7
Wages Act 1986	8.15

Table of EC Legislation

	PARA		PARA
Treaty of Amsterdam 1997	1.2	EC Directive 97/81 (Part-time Work Directive	8.1; 8.2; 8.3; 8.11
EC Directive 76/207 (Equal Treatment Directive	6.14	Annex	
EC Directive 77/187 (Acquired Rights Directive)	1.4; 10.7	Clause 1	8.3
		2(2)	8.4
EC Directive 92/85 (Pregnant Workers Directive)	6.1; 6.5; 6.14	3	8.4
		(2)	8.4
EC Directive 93/104 (Working Time Directive)	1.1	4	8.4
		(4)	8.4
EC Directive 94/45 (European Work Council Directive)	9.1	5(1), (2)	8.5
		3(a)	8.6
EC Directive 96/34 (Parental Leave Directive)	6.1; 6.16; 6.19; 6.21; 6.22; 6.24	(b)	8.7
		(c)	8.8
		(d)–(e)	8.9

xiii

Table of Cases

A

Associated British Ports v Palmer [1994] ICR 97, [1993] IRLR 336, [1993] 26 LS Gaz R 37, 137 Sol Jo LB 134, CA; revsd [1995] 2 AC 454, [1995] 2 All ER 100, [1995] 2 WLR 354, [1995] ICR 406, [1995] IRLR 258, [1995] 17 LS Gaz R 48, [1995] NLJR 417, HL.................................. 4.1, 4.2

Associated Newspapers Ltd v Wilson [1994] ICR 97, sub nom Wilson v Associated Newspapers Ltd [1993] IRLR 336, CA; revsd sub nom Associated Newspapers Ltd v Wilson [1995] 2 AC 454, [1995] 2 All ER 100, [1995] 2 WLR 354, [1995] ICR 406, [1995] IRLR 258, [1995] 17 LS Gaz R 48, [1995] NLJR 417, HL 4.1, 4.2

B

Blackpool and Fylde College v National Association of Teachers in Further and Higher Education [1994] ICR 648, [1994] IRLR 227, CA 3.1, 3.5

Booth v United States of America [1999] IRLR 16, 611 IRLB 9, EAT 8.14

Boyle v Equal Opportunities Commission: C-411/96 [1998] All ER (EC) 879, [1998] 3 CMLR 1133, [1999] ICR 360, [1998] IRLR 717, [1999] 1 FCR 581, [1999] 1 FLR 119, 608 IRLB 5, ECJ............................ 6.14

British Telecommunications plc v Ticehurst [1992] ICR 383, [1992] 15 LS Gaz R 32, 136 Sol Jo LB 96, sub nom Ticehurst and Thompson v British Telecommunications plc [1992] IRLR 219, CA........................ 5.16

Brown v Rentokil Ltd: C-394/96 [1998] ECR I-4185, [1998] All ER (EC) 791, [1998] 2 CMLR 1049, [1998] ICR 790, [1998] IRLR 445, [1999] 1 FCR 49, [1998] 2 FLR 649, [1998] Fam Law 597, 48 BMLR 126, [1998] 34 LS Gaz R 34, ECJ 6.12

C

Carmichael v National Power plc [1998] ICR 1167, [1998] IRLR 301, [1998] 19 LS Gaz R 23, 142 Sol Jo LB 140, 593 IRLB 12, CA 8.14

Carver (née Mascarenhas) v Saudi Arabian Airlines [1999] 3 All ER 61, [1999] IRLR 370, CA 1.4, 5.13

Clark v Oxfordshire Health Authority [1998] IRLR 125, CA 8.14

Connex South Eastern Ltd v National Union of Rail Maritime and Transport Workers [1999] IRLR 249, CA....................................... 3.9

Crees v Royal London Mutual Insurance Society Ltd [1998] ICR 848, [1998] IRLR 245, [1998] 15 LS Gaz R 33, 142 Sol Jo LB 94, 590 IRLB 11, CA... 6.12

E

Express and Echo Publications Ltd v Tanton [1999] ICR 693, [1999] IRLR 367, [1999] 14 LS Gaz R 31, CA 8.15

G

Goold (W A) (Pearmak) Ltd v McConnell [1995] IRLR 516, EA 7.2

Greater Glasgow Health Board v Carey [1987] IRLR 484, EAT............. 8.6

Gunning v Mirror Group Newspapers Ltd [1986] 1 All ER 385, sub nom Mirror Group Newspapers Ltd v Gunning [1986] 1 WLR 546, [1986] ICR 145, [1986] IRLR 27, 130 Sol Jo 242, CA 8.16

Table of Cases

H

Halfpenny v IGE Medical Systems Ltd [1999] ICR 834, [1999] IRLR 177, [1999] 1 FLR 944, 143 Sol Jo LB 38, CA.	6.12
Home Office v Holmes [1984] 3 All ER 549, [1985] 1 WLR 71, [1984] ICR 678, [1984] IRLR 299, 128 Sol Jo 645, EAT	8.6

I

Intercity West Coast Ltd v National Union of Rail, Maritime and Transport Workers [1996] IRLR 583, CA.	3.10

K

Kingston upon Hull City Council v Mountain [1999] ICR 715, EAT	5.10

L

Lavery v Plessey Telecommunications Ltd [1982] ICR 373, [1983] IRLR 180, EAT; affd [1983] ICR 534, [1983] IRLR 202, CA.	6.13
Lock v Cardiff Rly Co [1998] IRLR 358, 599 IRLB 6, EAT	7.1

M

Malik v BCCI SA (in liquidation) [1998] AC 20, [1997] 3 All ER 1, [1997] 3 WLR 95, [1997] ICR 606, [1997] IRLR 462, [1997] 94 LS Gaz R 33, [1997] NLJR 917, HL.	6.14
Mirror Group Newspapers Ltd v Gunning. See Gunning v Mirror Group Newspapers Ltd	
Morgan v Fry [1968] 2 QB 710, [1968] 3 All ER 452, [1968] 3 WLR 506, [1968] 2 Lloyd's Rep 82, 112 Sol Jo 671, CA.	5.16

S

Sheehan v Post Office Counters [1999] ICR 734, EAT	8.16

T

Ticehurst and Thompson v British Telecommunictions plc. See British Telecommunications plc v Ticehurst

W

Woolf (Lewis) Griptight Ltd v Corfield [1997] IRLR 432, EAT.	6.13

1 Introduction

BACKGROUND

1.1 When introducing the Employment Relations Bill in the House of Commons, the Secretary of State for Trade and Industry, Stephen Byers, stated that the intention was to produce 'an industrial relations settlement' which would last for 'the remainder of this Parliament'.[1] The Bill, based on the main proposals contained in the White Paper 'Fairness at Work' published in May 1998,[2] reflected some of the commitments made by the Labour Party in its manifesto for the 1997 general election. The manifesto commitments also included the introduction of the national minimum wage, the implementation of the Working Time Directive[3] and the intention to make the UK a signatory to the European Social Chapter.

---
[1] HC 2R, 9 February 1999, col 134.
[2] Cm 3968.
[3] Council Directive 93/104/EC.

Context of Act

1.2 It is important when considering the 'industrial relations settlement' referred to by the Minister to consider the 1999 Act in context with the provisions of the National Minimum Wage Act 1998 and the Working Time Regulations 1998, SI 1998/1833. The government's commitment to making the UK a signatory to the European Social Chapter was fulfilled at the Treaty of Amsterdam.[1]

---
[1] Operative from 1 May 1999.

Objectives

1.3 The Secretary of State identified three 'fundamental strands', first the promotion of family friendly policies, secondly the promotion of a new culture of partnership in the workplace and thirdly the desire to ensure equal and fair treatment for all at work.[1] These initial objectives can be seen as a response to a broad range of different pressures and influences. They demonstrate a desire not only to promote a change in the balance of power in the workplace and to comply with European Union Treaty obligations but also to tidy up some of the perceived weaknesses in the statutory framework without challenging the underlying basis of that framework.

---
[1] HC 2R, 9 February 1999, col 134.

PASSAGE OF THE BILL

1.4 The Bill was substantially amended throughout the parliamentary process—indeed more than 100 amendments were incorporated in the House of

1.4 Introduction

Lords alone. These amendments mainly took the form of technical amendments, in particular, to the detailed provisions relating to trade union recognition. In addition, new clauses were introduced during the later stages of the Bill dealing with a wide variety of matters including a fundamental rethink on the relationships of staff employed in the national security sector, the jurisdiction of employment tribunals following the decision of the Court of Appeal in *Carver v Saudi Arabian Airlines*,[1] enforcement matters overlooked in the National Minimum Wage Act 1998, and the introduction of specific regulatory powers to amend the Transfer of Undertakings (Protection of Employment) Regulations 1981, SI 1981/1794, as a result of changes to the Acquired Rights Directive (77/187/EEC). The Act as passed bears little resemblance in places to the Bill as it was first introduced into the House of Commons.

[1] [1999] IRLR 370.

1.5 It is also worth noting the extent to which the 1999 Act confers the power onto the Secretary of State to make subordinate legislation, a matter which raised some concerns on the Opposition benches. The government responded to these concerns by stating its intention to consult widely on the content of such regulations and to issue helpful guidance where appropriate.[1] At the time of writing it is difficult to ascertain the precise scope of the 1999 Act and this will have to await the specific regulations made under the Act. However, this book seeks to identify any expressed intentions as to the content of future regulations. As and when the regulations are issued they will be accessible on an associated website.[2]

[1] HC SC E, 16 February 1999, col 32.
[2] See http://www.butterworths.co.uk/content/products/publications, using the password given in the preface.

MAIN ELEMENTS OF THE 1999 ACT

1.6 There is little doubt that the 'headline' element of the 1999 Act is the introduction of the statutory right to recognition. The importance of this issue is reflected in the length of the final amended version of the 1999 Act, Sch 1, which deals with recognition. This covers some 59 pages, accounting for almost one half of the Act. However, this should not obscure the fact that the 1999 Act also includes radical reforms in a number of other important areas. These include the extension of rights to claim unfair dismissal for workers who are dismissed when on strike: this represents a significant departure from the previous practice of both former Labour and Conservative governments. Substantial regulatory powers have also been created to deal with the extension of employment rights to groups of 'atypical' and 'marginal' workers, continuing themes found in the legislation on working time and the national minimum wage.

1.7 As a result of the substantial amendments made throughout the parliamentary progress the 1999 Act, in its final form, includes far more than the three themes originally identified by the Minister. Although there is some degree of overlap, there are probably ten readily identifiable elements, summarised as follows—

(1) trade union recognition;
(2) support for collective bargaining in the form of protection for individual employees who wish to engage in the activities of a trade union or be covered by collectively agreed terms and other associated matters;
(3) protection for employees when taking lawful industrial action and the simplification of some of the previous provisions on industrial disputes;
(4) family friendly measures in the form of rights to maternity and parental leave and time off for domestic incidents;
(5) the extension of individual rights as regards disciplinary and grievance proceedings;
(6) further protections for part-time workers;
(7) the simplification of the rules on compensation for unfair dismissal and the raising of the cap on the levels of that compensation (which have to be seen in the context of the reduction in the qualifying period for such rights);
(8) major reforms to the structure of the regulatory bodies in the industrial relations field;
(9) the possible extension of employment rights to 'atypical' and 'marginal' workers; and
(10) miscellaneous elements including the treatment of employees in the national security sector and the regulation of employment agencies.

1.8 The government resisted several concerted attempts to include provisions in the Act dealing with discrimination on the basis of age and sexual orientation. These matters were canvassed in both the House of Commons and the House of Lords without success. The government, although expressing sympathy for the proposed amendments, indicated that it does not wish to proceed in such areas through primary legislation.[1]

[1] HC SC E, 23 March 1999, cols 568–577; HL Committee, 16 June 1999, col 340 and HL Official Report, 9 July 1999, col 1108.

COMMENCEMENT

1.9 The 1999 Act is to be brought into force by commencement orders. It is intended that this should take account of the need for further consultation and allow time for business, employees and trade unions to adapt to the new changes. Although the government has not committed itself to specific dates for implementation it should be noted that some of the elements of the Act regarding the 'family friendly' proposals are subject to European law time limits for implementation. These are December 1999 (maternity rights, parental leave) and April 2000 (domestic incidents and part-time work).[1] The government's intention of reducing the qualifying period for unfair dismissal rights has already been implemented in the case of dismissals occurring on or after 1 June 1999.[2]

[1] HC SC E, 23 March 1999, col 541.
[2] The Unfair Dismissal and Statement of Reasons for Dismissal (Variation of Qualifying Period) Order 1999, SI 1999/1436.

2 Recognition

GENERAL

2.1   Trade union recognition is a fundamental aspect of the 1999 Act and one that proved controversial during the passage of the Bill, prompting many heated debates. The provisions relating to recognition are contained in the 1999 Act, Sch 1 which inserts a new Sch A1 into the Trade Union and Labour Relations (Consolidation) Act 1992.

HISTORICAL CONTEXT

2.2   A statutory right to recognition had previously existed under both the Industrial Relations Act 1971 and the Employment Protection Act 1975. However, both schemes met with limited success for entirely different reasons. The provisions of the 1971 Act depended upon an application for recognition being made by a 'registered' trade union, and were therefore frustrated by the mass boycott of 'registration' conducted by the trade union movement. On the other hand the 1975 Act, ss 11–16, provided broad discretions to both ACAS and the Central Arbitration Committee (CAC) to consider recognition disputes. The weight of resultant legal disputes and poor legislative guidance on the role and responsibility of the relevant bodies resulted in general acrimony and the ultimate collapse of this system. Accordingly the repeal of those provisions of the 1975 Act by the Employment Act 1980 was met with widespread relief from both sides of industry.

2.3   Following this repeal and prior to the White Paper 'Fairness at Work'[1] the legal framework simply provided that recognition was a purely voluntary concept. If a trade union was voluntarily recognised by the employer a number of important legal implications would follow, but the employer was always free, subject to the balance of power in the workplace, to withdraw that recognition.

---
[1]   Cm 3968.

THE WHITE PAPER

2.4   In its manifesto for the 1997 general election the Labour Party gave notice of its intention to introduce a statutory right to recognition. This right would apply 'where a majority of the relevant workforce vote in a ballot for the union to represent them'. In view of the controversial nature of the proposal the social partners, the TUC and the CBI, were invited to prepare a joint statement on the issue prior to the publication of the White Paper. The resulting document only served to highlight the differences in approach of the two parties with many areas of disagreement.

2.5 The White Paper reiterated the government's commitment to introduce a legal right to recognition. It indicated that whilst the CAC would rule upon areas of disagreement the general aim of the legislation was that parties should reach voluntary agreements. The White Paper identified a number of core issues for clarification, namely—
- (a) the proper test to be applied in order to prevent frivolous applications;
- (b) the tests to be applied when determining the appropriate bargaining unit;
- (c) the test to be applied when determining whether a majority of the workforce desired recognition; and
- (d) which businesses, in terms of size, should be subject to the recognition procedure.

2.6 The government also considered that recognition procedures should not apply to businesses where 20 or fewer employees are employed in the relevant bargaining unit. In addition, for recognition to be imposed, not only should a majority of those voting be in favour of recognition but they must also equate to at least 40% of those entitled to vote.[1]

[1] Cm 3968, para 4.18.

THE GENERAL APPROACH TO THE LEGISLATION

2.7 It is apparent from even a cursory glance at the recognition provisions contained in the 1999 Act that the government has set out the relevant procedures in a most detailed manner. This is in many respects the most striking element of the legislation. The complexity is deliberate, the reasoning for it clearly stated by the Minister, Mr Wills, during Standing Committee in the House of Commons.[1] He stated that the government did not wish to repeat the mistakes of the 1975 legislation by providing only vague general guidance on the procedures and principles to be applied. Such vagueness was considered to be the downfall of the 1975 Act because so many steps taken by ACAS and the CAC were open to disagreement and challenge by way of judicial review. Accordingly the government now provides the maximum guidance possible for the CAC and defines the procedural steps in great detail.

[1] HC SC E, 16 March 1999, col 345.

2.8 The main features of the Bill as described by the Minister in Standing Committee can be summarised as follows—
- (a) the legislation would provide the greatest possible scope for voluntary arrangements to be reached. Compulsion would be seen as a last resort reserved for only the most recalcitrant of employers;
- (b) the threshold for frivolous complaints would be set at 10% of the relevant workforce;
- (c) the crucial test when determining the appropriate bargaining unit would be effective management, and fragmentation of the workplace was to be avoided;
- (d) if more than 50% of the workforce were already members of the relevant trade union a simplified procedure for recognition would operate;

2.8   *Recognition*

>   (e) if no voluntary agreement was reached the dispute would be determined by the CAC;
>   (f) the CAC's determination would be binding but would only relate to procedural matters: there would be no legal requirement to agree on matters of substance or for binding arbitration to take place; and
>   (g) existing arrangements should, where possible, be left untouched.[1]

---

[1]   HC SC E, 16 March 1999, cols 344–410.

2.9   These basic features remained intact throughout the parliamentary process although a substantial number of technical amendments were introduced at various stages. A number of significant issues, however, were canvassed and are worthy of comment. Among these were attempts made in the House of Lords to include an element of compulsion to negotiate in good faith or to impose a requirement on the parties to reach agreement on certain matters. These proposals were rejected by the government which stressed the desire to secure voluntary arrangements and the requirement to avoid time-consuming and unproductive litigation.[1] Attempts to introduce some form of binding arbitration were also resisted.[2]

---

[1]   HL Committee 7 June 1999, col 1276.
[2]   Ibid, cols 1279–1280.

2.10   The role of the CAC was also debated at length, in particular whether it should be permitted to make binding decisions relating to matters beyond pay, hours and holidays. The government for the most part resisted these proposals but did make provision to enable the parties to extend the subject matter of collective bargaining by agreement.[1] Proposals to increase participation in the ballot were also rejected but protections were inserted to prevent obstruction of the balloting process by the employer.[2] Amendments were also introduced into the Bill so that trade unions which already have some voluntary arrangements in place should not be forced to give up such arrangements before a formal application for recognition is commenced.[3]

---

[1]   HL Committee, 7 June 1999, col 1146 and HC 3R, 31 March 1999, col 1168. See para 2.15.
[2]   HL Committee, 7 June 1999, col 1198. See para 2.15.
[3]   HL Official Report, 8 July 1999, at col 1039.

SCHEDULE A1

2.11   As stated above the provisions contained in the 1999 Act dealing with recognition are extremely detailed, and are contained in Sch 1 which inserts a new Sch A1 into the Trade Union and Labour Relations (Consolidation) Act 1992.

2.12   Schedule A1 is divided into nine Parts, as follows—

>   Part I   deals with the statutory process for recognition. It provides a number of opportunities for the parties to agree voluntary arrangements but if such agreement is not forthcoming it provides for the CAC to determine any relevant disputes.

Part II	deals with voluntary recognition.
Part III	deals with changes which may have occurred attendant on alterations in the relevant bargaining unit.
Part IV	deals with derecognition of a union in circumstances in which that recognition has arisen under Pt I but in which 'automatic' recognition has not occurred.
Part V	deals with the derecognition of 'automatically' recognised unions.
Part VI	provides for workers to be able to invoke a derecognition procedure in the case of 'sweetheart' unions.
Part VII	deals with the process to be adopted when a trade union loses its independence.
Part VIII	introduces employment protection measures to enable individuals to take part in the recognition process without fear of victimisation.
Part IX	deals with various miscellaneous general matters.

2.13 In view of the detail contained in Sch A1 it is beyond the scope of this work to provide a line by line assessment of the provisions. This chapter seeks to identify the broad themes and thus concentrates mostly on Sch A1, Pt I.

Procedure for recognition

2.14 Schedule A1, Pt I contains the major provisions relating to the recognition procedure. Although it seeks to encourage agreement between the parties it also provides a procedure for the CAC to impose a binding structure for collective bargaining. It deals with the central question as to whether the union should be recognised and how collective bargaining should be conducted.

2.15 Schedule A1, Pt I, para 1 provides that one or more trade unions may make a request for recognition. The issues which may be subject to the compulsory recognition procedure are identified in para 3 as being 'negotiations relating to pay, hours and holidays' (para 3(3)). Importantly, para 3(4) provides that, so long as the parties agree, the ambit of collective bargaining may be extended to other matters, and thus the parties may extend the scope of the statutory procedure. This represents a fundamental amendment to the original Bill as presented to Parliament.

2.16 Paragraph 6 states that the union must be independent in order for a request for recognition made under para 4 to be valid. In keeping with the government's aim of promoting voluntary arrangements the initial request under para 4 is made to the employer. The exclusion from the procedure for employers which employ at least 21 employees is included in para 7 which also provides a formula for calculating the relevant figure (para 7(2)). If the parties are able to reach agreement for recognition para 10 provides for the procedure under Sch A1, Pt I to cease. If agreement cannot be reached or if negotiations fail the formal application procedure applies and the CAC becomes formally involved in the process (paras 11–13).

2.17 In order to prevent frivolous applications para 14(4) provides that for the procedure to continue the '10% test' must be satisfied. This provides that at least 10% of the workers constituting the relevant bargaining unit must be members of the relevant union or unions (para 14(5)).

2.18   *Recognition*

Bargaining units

2.18 The bargaining unit is a fundamental part of the statutory procedure. In accordance with the preference for voluntary arrangements para 18 provides an opportunity for the parties to reach agreement on what should be the appropriate bargaining unit. If agreement cannot be reached the CAC must decide the appropriate bargaining agreement in accordance with para 19. In making this determination the CAC must take into account the need for the unit to be compatible with effective management (para 19(3)(a)). It must also take into account certain factors including the views of the parties, existing bargaining arrangements, the desirability of avoiding 'small fragmented bargaining units within an undertaking' and the location of workers (para 19(4)).

2.19 Once the bargaining unit has been identified the CAC has to consider whether there is sufficient support for collective bargaining to make the relevant order. Recognition can be reached by means of a short cut available under para 22 where the CAC is satisfied that a majority of the workers in the bargaining unit are members of the relevant trade union (para 22(1), (2)). However para 22(3) provides an option for the CAC to nevertheless hold a ballot if it considers either that such a ballot is in the interests of good industrial relations, or if a significant number of union members do not wish to have the collective bargaining conducted on their behalf by the unions, or if there is some concern that the union membership figures are incorrect or misleading (s 22(4)). If the union membership figures are insufficient to trigger the short cut a ballot needs to be held in any event (s 23).

Ballots

2.20   If a ballot needs to be held detailed procedures are set out in paras 24–28.

2.21 If the result of a ballot where a majority of the workers voted and at least 40% of the workers constituting the bargaining unit support the union's application the CAC must make a declaration that the union is entitled to conduct collective bargaining on behalf of the bargaining unit (para 29(3)). The consequences of recognition are dealt with in para 30 which provides that unless the parties can reach agreement as to how collective bargaining should be conducted the parties may apply to the CAC for assistance (s 30(3)). If the CAC cannot assist the parties to reach a voluntary agreement on such matters it must specify the method by which the collective bargaining should be conducted (para 31(3). This determination shall have effect as if contained in a legally enforceable agreement between the parties (para 31(4)) unless the parties agree otherwise (para 31(5)). Specific performance is the only remedy available to the parties (para 31(6)).

2.22 Paragraph 32 states that the CAC should provide assistance in cases in which a method for collective bargaining has been agreed but one of the parties fails to comply with that agreement. Schedule A1 also deals with matters such as admissibility (paras 33–42), validity (paras 43–50), and competing applications (para 51).

Voluntary recognition

2.23 Schedule A1, Pt II (paras 52–63) deals with issues relating to voluntary recognition. Paragraph 52 specifies the conditions to be fulfilled in order for an agreement to be an agreement of recognition for the purposes of Sch A1, Pt I. These conditions are essentially met if the agreement is reached as a result of an application for recognition under para 4 where either the parties have reached agreement under the procedures set out at paras 5–9 or where agreement has subsequently been reached in accordance with para 17 after the employer had initially rejected the original request. If a dispute arises as to whether an agreement satisfies the conditions set out at para 52 an application may be made to the CAC to consider the status of the agreement (para 55). The CAC must reach its decision in accordance with para 55(6).

2.24 In circumstances where an agreement for recognition exists the employer is entitled to terminate that agreement although not before the end of the period of three years starting with the day after the date of the agreement (para 56(1), (5)). The time restriction does not apply in circumstances in which the union consents to the termination, and in addition the union may also terminate the agreement at any time without the consent of the employer (para 56(3)). These provisions are designed to provide the union with a degree of initial protection and security whilst also providing more flexible arrangements for the parties to terminate the recognition agreement. This flexible approach to derecognition is designed to encourage voluntary recognition arrangements.[1]

[1] HL Official Report, 8 July 1999, col 1053.

2.25 Applications may also be made to the CAC when the parties cannot agree on the method of collective bargaining (para 58) or where, although a method has been agreed, one or more of the parties fails to carry out that method (para 59). The relevant procedural requirements relating to such an application are set out in paras 60–62. On receipt of a valid application the CAC must first try to assist the parties to reach agreement on the matters in dispute (para 63(1)). If agreement is not forthcoming the CAC can specify the relevant method of collective bargaining (para 63(2)) which will have effect as if contained in a legally binding agreement between the parties (para 63(3)). Specific performance is the only available remedy for breach of such an agreement (para 63(5)).

CHANGES AFFECTING THE BARGAINING UNIT

2.26 Part III (paras 64–95) deals with changes affecting the bargaining unit after a recognition agreement has been put in place either voluntarily or through the mechanism of an application to the CAC. As has previously been stated a fundamental objective of the legislative scheme is to ensure that any relevant bargaining unit is compatible with effective management.[1] In furtherance of this objective Pt III sets out a detailed scheme for dealing with circumstances in which changes are alleged to have taken in place in the bargaining unit which necessitate corresponding changes to the collective bargaining structure.

[1] HC SC E, 16 March 1999, col 347.

DERECOGNITION

2.27 Schedule A1, Pts IV–VI deal with derecognition. It is important to distinguish between these provisions and the ability of the parties to terminate voluntary recognition agreements (see para 2.24). Part IV covers derecognition in general. Part IV, para 99 deals with the situation in which the relevant number of employees falls below the threshold requirement of 21 employees. In such circumstances the employer can apply to the CAC to have the relevant unions derecognised under the procedures set out at paras 100–103. Even if the threshold requirement is met the employer can still apply for derecognition and paras 104–111 deal with the procedure to be followed in such circumstances. Paragraph 105 encourages the parties to arrive at a negotiated settlement, in line with the general aim of achieving voluntary agreements. If this does not prove possible the employer can then apply to the CAC for a ballot to be held on the issue of derecognition (para 106). Similarly paras 112–116 deal with circumstances in which the request for derecognition comes not from the employer but from the relevant employees. If the CAC accepts an application to hold a ballot on the derecognition issue such a ballot must be conducted in accordance with the detailed requirements set down in paras 117–120. When the CAC is aware of the result of the ballot it must make the relevant declarations in accordance with para 121.

2.28 Schedule A1, Pt V (paras 122–133) contains special provisions which apply to requests for derecognition in circumstances in which the 'short cut' to recognition has previously been achieved on the basis that more than 50% of the relevant workers are union members in accordance with para 22(2). Paragraphs 127–132 set out the procedure to be followed by the CAC if it receives an application from the employer to derecognise in such circumstances. If the CAC considers the employers' request to be valid it must ensure that a secret ballot is held under para 133. The protections in place to ensure that the ballot is fair (as contained in paras 118–121) also apply in such circumstances (para 133).

2.29 Schedule A1, Pt VI (paras 134–148) deals with derecognition in circumstances where the union concerned is not independent, and there is a risk that the union in question is a 'sweetheart union'. Paragraph 147 gives the CAC the power to hold a ballot in such circumstances. Similarly Pt VII (paras 149–155) deals with circumstances in which a previously independent union loses its independent status.

Victimisation

2.30 Schedule A1, Pt VIII introduces a right not to suffer detriment or dismissal for certain protected activities associated with recognition. These are identified in para 156 and cover diverse matters ranging from voting in the ballot to seeking to influence other individuals in the way in which they should vote. Protections are also provided in the case of dismissal in para 161. The interim relief procedure applies to such cases under the 1999 Act, s 6.

TRAINING

2.31 One further element of the 1999 Act is worthy of mention. Section 5 amends the Trade Union and Labour Relations (Consolidation) Act 1992, Pt I, Ch VA, by inserting a new s 70B. The purpose of the provision is to extend collective bargaining to include discussions relating to training. These reforms were uncontroversial.

3 Industrial action

GENERAL

3.1 In its election manifesto the Labour Party indicated that it would not interfere with the substantive law on industrial action and that the main statutory provisions relating to ballots and other associated matters would remain intact. Accordingly the amendments in this area made by the 1999 Act are relatively minor, and for the most part are necessitated by other amendments within the Act, for example the alterations to the 'government health warning' on ballot papers arise from the extension of unfair dismissal rights to certain workers engaged in industrial action. Further amendments were introduced to remedy the perceived injustices resulting from the notification provisions contained in the Trade Union and Labour Relations (Consolidation) Act 1992 ('the 1992 Act') as highlighted by the decision of the Court of Appeal in *Blackpool and Fylde College v National Association of Teachers in Further and Higher Education*[1] and to secure clarification and simplification of the law in a number of other areas.

[1] [1994] ICR 648.

THE WHITE PAPER

Collective rights

3.2 The limited nature of the government's intentions were set out in the White Paper 'Fairness at Work'. They include the desire to simplify the unduly complex nature of existing arrangements which it was claimed led to the escalation of disputes.[1] The White Paper also gave notice that the government intended to reform the law regarding the provision of notices contained in the 1992 Act, ss 226A and 234A, in order to protect the confidentiality of trade union membership. The government's proposal was to amend the existing law so that while the notices provided by a trade union to an employer should still identify as accurately as reasonably practicable the group or category of employees concerned, it need not contain the specific names and addresses of the individuals involved.

[1] Cm 3968, para 4.26.

BALLOTS AND NOTICES

Accidental failures

3.4 The 1999 Act, Sch 3, amends the 1992 Act by introducing a potentially significant defence against certain failures to comply with provisions for a trade union

3.4 *Industrial action*

which has organised industrial action. Schedule 3, para 9 inserts into the 1992 Act a new s 232B, which requires a court to disregard small accidental failures when considering whether the industrial action in question has the support of a ballot under the 1992 Act, s 226. The criteria to be applied under the new section is that failures to comply should be disregarded if they are accidental and on a scale which is unlikely to affect the result of the ballot.

Notification

3.5 As indicated in the White Paper[1] the government proposed to amend the notification provisions contained in the 1992 Act, ss 226A and 234A. The controversial nature of these provisions was highlighted by the decision of the Court of Appeal in *Blackpool and Fylde College v National Association of Teachers in Further and Higher Education*.[2] In this case the employer had succeeded in obtaining an interlocutory injunction on the basis that the information provided by the union in the relevant notices served in accordance with the 1992 Act was insufficient and the names and addresses of the relevant employees should have been provided. The 1999 Act has amended the existing provisions so that a trade union is only obliged to provide the number, category or workplace of the employees concerned. The failure to name employees in the relevant notice shall no longer be a ground for holding that it does not comply with the relevant requirements of the 1992 Act.

---

[1] Cm 3968.
[2] [1994] ICR 648.

3.6 The limited nature of this amendment was criticised by Lord Wedderburn of Charlton during the Committee stage in the House of Lords. Although he welcomed the specific removal of the requirement to provide the names of the relevant employees he considered it absurd that the trade union should have to provide any information at all to the employer in the context of an industrial dispute.[1] Lord McIntosh reiterated the government's manifesto commitment to leave the existing statutory framework essentially untouched and indicated that the government felt that the right balance had been struck.[2] A trade union is thus still subject to a requirement to provide significant information to the employer and, if it has such information, to provide details of the number and type of employees likely to be involved in the action along with information regarding type of work and the workplace concerned. Any attempt to mislead the employer or to misrepresent information by the trade union would result in the loss of protection for the action.[3]

---

[1] HL Committee, 16 June 1999, col 297.
[2] Ibid, cols 298, 300, 301, 302.
[3] HC SC E, 18 March 1999, cols 464 and 467.

Effectiveness of the ballot

3.7 An important but uncontroversial amendment was also introduced to extend the period of a ballot's effectiveness for the purposes of the 1992 Act, s 234. The 1999 Act, Sch 3, para 10, amends s 234 so that the initial period of four weeks for the effectiveness of the ballot may be extended for a further period as agreed between the employer and the trade union subject to a maximum extension of eight weeks. This amendment was designed to avoid the 'absurd' position in which a union may be forced to take action in the four-week period in order to prevent losing the protection of the ballot even though the dispute may be close to resolution.[1]

[1] HC SC E, 9 March 1999, col 330.

Voting papers

3.8 The introduction in the 1999 Act of the right for workers who take part in industrial action to claim unfair dismissal is reflected in Sch 3, para 6(3),[1] which amends the so-called 'government health warning' which is required to be included on voting papers under the 1992 Act, s 229. The existing wording is qualified by stating that if the employee is dismissed when taking part in official action 'the dismissal will be unfair if it takes place fewer than eight weeks after you started taking part in the action, and depending on the circumstances may be unfair if it takes place later.'

[1] For a more detailed discussion of these reforms see Ch 5.

3.9 Further amendment to the voting paper is made by Sch 3, para 6(2), which specifically defines an overtime ban and a call-out ban as constituting 'action short of a strike' for the purposes of the balloting provisions. This amendment was introduced in response to arguments advanced by Lord Wedderburn of Charlton during the Committee stage in the House of Lords relating to the possible ramifications of the decision of the Court of Appeal in *Connex South Eastern Ltd v National Union of Rail, Maritime and Transport Workers*.[1] In that case the employer had unsuccessfully attempted to exploit the lack of definition in the 1992 Act regarding the distinction between 'strike action' and 'action short of a strike'. The 1999 Act now removes any ambiguity in order to prevent such technical arguments being advanced in the future.[2]

[1] [1999] IRLR 249.
[2] HL Official Report, 8 July 1999, col 1076.

Other amendments

3.10 Further technical amendments are also introduced in order to simplify the law in relation to separate workplace ballots, and single and aggregate ballots (Sch 3, para 5). The 1999 Act introduces new ss 228, 228A to the 1992 Act, in part to simplify the definition of a 'place of work'. This simplification was considered necessary after the decision of the Court of Appeal in *Intercity West Coast Ltd v National Union of Rail, Maritime and Transport Workers*[1] in which the employers had (albeit unsuccessfully) attempted to exploit the vague definition of 'place of work' in the 1992 Act by arguing that the term 'occupation' in s 228(4) should be accorded a technical meaning in keeping with the law of property. Although this argument found favour at first instance it was rejected by the Court of Appeal which held, by a majority, that the term 'occupation' in s 228(4) must be construed in the context of legislation dealing with industrial relations and the conduct of trade unions. As such

3.10   *Industrial action*

the term should be given a broad and not overly technical meaning. The amendments introduced by the 1999 Act are designed to prevent any such arguments being advanced by employers in future.

[1]   [1996] IRLR 583. See HL 3R, 15 July 1999, col 575.

Inducement

3.11 In one respect the amendments introduced by the 1999 Act introduce an additional statutory hurdle to overcome in order for industrial action to enjoy the support of a ballot. Schedule 3, para 8 inserts a new s 232A into the 1992 Act which specifically provides that the action loses support of the ballot if the trade union induces to take part in the action a member who was not accorded an entitlement to vote in the ballot but who it was nevertheless reasonable at the time at which the ballot was held for the trade union to believe would be induced to take part in the action. Interestingly this proposal did not appear in the White Paper and was not debated at length during the parliamentary passage of the Bill. It is also important to note that it is not subject to the overriding defence set out in the new s 232B which only applies to ss 227(1), 230(2), (2A).

4 Victimisation

INTRODUCTION

4.1 The statutory right to 'recognition' is reflected in other areas of the structure of the 1999 Act. Increased protection for individuals who wish to be members of and participate in the activities of trade unions are supported by a number of provisions. Three of those provisions are considered in this chapter. The first relates to the government's intention to overrule the perceived injustice arising from the decision of the House of Lords in the cases of *Associated Newspapers Ltd v Wilson* and *Associated British Ports v Palmer*.[1] The second is a regulation-making power creating the right not to be victimised where an individual refuses to enter into an individual contract with different terms to those enjoyed under a collective agreement. The third outlaws the practice of the compilation and use by employers and other individuals of blacklists of trade union activists.

[1] [1995] IRLR 258. For a detailed analysis of this decision see *Harvey on Industrial Relations and Employment Law* N [683] ff.

DETRIMENT RELATED TO TRADE UNION MEMBERSHIP

4.2 The Trade Union and Labour Relations (Consolidation) Act 1992 ('the 1992 Act') permitted action short of dismissal to be taken against trade union members and activists if the employer's purpose in taking such action was to 'further a change in his relationship with all or any class of his employees' (s 148(3)). This provision was introduced by the Conservative government in 1993 by way of a late amendment ('the Ullswater amendment') to the Trade Union Reform and Employment Rights Act 1993, s 13, which added the 1992 Act, s 148(3)–(5). The reasoning behind the amendment, which was introduced before the *Wilson* case reached the House of Lords, was to counter the decision of the Court of Appeal in that case that the action of an employer in restricting pay increases to non-union members was unlawful under the provisions of the 1992 Act, s 146 (see *Wilson v Associated Newspapers Ltd* and *Palmer v Associated British Ports*).[1] Somewhat ironically, after the Ullswater amendment had been introduced into the 1993 Act, the House of Lords, by a majority, controversially overturned the decision of the Court of Appeal on the basis that the word 'action' in the 1992 Act, s 146, did not cover the omission of an employer to pay an increase in wages to an employee.[2]

[1] [1993] IRLR 336.
[2] [1995] IRLR 258.

THE WHITE PAPER

4.3 In the White Paper 'Fairness at Work' the government stated its belief that the discrimination permitted by the 1992 Act, s 146(3), was contrary to its commitment

4.3 Victimisation

to ensuring that individuals are free to choose whether or not to join a trade union, and that it was important that trade union representatives were active in promoting effective dialogue with employees. The government's considered view was that the law as it stood might deter employees from being involved in such activity and it therefore proposed to make it unlawful to discriminate by omission on grounds of trade union membership, non-membership or activities.[1]

[1] See Cm 3968, para 4.25.

Detriment through omission

4.4 The relevant provisions regarding detriment through omission are contained in the 1999 Act, Sch 2, which makes a number of amendments to the 1992 Act, s 146, The most important amendment is the substitution of the phrase 'have action short of dismissal taken against him as an individual by his employer' with the phrase 'be subjected to any detriment as an individual by any act, or any deliberate failure to act, by his employer if the act or failure takes place' (Sch 2, para 2(2)). The remaining amendments contained in Sch 2 are effectively procedural in nature and stem from this alteration.

4.5 It is striking that the amendments made by the 1999 Act do not include the removal of the 'Ullswater amendment' introduced by the Trade Union Reform and Employment Rights Act 1993. In particular the 1992 Act, s 148(3) is retained.

The debate in Parliament

4.6 During the Standing Committee debate in the House of Commons the Opposition proposed to amend the Bill by creating a 'wilful determination' test to be imposed before liability could be established, the key point being the addition of the word 'wilful'. This amendment was withdrawn after the Minister for Small Firms, Trade and Industry, Michael Wills, stated that the government believed that the use of the word 'deliberately' in the Act was sufficient to signify the requirement for intent and that this was the 'key test'.[1] This passage is significant in that the 'intention' test is an integral part of the 1992 Act, s 148(3), as inserted by the 'Ullswater amendment'.

[1] HC SC E, 18 March 1999, col 444.

4.7 An attempt was made by Lord Wedderburn of Charlton, who was concerned at the limited nature of the amendment, to remove the 'Ullswater amendment' in its entirety during the Committee stage of the Bill in the House of Lords. Lord Wedderburn expressed concern at the retention of the reasonable employer test implied by that provision.[1] In rejecting this attempt Lord McIntosh of Haringey explained that the government considered that wholesale removal of the Ullswater amendment would 'reintroduce uncertainty'. The reform had to be viewed in the context of the other rights contained in the Bill including the right to recognition, and the introduction of regulatory powers preventing employees from being victimised if they do not consent to the transfer from collective agreements to individual contracts. As such the government viewed the 1992 Act, s 148(3) as serving a 'useful purpose' in this new statutory context and proposed its retention.[2]

[1] HL Committee, 7 June 1999, col 1283.
[2] Ibid, col 1286.

4.8 The position was revisited at a later stage in the House of Lords when the Opposition expressed concern that under the 1999 Act an employer who wished to pay an increase in wages to an employee who had agreed to take on more flexible duties would have to pay the same increase to an employee who did not agree to those more flexible terms simply because they were covered by a collective agreement.[1] Replying on behalf of the government Lord McIntosh of Haringey stated that the fact that one worker benefits from better terms under an individual contract did not constitute a detriment for those who remain covered by the collective agreement. However the government's view was that it would not be permissible for employers to offer better terms conditional on workers leaving or not joining a trade union. After referring to the *Wilson* and *Palmer* decisions, Lord McIntosh clarified the government's position further by stating that the government was—

> 'ensuring that an omission intended to deter trade union membership will be unlawful, but we shall maintain the right to change bargaining arrangements where there is no intention to prevent or deter union membership.'[2]

[1] HL Committee, 16 June 1999, col 356.
[2] Ibid, col 359.

4.9 Uncertainty remains about the real nature of the changes introduced by the 1999 Act. Indeed, as Lord McCarthy commented,[1] it appears as if the government's proposals still permit the type of activity which was the subject of the decisions in the *Wilson* and *Palmer* cases. This is certainly arguable, since the offer of pay increases in those cases was dependent not upon the individual giving up their right to trade union membership but upon their agreement to move from collectively negotiated terms to individual contracts. Against this background it appears as if the intention of the 1999 Act is simply to remove the arbitrary distinction between acts and omissions contained in the 1992 Act. It is ironic that the outcome of the *Wilson* and *Palmer* cases would almost certainly have been the same even after the enactment of the 1999 Act. In those cases a majority in the House of Lords held that the intention of the employers was not to discourage trade union membership as such but to move away from collective bargaining and towards individual contracts. Since the material parts of the 1992 Act, s 148(3) are unamended, those employers are likely to pass the same test now. These conclusions are further supported by the nature of the regulatory power which has been created by the 1999 Act to deal with detriment and dismissal in the context of collective agreements.

[1] HL Committee, 16 June 1999, col 359.

COLLECTIVE AGREEMENTS: DETRIMENT AND DISMISSAL

4.10 The 1999 Act, s 17 introduces a power for the Secretary of State to introduce regulations prohibiting a worker from being subjected to detriment or dismissal on

4.10 *Victimisation*

the grounds that 'he refuses to enter into a contract which includes terms which differ from the terms of a collective agreement which applies to him' (s 17(1)). However, the 1999 Act, s 17(4) effectively provides that discrimination in the form of pay will not constitute a detriment unless the enhanced payment is linked to a contractual term which prohibits the worker from being a member of any trade union and the additional payment does not reasonably relate to the services provided by the worker under that contract.

4.11 The provisions relating to detriment contained in the 1999 Act are certainly open to criticism. Although the arbitrary distinction between acts and omissions contained in the 1992 Act, s 146 has been removed, substantial leeway remains for an employer to offer financial incentives to employees in order to encourage them to reject collectively agreed terms. In such circumstances it is notoriously difficult to ascertain whether hostility is merely directed at the collective agreement itself or to the trade union which negotiated that agreement. Such concerns were expressed by Lord McCarthy in the House of Lords.[1]

---

[1] HL Committee, 16 June 1999, col 359.

BLACKLISTS

4.12 The White Paper also set out the government's intention to introduce a prohibition on the compilation and use of blacklists of trade union members.[1]

---

[1] See Cm 3968, para 4.25.

4.13 The 1999 Act, s 3, gives the Secretary of State the power to make regulations prohibiting the compilation, use and sale of blacklists.

4.14 The introduction of such a regulatory power was uncontroversial although the precise ambit and extent of the power was the subject of some debate. Limited indications were given by the government as to the likely content of any regulations. For example the government indicated its wish to consider the use of employment tribunals as a mechanism of enforcement as well as the possibility of introducing procedural rules permitting trade unions to bring proceedings on behalf of their members. The regulations may also provide for proceedings to be commenced against parties other than employers.[1] The regulations may also include the power to create criminal offences.

---

[1] HL Official Report, 8 July 1999, col 1075.

CRIMINAL SANCTIONS

4.15 The subject of criminal sanctions raised concerns from both sides during the debate. The opposition were concerned that the presence of criminal sanctions was an overreaction, and an unsuccessful attempt was made to remove the power to create criminal offences from the Bill.[1] On the other hand Lord Monkswell was concerned at the absence of a power to create an offence punishable by imprisonment, as he felt that the type of person who was likely to challenge the Bill would be 'a rich individual' rather than an employer, and therefore merely to impose a fine would be 'risible'. In the circumstances he felt the absence of a power to imprison would undermine the protection afforded in the Bill.[2] The government ultimately stood firm on its original proposals which were based upon the powers in relation to criminal sanctions contained in the Data Protection Act 1998.[3]

---

[1] HC Report, 30 March 1999, col 986.
[2] HL Committee, 16 June 1999, col 290.
[3] Ibid, col 288.

5 Unfair dismissal

GENERAL

5.1 The 1999 Act introduces substantial amendments to the law of unfair dismissal, with a number of objectives including the addition of substantial new rights and the extension and simplification of the existing law.

WHITE PAPER

5.2 The White Paper 'Fairness at Work' set out the government's intention to reduce the qualifying period for unfair dismissal protection from two years to one year and to lift the cap on the compensatory award for unfair dismissal.[1] The government considered the existing two year qualifying period to be a barrier to labour market flexibility, since employees were reluctant to move from one employer to another because they stood to lose the right to unfair dismissal protection for a relatively substantial period. The removal of the cap on compensation was seen as a matter of industrial justice and reflected the seriousness with which the loss of employment as a result of an unfair dismissal was viewed by a substantial proportion of the working population. Both proposals were the subject of substantial consultation and, by the time the Bill was presented to Parliament, the latter had been significantly amended with the government having been persuaded to retain the compensation cap but at an increased level of £50,000. Further consultation was invited, however, on whether the cap should nevertheless be abolished in certain limited cases such as those involving 'whistleblowing'.

[1] Cm 3968, Ch 3.

5.3 The White Paper also set out the government's intention to simplify the existing system of special and additional awards and to provide for the indexation of relevant benefits.[1] It also indicated its intention to restrict the right for employees and employers to exclude unfair dismissal and redundancy rights through the mechanism of fixed term contracts[2] and proposed an extension of the right to claim unfair dismissal to individuals dismissed after taking lawful industrial action.[3]

[1] Cm 3968, paras 3.6, 3.7.
[2] Ibid, para 3.8.
[3] Ibid, paras 4.21, 4.22.

REDUCTION OF QUALIFYING PERIOD

5.4 The qualifying period for unfair dismissal rights has enjoyed something of a chequered history. The right to claim unfair dismissal was first introduced in the

Industrial Relations Act 1971 and the qualifying period was originally set at two years. This was reduced to one year in 1974 and to six months in 1975 by the Trade Union and Labour Relations Act 1974. In 1979 the limit was increased to one year and then, in 1980, to two years for employees in undertakings with fewer than 21 employees. In 1985 the limit was raised to two years in all cases.[1]

---

[1] Unfair Dismissal (Variation of Qualifying Period) Order 1985, SI 1985/782.

The qualifying period order

5.5 The Unfair Dismissal and Statement of Reasons for Dismissal (Variation of Qualifying Period) Order 1999, SI 1999/1436 gave legislative effect to the government's intention to reduce the qualifying period for the right to claim unfair dismissal from two years to one year for all dismissals occurring on or after 1 June 1999.

COMPENSATION CAP

5.6 By the time the Bill was presented to Parliament the government's original proposal to abolish the cap on unfair dismissal compensation had been modified by the proposal to retain the cap but at the increased level of £50,000 (see para 5.2). If the original cap on compensation contained in the Industrial Relations Act 1971 had been increased in line with average earnings it would have been fixed at £52,800.[1] The raising of the cap has been implemented by the 1999 Act, s 34(4), which substitutes the sum specified in the Employment Rights Act 1996, s 124(1), with the sum of £50,000.

---

[1] House of Commons Research Paper 98/99.

COMPENSATION CAP—SPECIAL CASES

5.7 Although the compensation cap remains for standard unfair dismissal cases it has been removed completely for certain specified cases, namely those where the reason for the dismissal relates either to health and safety reasons or to the whistleblowing activities of the worker concerned. The decision to remove the cap altogether in such cases represents the importance attached to such activities by the government and did not prove controversial.[1] These amendments are set out in the 1999 Act, s 37, which removes the cap in circumstances in which the dismissal has taken place for certain specified reasons, ie those covered by certain provisions of the Employment Rights Act 1996, namely: ss 100, 105(3) (health and safety cases), and ss 103A, 105(6A) (whistleblowing cases).

---

[1] HC Report, 30 March 1999, col 875.

5.8   *Unfair dismissal*

SPECIAL AND ADDITIONAL AWARDS

5.8   In the White Paper the government indicated its intention to reform the system of special awards which were payable in circumstances in which an individual had been dismissed for reasons relating to trade union activities or membership, health and safety activities and other similar cases.[1] By the time the Bill was presented to the House of Commons this proposal had been extended to incorporate reforms to the system of additional awards which were payable in circumstances in which orders for re-engagement or re-instatement were not complied with. Once again these proposals did not prove to be controversial. The 1999 Act now incorporates additional and special awards into a single code. Special awards are abolished by the 1999 Act, s 33(1), and the level of additional awards is correspondingly increased to the sum of 52 weeks' pay by s 33(2).

---

[1]   Cm 3968, para 3.7.

INDEXATION

5.9   There was general approval for the government's proposals to provide for the automatic indexation of certain sums which are relevant to the unfair dismissal jurisdiction. The White Paper indicated the government's general desire to ensure that the relevant sums did not become devalued by inflation over time (as had occurred with the cap on compensation for unfair dismissal). In addition the existing practice of reviewing the limits each year was felt to be inefficient and time-consuming.[1] Accordingly the Bill contained the necessary provisions for the automatic indexation of these relevant amounts. The amendments are contained in the 1999 Act, s 34, with similar provisions for guarantee payments in s 35.

---

[1]   Cm 3968, para 3.8.

AGREEMENTS TO EXCLUDE UNFAIR DISMISSAL RIGHTS

5.10   The White Paper also contained important proposals relating to fixed term contracts. Although the advantages of such contracts and the flexibility which they offer was recognised, concern was expressed at the ability of employees to waive their rights to unfair dismissal and statutory redundancy payments contained in the Employment Rights Act 1996, s 197(1), (3). The government was concerned that the flexibility of this system was being abused by employers who were deliberately recruiting employees on fixed term contracts with waivers when, in reality, the work they performed was open ended.[1] As such the law permitted the widespread denial of basic employment rights and the government therefore invited reactions on proposals to restrict the ability of the parties to agree such waivers whilst retaining the flexibility of the system.[2]

---

[1]   For a stark example of the injustice of the system see *Kingston upon Hull City Council v Mountain* [1999] ICR 715.
[2]   Cm 3968, paras 3.10–3.13.

5.11 The Bill was based upon a compromise proposal under which the right to waive unfair dismissal rights would be abolished but parties would be free to exclude the right to a redundancy payment at the expiry of the contract. This proposal was supplemented by specific provisions which were introduced during the passage of the Bill through Parliament to provide retrospective protection for employees who had entered into fixed term contracts containing waiver clauses but were dismissed on the grounds of pregnancy, maternity or if they had asserted a statutory employment right.[1]

[1] HL Committee, 16 June 1999, col 376.

5.12 The various reforms to the law on fixed term contracts are contained in the 1999 Act, s 18, which entirely removes the reference to unfair dismissal rights from the Employment Rights Act 1996, s 197. Consequential amendments have also been made to the National Minimum Wage Act 1998 and the Tax Credits Act 1999.

JURISDICTION

5.13 During the passage of the Bill in the House of Lords the government introduced a series of amendments to deal with the jurisdiction of employment tribunals, particularly in the context of workers who perform duties outside the UK. The different nature of the jurisdictions for discrimination and unfair dismissal cases were strikingly illustrated in the Court of Appeal decision in *Carver v Saudi Arabian Airlines*.[1]

[1] [1999] IRLR 370. See para 10.5.

5.14 Introducing the relevant amendments, Lord Simon of Highbury indicated that the government considered that the established principles of international and domestic law were sufficient to resolve jurisdictional disputes of the nature which arose in *Carver*. A proper connection with the UK must be shown in order for a tribunal to accept jurisdiction. It was also stated that the amendments would have the additional advantage of fulfilling the UK's obligations under European law relating to the posted workers Directive.[1]

[1] HL Official Report, 8 July 1999, col 1089.

5.15 Amendments contained in the 1999 Act, s 32, effectively abolish the exception relating to working outside Great Britain contained in the Employment Rights Act 1996, s 196 (s 32(3)). Jurisdictional questions before employment tribunals in unfair dismissal cases are now likely to be determined by reference to normal conflict of law principles.

5.16   *Unfair dismissal*

UNFAIR DISMISSAL PROTECTION FOR STRIKING WORKERS

5.16   The most controversial new measure concerning unfair dismissal in the 1999 Act creates the ability for workers to claim unfair dismissal in circumstances in which they are dismissed when taking part in industrial action. Although there was a brief flirtation with the 'suspension' theory of industrial action[1] the general rule at common law has invariably been that an employee who participates in industrial action is committing a repudiatory breach of contract and can be lawfully dismissed without notice. Furthermore an employee who threatens to take such action in the future may also be in breach of their contract of employment and thereby lose the right to be paid (see for example *Ticehurst and Thompson v British Telecommunications plc*).[2]

---

[1]   See *Morgan v Fry* [1968] 2QB 710.
[2]   [1992] IRLR 219. For a full discussion on this topic see *Harvey on Industrial Relations and Employment Law* N [1887].

5.17   In addition to the common law rules the general policy of both previous Labour and Conservative governments had been to avoid interfering in the merits of industrial disputes. The right to complain of unfair dismissal in such situations was therefore extremely limited. The Industrial Relations Act 1971, which first introduced the right to claim unfair dismissal, excluded the jurisdiction of tribunals to consider whether a dismissal was unfair in an industrial action context unless it could be shown that the employer had selectively dismissed or re-engaged those taking part in the action and that the reason for the dismissals was the union membership or activities of the individuals involved. Minor modifications were made in the Employment Protection Act 1975 but the general principle of excluding jurisdiction remained intact. Further modifications were introduced by the Employment Act 1990 which were then consolidated in the Trade Union and Labour Relations (Consolidation) Act 1992 ('the 1992 Act'), ss 237, 238. These provisions excluded jurisdiction completely in cases which involved unofficial action and introduced a slightly more lenient regime in relation to workers who were participating in official action. However, the employer was still permitted to selectively re-engage or dismiss so long as a three month waiting period had been satisfied.

5.18   Statutory and common law frameworks therefore placed significant barriers on the ability of an individual to strike. From 1980 onwards this imbalance was accentuated by the legal obstacles which were placed in the way of a trade union which was organising industrial action. These developments led to the censure of the UK by the International Labour Organisation for a failure to protect and recognise the right to strike in domestic law.

The White Paper

5.19   The White Paper outlined the government's intention to correct the anomaly between the substantial hurdles which had to be overcome for industrial action to be lawful in the collective sense on the one hand and the almost total lack of legal protection for the employee participating in that action on the other. The government indicated that it had no plans to change the position in relation to individuals dismissed for taking unofficial action but that it intended to grant employees who took part in lawfully organised official industrial action the right to complain of unfair dismissal.[1]

[1] Cm 3968, paras 4.21, 4.22.

The Bill

5.20 The proposals relating to the granting to workers dismissed while engaged in industrial action the right to claim unfair dismissal were controversial and the subject of much debate during the passage of the Bill. The Opposition benches saw these provisions as an attack on the fundamental right of the employer to dismiss a worker who is seeking to damage the employer's economic interests.[1] The government, however, reiterated its view that the right to withdraw labour was a fundamental human right and that the proposed legislation was to correct the present imbalance in the law on industrial action.[2]

[1] HC SC E, 9 March 1999, col 294.
[2] Ibid, col 288.

5.21 It is important to realise that the new provisions fall short of enshrining a 'right to strike' in domestic law. As Lord Wedderburn noted in the House of Lords the proposals are intended to bring the UK in line with other European states, where industrial action results in a suspension rather than a termination of the employment contract.[1] The government's approach incorporated certain restrictions and these were highlighted during the passage of the Bill. The Bill set out to create a dual set of obligations: upon the unions to organise any industrial action lawfully and, if they do so, a corresponding obligation on the employer to enter into serious negotiations before taking the step of dismissing the workers.[2] In order to meet these objectives workers who are engaged in lawfully organised industrial action may complain of unfair dismissal if they are dismissed within an initial eight week period. This period was felt to be sufficient to enable the parties to enter into serious negotiations or call upon the assistance of third parties such as ACAS.[3] If dismissals occur after the initial eight week period different rules apply depending upon the merits of the procedural steps taken by the parties. The Bill therefore places great emphasis on the procedural aspects of the dispute.

[1] HL 2R, 10 May 1999, col 1016.
[2] HC SC E, 9 March 1999, col 289.
[3] Ibid.

The 1999 Act

5.22 The relevant provisions on unfair dismissal are contained in the 1999 Act, Sch 5. As has been stated at para 5.21 the purpose of the amendments is to encourage dialogue between the trade union and the employer to ensure that dismissal is viewed as a last resort. If the employer acts in a precipitate manner without seeking to resolve the dispute unfair dismissal complaints may result. The 1999 Act concentrates upon the procedural merits of the dispute and the government was quick to confirm that employment tribunals should have no part in ascertaining or adjudicating the underlying merits of the dispute itself.[1]

[1] HC SC E, 9 March 1999, col 290.

5.23   *Unfair dismissal*

5.23 Schedule 5 amends the 1992 Act so as to apply the concept of 'protected industrial action'. If an employee is dismissed as a result of taking part in such action the dismissal will be unfair if the employer fails to show that proper attempts were made to resolve the dispute. Schedule 5, para 3 inserts a new s 238A into the 1992 Act to provide that the dismissal will be unfair in certain circumstances as follows—

(a) where the dismissal takes place within the period of eight weeks beginning with the day on which the action commenced (s 238A(3)),

(b) if it takes place after that eight week period but the employee had previously stopped taking action within the eight week period (s 238A(4)),

(c) if the employee had continued taking action after the eight week period but the employer had not taken 'such procedural steps as would have been reasonable for the purposes of resolving the dispute' before electing to dismiss (s 238A(5)).

5.24 The government was keen to ensure that specific guidance should be given to employment tribunals on what procedural steps will be considered as reasonable,[1] and these steps are set out in the 1992 Act, s 238A(6), as inserted by the 1999 Act, Sch 5, para 3. The employer will be expected to comply with any dispute resolution procedures established by collective agreement, to have made offers to enter into negotiations and not to have unreasonably refused to enter into conciliation or mediation procedures.

---

[1]   HC SC E, 9 March 1999, col 289.

5.25 The government's declared intention that the merits of the dispute shall not be considered by the tribunal is now embodied in the 1992 Act, s 238(7), as inserted by the 1999 Act, Sch 5, para 3. It follows that, as was stated by the Minister in the House of Commons, the 'test of fairness is whether an employer has taken all reasonable procedural steps to resolve the dispute.'[1]

---

[1]   HC SC E, 9 March 1999, col 333.

5.26 Important procedural matters are also dealt with by the amendments contained in the 1999 Act, Sch 5. These include provisions to ensure that reinstatement or re-engagement orders cannot be made during the currency of the dispute and a general encouragement of the use of pre-hearing reviews to express initial opinions as to the merits of any claims to facilitate negotiation between the parties.[1]

---

[1]   HC SC E, 9 March 1999, col 290.

OTHER CHANGES TO THE LAW OF UNFAIR DISMISSAL

5.27 The 1999 Act also incorporates further substantive changes to the law of unfair dismissal, which are considered in detail elsewhere in this book. These measures relate to dismissal in relation to trade union recognition (Sch 1); dismissal in relation to trade union blacklists (s 3); interim relief in relation to trade union recognition dismissals (s 6); dismissal in relation to disciplinary and grievance hearings and representation (s 12); and dismissal in relation to collective agreements (s 17).[1]

---

[1]   See paras 2.30, 4.13, 2.30, 7.14, 4.10 respectively.

6 Maternity rights, parental leave and time off for dependants

INTRODUCTION

6.1 The government has placed considerable emphasis on 'family friendly policies'.[1] Maternity leave has been a statutory right since the Employment Protection Act 1975, but has steadily grown in complexity, with amendments in the 1980s, the interaction with statutory maternity pay and the addition of the 'basic' maternity leave provision (for 14 weeks) required by the Pregnant Workers Directive (92/85/EEC). Two principal criticisms prior to the 1999 Act were the complexity of the resulting accretion of rules, time scales and obligatory notices, and the harsh results of failure to comply with these technicalities, often involving complete loss of rights. The government's aim was to simplify these provisions and to lessen the harsh results for both employer and employee. The initiative for doing so arose from the obligation to implement the Parental Leave Directive (96/34/EC), which requires member states to enact legislation giving rights to both spouses ensuring a minimum level of unpaid time off work for childcare purposes, and a basic, residual right to unpaid time off work for what have loosely been referred to as 'domestic emergencies'. This has been achieved in the 1999 Act by giving regulation-making powers to the Secretary of State (even in areas such as the major maternity rights which were previously contained in the primary legislation). At the time of writing, the government had issued a public consultation document 'Parental and Maternity Leave' (URN/99/1043), which provides initial thoughts on this area.[2] The document states that draft regulations are due to be produced at the beginning of September 1999. When these are put into final form and passed by Parliament, they will be available on this book's associated website.[3]

---

[1] See the White Paper 'Fairness at Work', Cm 3968, Ch 5.
[2] See para 6.5.
[3] See http://www.butterworths.co.uk/content/products/publications.

MATERNITY LEAVE

The background

6.2 The reforms to maternity leave are to be implemented entirely by secondary legislation.[1] The regulations will however be subject to the positive resolution procedure.[2] It will be a distinct advantage to have all the maternity provisions (except those relating to statutory maternity pay) in one place; in the past, they developed 'piecemeal' and with a level of complexity which, the White Paper noted, has been criticised by 'employers, employees, the judiciary and the House of Commons Employment Committee'.[3] The principal aims stated in the White Paper were—
  (a) simplification of the system, to produce more internal coherence between the maternity provisions, and also consistency with the two new rights to parental leave and time off for domestic emergencies;

6.2 Maternity rights, parental leave and time off for dependants

(b) extension of what is to be called 'ordinary maternity leave' (the day-one right) from 14 weeks to 18 weeks (to rationalise it with statutory maternity pay);
(c) streamlining of the notice-giving requirements;
(d) lowering the qualifying period for what is to be known as 'additional maternity leave' (the original 1975 right to 'return to work') from two years to one year (to bring it into line with the new parental leave right);
(e) to set out in legislation what is to happen to the contract of employment during additional maternity leave.

---

[1] Previously the legislation was contained in the Employment Rights Act 1996, Pt VIII.
[2] HC SC E, 25 February 1999, col 148. This is achieved through the amendment of the Employment Rights Act 1996, s 236 (orders and regulations), by the 1999 Act, Sch 4, para 42.
[3] Cm 3968, para 5.13.

The contract of employment

6.3 The issue of the contract of employment (sub-para (e) above) has been particularly troublesome. The right to return to work, as stated in the Employment Protection Act 1975, was specifically drafted so as not to rely on the uncertainties of common law contract principles. The statutory scheme was enacted with definite statutory 'trigger' requirements (for example the various notices that the employee had to provide to the employer). When these were viewed as over-complex and harsh (eg the penalty for failure to comply being total loss of the right to return), lawyers argued for a 'contractual' right to return, paralleling statutory guidelines, where it was arguable that the absent employee's contract actually subsisted. This was clearly inconsistent with the original statutory scheme which sought to avoid the influence of common law principles. The position became even more complex in 1993 when the new, 'basic' maternity leave right stated that (for the purposes of *this* right) the contract was deemed to subsist. Rationalisation of the position between the contract of employment and the statutory scheme is highly desireable.

ORDINARY MATERNITY LEAVE

6.4 The 1999 Act, Sch 4, Pt I substitutes the Employment Rights Act 1996, Pt VIII, Ch I (ss 71–75), entitled 'Maternity Leave'. Much of it repeats the existing provisions (and the Parliamentary debates on this part of the Act were not particularly illuminating), though in a manner that is far more reliant on the use of regulatory powers. The new s 71 sets out the right to 'ordinary maternity leave'; the conditions for and length of this are to be prescribed in regulations, but a minimum length of 18 weeks is provided, and the regulations may allow the employee to choose the start date (subject to any prescribed restrictions) (s 71(1), (2)). An employee who exercises this right is—

(a) entitled to the benefit of the terms and conditions of employment which would have applied if she had not been absent,
(b) bound by any obligations arising under those terms and conditions (except in so far as they are inconsistent with the right to leave), and
(c) entitled to return from leave to the job in which she was employed before her absence (s 71(4)).

'Terms and conditions of employment' are defined as including matters connected with an employee's employment whether or not they arise under her contract of employment, but it does not include terms or conditions about remuneration (s 71(5)). Regulations may define what matters are, or are not, to be treated as remuneration for these purposes (a potentially useful clarification) (s 71(6)). The employee has a right to return to her previous job with her seniority, pension rights and similar rights as they would have been if she had not been absent,[1] ie the period off work counts for these purposes, the contract is not merely suspended. In addition she must return on terms and conditions no less favourable than those which would have applied if she had not been absent (s 71(7)). This last point could cause problems if, for example, there had been a disadvantageous change to the terms and conditions of her fellow employees on similar contracts during her absence. It would be a question of fact whether her contract had also changed, depending on such factors as whether she was bound contractually by any new collective agreement or whether she was on an individual contract requiring her personal assent to any variation in terms.

[1] Subject to the provisions of the Social Security Act 1989, Sch 5, para 5, on equal treatment under pension schemes, which has its own maternity provisions, see *Harvey on Industrial Relations and Employment Law* Q [212].

COMPULSORY MATERNITY LEAVE

6.5 Compulsory maternity leave (of two weeks after the day of childbirth) was also introduced in 1993 along with ordinary maternity leave (in order to comply with the Pregnant Workers Directive (92/85/EEC). This is now contained in the 1996 Act, s 72 (as substituted) which states that an employer shall not permit an employee who satisfies prescribed conditions to work during a compulsory maternity leave period (itself to be defined in regulations, but to be not less than two weeks, and to fall within an ordinary maternity leave period) (s 72(1)–(3)). Although this re-enacts similar wording, concern arose on this point from the Opposition in committee in the House of Commons, centring on the word 'permit', which clearly places an obligation of enforcement of this requirement on the employer. This concern was increased by the fact that an employer permitting work[1] during this period is subject to criminal prosecution under the Health and Safety at Work Act 1974, though with the substitution of a lower level of penalty (a fine not exceeding level 2 on the standard scale, on summary conviction (s 72(4), (5)). However, a proposed amendment to substitute the phrase 'an employer shall not *require* an employee to work' (thus only covering a positive breach by the employer) was not accepted.[2]

[1] The definition of 'work' could be problematic. Would an employer breach this provision by phoning the employee at home during this period to ask where a filing cabinet key was kept?
[2] HC SC E, 23 February 1998, cols 50–68.

ADDITIONAL MATERNITY LEAVE

6.6 The longer-term maternity leave (the original 'right to return' up to 29 weeks after childbirth) is now termed 'additional maternity leave' and is dealt with in the

6.6 *Maternity rights, parental leave and time off for dependants*

1996 Act, s 73 (as substituted). The details, as to qualifying conditions, calculation of period and the right for the employee to choose the start date are to be prescribed by regulations (s 73(1)–(3)); note, however, the intention to fix the qualifying period at one year's continuous employment (the previous period was two years) (see para 6.2). The remainder of s 73 follows the scheme of the provisions on ordinary maternity leave (see para 6.4), for improved consistency of approach. Section 73(4) states that an employee exercising the right to additional maternity leave is—

    (a) entitled to the benefit of the terms and conditions of employment[1] which would have applied is she had not been absent (for such purposes and to such extent as may be prescribed),

    (b) bound by obligations arising under those terms and conditions (for such purposes and to such extent as may be prescribed), except in so far as they are inconsistent with the right to leave, and

    (c) entitled to *return* from leave to a job of a prescribed kind.

The outline structure of this right is similar to that of ordinary maternity leave, but more of the detail is to be set out in future regulations. In addition questions relating to seniority, pensions and similar rights and also to terms and conditions of employment on return are left to regulations (s 73(7)).

---

[1] 'Terms and conditions of employment' include matters connected with an employee's employment whether or not they arise under her contract, but it does not include terms and conditions about remuneration (s 73(5)). Regulations may define what matters are, or are not, to be treated as remuneration for these purposes (s 73(6)).

REDUNDANCY AND DISMISSAL, SUPPLEMENTAL

6.7 Regulations may be made, relating to both ordinary and additional maternity leave, covering questions of redundancy during the relevant period and dismissal other than by reason of redundancy (s 74(7)). In relation to both maternity leave and the compulsory element, a wide power is given to make consequential provisions, in particular relating to the notices that are to be given (s 75).

THE CONSULTATION DOCUMENT

6.8 The regime proposed in the consultation document[1] is as follows.

---

[1] Parental and Maternity Leave (URN 99/1043, August 1999).

Procedural steps

(i) Starting ordinary and additional maternity leave

6.9 An employee would be required to inform her employer (at least 21 days before she wished to start maternity leave, or as soon as reasonably practicable) that she is pregnant, the expected week of childbirth (with a medical certificate if the employer requests it), and when she wishes to start leave (in writing if the employer requests it).

(ii) Returning to work

6.10 Ordinary maternity leave ends automatically after 18 weeks, so there will be no need for return notification. Additional maternity leave depends on the actual date of childbirth (finishing 29 weeks after that), in which case there would be a requirement on the employee to notify the employer of the date of birth. If that were not done, the employer could write to her (no earlier than 21 days before the end of ordinary maternity leave) asking her to confirm the date of birth and her intention to return to work. The employee must then respond within 21 days, and the employer would then confirm the last possible date for return.

(iii) Early return

6.11 An employee could return early (from either type of leave) by giving 21 days' notification in writing of her intended return date (failure to do so would permit the employer to postpone her return for 21 days).

(iv) Postponement of return

6.12 There would be no further postponement powers on either side. The previous provisions allowing an ill employee a one-off four week postponement of return date would no longer be necessary because an employee still ill at the return date would simply be deemed to return subject to the firm's normal sick leave procedures. In so providing, the consultation document takes up the views of the Court of Appeal in their ground-breaking decisions in *Crees v Royal London Mutual Insurance Society Ltd*[1] and *Halfpenny v IGE Medical Systems Ltd*[2] reinterpreting the maternity provisions so that the employee still ill at the date of return did not lose her rights, but instead should be deemed to have returned to work but immediately taken sick leave. One refinement of this under EC law is that the employer's ordinary illness/sickness absence rules should not count in any illness absence while the employee was pregnant: *Brown v Rentokil Ltd*.[3]

---

[1] [1998] ICR 848, [1998] IRLR 245.
[2] [1999] IRLR 177.
[3] C-394/96 [1998] IRLR 445, ECJ.

(v) Penalty for failure to comply with notice requirements

6.13 Instead of the previous draconian penalty for not giving the proper notices (loss of the right altogether), the proposal in the consultation document is that failure to give the required notifications for the start of maternity leave would lead to a 21 day delay of the start, and that failure to give any of the other notifications would be treated as an ordinary disciplinary matter by the employer. It was primarily the harshness of the previous rule which removed maternity leave rights completely where proper notification was not given (even where such failure was technical) that was most heavily criticised (see particularly the trenchant remarks of Browne-Wilkinson P in *Lavery v Plessey Telecommunications Ltd*,[1] which were endorsed by the Court of Appeal[2]), and led to more and more inventive arguments trying to erect a contractual right to return due to the argued continuing existence of the contract, as for example in *Lewis Woolf Griptight Ltd v Corfield*.[3] It is hoped that the proposed new regime will

6.13 Maternity rights, parental leave and time off for dependants

render such arguments otiose and that it will be possible to return to what was initially intended, namely a statutory maternity scheme operating on its own terms and in an entirely self-contained manner.

[1]   [1983] IRLR 180, EAT, at 182.
[2]   [1983] IRLR 202.
[3]   [1997] IRLR 432, EAT.

(vi)   Contract of employment and remuneration

6.14   The contract of employment would be deemed to continue throughout both ordinary *and* additional maternity leave, unless ended by either party or expiring. During ordinary maternity leave it would continue for the purposes of all terms and conditions other than those relating to remuneration, ie monetary wages or salary. More restrictively and perhaps controversially, during additional maternity leave the only terms of the contract continuing to apply would be the employer's obligations of trust and confidence[1] and the employee's obligation of good faith.[2]

[1]   The implied term of trust and respect in all contracts of employment evolved over many years as an essential adjunct to the law of constructive dismissal, and was finally given the approval of the House of Lords in *Malik v BCCI SA (in liq)* [1997] ICR 606, [1997] IRLR 462.
[2]   This approach of preserving accruing rights during the ordinary maternity leave (required by the Pregnant Workers Directive, 92/85/EC: see para 6.5) but not during the extra period of the additional maternity was held by the ECJ (in the context of a contractual maternity scheme used widely in the public sector) *not* to infringe the Pregnant Workers Directive or the Equal Treatment Directive 76/207/EEC: *Boyle v Equal Opportunities Commission* C-411/96 [1999] ICR 360, [1998] IRLR 717.

Maternity leave plan

6.15   The other interesting development in the consultation document is the proposal to have a pro forma 'Maternity leave plan' which sums up the procedure and the notices to be given. The parties would not have to use this, but it could be very useful. Its potential use was one of the matters on which the government sought comments, along with other key elements of the proposed scheme such as the relevant notifications, the penalties for failure to give them, and the proposals on continuation of contracts. As stated in para 6.1 above, it will be essential for the reader to consult the associated website for this book,[1] to check the final form of the regulations on these vital matters.

[1]   See http://www.butterworths.co.uk/content/products/publications.

PARENTAL LEAVE

The Parental Leave Directive

6.16   Council Directive 96/34/EC adopts the framework agreement reached by the social partners (UNICE, CEEP, and ETUC) on parental leave.[1] Its aim is to lay down 'minimum requirements designed to facilitate the reconciliation of parental and professional responsibilities for working parents.' Clause 2 of the agreement grants to men and women workers an individual, non-transferable,[2] right to (unpaid) parental leave on the grounds of the birth or adoption of a child to enable them to take care of that child, for at least three months, until a given age up to eight years old. Most matters of implementation are left up to member states and/or management and labour, in particular in deciding in what time blocks leave may be taken, whether there should be a service qualification (maximum one year), how it is to apply to adoption, what administrative arrangements are to apply, whether and if so how an employer can defer a request, and to take into account any particular requirements of small firms. Employment protection must be provided for those taking parental leave, and the employee has a right to return to the same job or, if that is not possible, to an equivalent or similar job. Acquired rights are preserved and are to revive at the end of the leave, but it is left to member states to determine what is to happen to the contract of employment and any social security entitlements during the leave. The White Paper welcomed these developments,[3] and envisaged linking as many of them as possible into the reformed rules for maternity leave (see paras 6.4–6.15).

---

[1] The Directive is set out in *Harvey on Industrial Relations and Employment Law* P [516].
[2] Non-transferability was thought important in order to encourage greater participation of men and women in child rearing, and to avoid the position of the man simply transferring his entitlement to the woman.
[3] Cm 3968, paras 5.11 ff.

Entitlement to and rights concerning parental leave

6.17 The 1999 Act, Sch 4, Pt I substitutes the Employment Rights Act 1996, Pt VIII, Ch II (ss 76–80) entitled 'Parental Leave'. Except in relation to enforcement (s 80), it operates entirely by conferring regulation-making powers on the Secretary of State. Under s 76 he may make regulations entitling an employee who satisfies specified conditions (as to duration of employment and as to having, or expecting to have, responsibilities for a child) to be absent from work on parental leave for the purpose of caring for a child. In committee in the House of Commons, the Minister for Employment accepted that the concept of 'responsibility for a child' was likely to be a difficult one, for example in relation to absent parents and foster parents, and could only state that these were important matters for consultation, which was promised in full.[1] The deletion of the phrase 'expecting to have' was also proposed in committee, but it was eventually retained because of the importance for fathers to have the right to take time off work at the time of the birth.[2] The regulations are to provide for the length of the leave (with a minimum of three months) and when it may be taken (either in relation to the child's age or a specified period of time from a specified event, eg, adoption). Specific regulatory powers cover questions such as whether, and if so when, the leave is to be taken, either in one continuous period or in separate periods. They will also determine what are and are not things done for the purpose of caring for a child, and also when an employer is to be able to postpone requested leave. Section 77 requires regulations to provide for—
    (a) the extent to which the person taking leave is to retain the benefit of terms and conditions of employment (other than remuneration, which may be defined) which would have applied if they had not been absent,
    (b) the extent to which the employee remains bound by the obligations under the contract of employment, and

6.17 Maternity rights, parental leave and time off for dependants

(c) the employee to return from leave to a job of such kind as may be specified (with regulations making further provision as to seniority, pension rights and similar rights, and terms and conditions of employment on return).

---

[1] HC SC E, 23 February 1999, col 97 (Ian McCartney).
[2] HC SC E, 23 February 1999, cols 81, 96.

Special cases, supplemental

6.18 Sections 78 and 79 provide for regulation-making powers in relation to 'special cases' such as—

(a) redundancy and other dismissals during leave,
(b) whether any leave can be taken in the form of modified hours under the contract,
(c) transfer of rights to another employee,
(d) the ability to conclude collective or workforce agreements containing alternative forms of parental leave,[1]
(e) notices to be given (and consequences of failure),
(f) record keeping, and
(g) how contractual parental leave schemes are to be dealt with.

Remedies are set out in s 80. An employee may present a claim to an employment tribunal that the employer has unreasonably postponed a period of parental leave requested or has prevented or attempted to prevent the taking of such leave.[2] If the complaint is upheld the tribunal is to make a declaration to that effect and may award such compensation as it considers just and equitable. It should take account of the employer's behaviour and any loss sustained by the employee which is attributable to the matters complained of (s 80(3), (4)).

---

[1] This was viewed by the government as an important way of ensuring desirable flexibility in the application of the Directive's requirements: HL Official Report, 8 July 1999, col 1079 (Lord Sainsbury of Turville).
[2] The time limit applies of three months for the complaint to be presented starting from the date (or last date) of the matters complained of, or within such further period as the tribunal considers reasonable in a case where it is satisfied that it was not reasonably practicable for the complaint to be presented in that time (s 80(2)). The well-established case law on the unfair dismissal time limit (Employment Rights Act 1996, s 111(2) from which this formulation is taken) would apply; see *Harvey on Industrial Relations and Employment Law* Q [735] and T [186].

The Consultation Document

6.19 The consultation document[1] stresses that parental leave should be introduced in as flexible a manner as possible. It emphasises that the parties themselves should come to an agreement on how parental leave should operate. A parental leave scheme can be contained in a collective or workforce agreement (to be defined). This will outline the employee's rights, provided it does not reduce the basic rights granted by the legislation and is given force by being lawfully incorporated into the individual employee's contract of employment. In default of such agreement, the employee's rights will be set out in a 'model scheme' to be set out in the regulations. This will apply to an employee with a minimum of one year's continuous employment who—

(a) is the parent (named on the birth certificate) of a child born after 15 December 1999 who is under five years old,[2] or
(b) has adopted, after 15 December 1999, a child under the age of 18,[3] or
(c) has acquired formal parental responsibility for a child born after 15 December 1999 who is under five years old.

---

[1] Parental and Maternity Leave (URN 99/1043, August 1999).
[2] The proposal is to restrict it to the first five years (ie up to normal school age); the Directive allows up to eight years. The purpose of the leave is to look after the child or to make arrangements for the good of the child; it need not be related to the child's health, and indeed unforeseen health problems could qualify separately for emergency leave, see para 6.21.
[3] In this case, the right lasts for five years from the date on which the child is placed for adoption or until the child's 18th birthday, whichever is the sooner.

The scheme

6.20 The major elements of the proposed scheme are as follows—
(i) The entitlement will be to 13 weeks in total for each child (including children in multiple births), on a pro rata basis for those working part-time.
(ii) The employee will remain employed while on leave, but there will be *no* obligation for them to be paid, and the only contractual terms continuing to bind them will be the terms of good faith and confidentiality.
(iii) Leave will have to be taken in blocks of a week, with the possibility of providing for a maximum of four weeks in any year—views were particularly invited on this question.
(iv) The employee will have to give at least four weeks' notice or, if more than four weeks' leave is allowed in one block, twice the length of the leave requested.[1]
(v) The employer will be able to postpone leave where the needs of the business or the quality of the service so require, to an agreed later date but in any event for no more than six months.
(vi) No particular form of records will need to be kept, but note that an employee changing employer will have to requalify and will only be able to claim against the new employer the amount of the 13 weeks unclaimed against the previous employer.
(vii) The employee must be able to return to the old job or, if that is not possible, a job with the same or better status, terms and conditions. Seniority, etc, will be preserved as at the time of taking the leave; in a case of redundancy, the employee on leave will have to be treated as if still working.

It will be necessary for the reader to consult the associated website for this book[2] to check the eventual form of the regulations.

---

[1] This will not be possible where a father-to-be wants to arrange leave to cover the birth and period shortly thereafter, because the actual dates will not be known. In such a case, the proposal is that such leave should be available on giving the employer three months notice of the week in which the birth is expected; a similar regime would apply to adopting a child when the date of adoption is not known precisely. This form of leave would not be subject to postponement by the employer.
[2] See http://www.butterworths.co.uk/content/products/publications.

6.21   *Maternity rights, parental leave and time off for dependants*

TIME OFF FOR DEPENDANTS

The Parental Leave Directive

6.21   Council Directive 96/34/EC requires member states to have provisions for unpaid leave for what have been loosely termed 'domestic emergencies'. It specifies that member states and/or management and labour should take necessary measures to entitle workers to time off on grounds of *force majeur* for urgent family reasons in case of sickness or accident making the immediate presence of the worker indispensable. The Directive allows conditions of access and detailed rules for this right, and limits on the amount of time allowed per year and/or per case.

The debate in Parliament

6.22   This apparently simple requirement for unpaid leave caused considerable problems during the passage of the Bill. It was considered too brief to allow anything like a simple 'copy-out' technique (especially as *force majeur* is not defined in the Directive). The intention in the Bill as originally drafted was to implement the scheme through an extensive regulatory power regime, similar to that applying to maternity and parental leaves, with the ability to opt out or supplement by collective or workforce agreement. However, in the light of considerable criticism in both Houses of Parliament[1] the whole scheme was replaced at Report stage in the House of Lords with the scheme that was eventually enacted.[2] This takes the opposite form, laying down the right to unpaid leave relatively briefly and in principle, in the primary legislation itself, without including the ability to opt out or supplement by collective or workforce agreement.

---

[1]   Some of the criticism centred around employers' fears that any eventual regulations could be so broadly drafted ('gold-plating the Directive' in the current Parliamentary jargon) that employees could claim time off work to get their washing machine mended (a 'domestic incident'?).

[2]   HL Official Report, 8 July 1999, col 1083. The government stressed that under the new provisions the right to time off remained *unpaid*: ibid, col 1088.

Entitlement to time off

6.23   Schedule 4, Pt II of the 1999 Act inserts the Employment Rights Act 1996, ss 57A and 57B entitled 'Time off for dependants'[1] and 'Complaint to employment tribunal' respectively. Section 57A(1) states that 'an employee is entitled to be permitted by his employer to take a reasonable amount of time off during the employee's working hours in order to take action which is necessary—

   (a)   to provide assistance on an occasion when a dependant[2] falls ill,[3] gives birth or is injured or assaulted;
   (b)   to make arrangements for the provision of care for a dependant who is ill or injured;
   (c)   in consequence of the death of a dependant;
   (d)   because of the unexpected disruption or termination of arrangements for the care of a dependant;[4] or
   (e)   to deal with an incident which involves a child of the employee and which occurs unexpectedly in a period during which an educational establishment which the child attends is responsible for him.'

The employee must tell the employer the reason for the absence as soon as reasonably practicable and for how long he expects to be absent (s 57A(2)). The decision not to set a limit on the amount of time was a deliberate one, partly because as an emergency right it would be impractical, and partly because of the danger that any stated minimum might become viewed as an entitlement. It is envisaged by the government that in most cases, whatever the problem, one or two days will be the most needed to deal with the immediate issues and sort out longer-term arrangements if necessary.[5] It is not expected that the time off is itself to be part of those arrangements. The new section 57B allows an employee to present a complaint to an employment tribunal that his employer has unreasonably refused to permit him to take time off as required by section 57A.[6] On upholding such a complaint, the tribunal is to make a declaration to that effect and may award such compensation as it considers just and equitable, having regard to the employer's default in refusing to permit the time off and any loss sustained by the employee which is attributable to the matters complained of.

[1] Interestingly s 8, which enacts Sch 4, Pt II, is entitled 'Time off for domestic incidents', which was its original title in the Bill as first drafted, before the substitution of all the substantive provisions in the House of Lords. Presumably this was an oversight and should be ignored, since the phrase 'domestic incidents' appears nowhere in the new section 57A.
[2] 'Dependant' means the employee's spouse, child or parent, or a person who lives in the same household as the employee (other than as an employee, tenant, lodger or boarder) (s 57A(3)). For the purposes of points (a) and (b), it also includes any person who reasonably relies on the employee either for assistance on an occasion when the person falls ill or is injured or assaulted, or to make arrangements for the provision of care in the event of illness or injury (s 57A(4)).
[3] Illness or injury includes mental illness or injury (s 57A(6)).
[4] For the purposes of point (d), dependant includes any person who reasonably relies on the employee to make arrangements for the provision of care (s 57A(5)).
[5] HL Official Report, 8 July 1999, col 1085.
[6] The same time limit of three months applies from the date when the refusal occurred (*quaere* whether this means the date of the employer's refusal, or the date of the refused leave, if they are different; it probably means the former), or within such further period as the tribunal considers reasonable in a case where it is satisfied that it was not reasonably practicable for the complaint to be presented in that time (s 57B(2)). See para 6.18, note 2, above.

6.24 The right to take time off under s 57A is novel, with little guidance to be gained from the Directive it seeks to implement. It will need interpreting *de novo*, and to that end it is worth citing in full two passages from Lord Sainsbury of Turville in introducing the amended form of the right at Report stage in the House of Lords—

> 'These amendments will put the provision back on a proper footing and cut out the risk of abuse by those who may seek to take time off to deal with running repairs to the home. The statutory right will be limited to urgent cases of real need. The emergency must involve a dependant who is either a family member or someone who relies upon the employee for assistance in the particular circumstances. By 'family member' I mean a child, parent, husband, wife, partner or other household member, but not someone who is in the household because he or she is the employee, tenant, lodger or boarder of that employee. By 'someone who relies upon the employee for assistance' I mean an individual for whom the employee has primary caring responsibility or someone who is involved in a serious emergency where the employee is the only person who can help; for example, an elderly neighbour living alone who falls and breaks a leg.'[1]

> 'Let me spell out what the amendment is intended to cover. We intend the right to apply where a dependant becomes sick or has an accident, or is assaulted, including where the victim is distressed rather than physically injured. It provides for reasonable time off, if an employee

suffers a bereavement of a family member, to deal with the consequences of that bereavement, such as making funeral arrangements, as well as to take time off to attend the funeral.

Employees will be able also to take time off in the event of the unexpected absence of the carer, where the person is a dependant of the employee. So if the childminder or the nurse does not turn up, the employee will be able to sort things out without fearing reprisals at work.

Employees may have to take time off to attend to a problem arising at their children's school or during school hours—for example, if the child has been involved in a fight, where the child is distressed, or if the child has committed a serious misdemeanour which could lead to expulsion. Again, the provision will secure their right to do so.

A father will have the right to be on hand at the birth of his child. After the birth, the father may be able to take parental leave to care for his child—but that is a matter which we will leave for the time being to the parental leave consultation.

I hope everyone can agree that all these are sensible, limited circumstances in which every employee should be able to take a reasonable amount of time off if necessary in order to deal with the matter.'[2]

---

[1] HL Official Report, 8 July 1999, col 1084.
[2] Ibid, 8 July 1999, cols 1084, 1085.

EMPLOYMENT PROTECTION

6.25 To complete the reforms, the 1999 Act, Sch 4, Pt III enacts specific employment protection for those claiming the rights mentioned above, in two particular ways. The first is the insertion of the Employment Rights Act 1996, s 47C (by Sch 4, Pt III, para 8), giving an employee a right not to be subjected to any detriment (by any act or failure to act by his employer) for a prescribed reason relating to—

(a) pregnancy, childbirth or maternity,
(b) ordinary, compulsory or additional maternity leave,
(c) parental leave or
(d) time off under section 57A (dependants).1

The second is the substitution of the 1996 Act, s 99 (by Sch 4, Pt III, para 16). This section was originally entitled 'unfair dismissal: pregnancy and childbirth',[2] and is now entitled 'leave for family reasons'. Section 99 provides that it is automatically unfair to dismiss an employee if the reason or principal reason is of a prescribed kind or the dismissal takes place in prescribed circumstances. Regulations will be made in due course to prescribe various circumstances covering the same points (a) to (d) as in s 47C above. Once again, the reader will need to consult the associated website[3] for this book to check the details of those rights once the regulations are enacted.

---

[1] Complaint will lie to an employment tribunal in the normal way under the 1996 Act, s 48.
[2] Also, the 1996 Act, s 96 is repealed (by Sch 4, Pt III, para 13); this used to declare a refusal to permit return to work after childbirth to be a 'dismissal' for the purposes of unfair dismissal law, but given the simpler formulation of the new s 99, that became otiose.
[3] See http://www.butterworths.co.uk/content/products/publications.

7 Disciplinary matters

GENERAL

7.1 The right of a worker to be accompanied at grievance and disciplinary hearings was described by Lord Wedderburn of Charlton as 'the most practically important innovation' contained in the Bill.[1] Various versions of the ACAS Code of Practice 1 Disciplinary Practice and Procedures in Employment[2] have recommended that employees should have the right to be accompanied during grievance and disciplinary procedures by a trade union representative or by a fellow employee of their choice, however there was no statutory right to such representation. Although employment tribunals are technically under an obligation to consider the ACAS Code of Practice where relevant[3] there is no reported instance of such a tribunal concluding that a dismissal was unfair because of a lack of such representation, so long as the procedure as carried out was still essentially fair.

[1] HL 2R, 10 May 1999, col 1015.
[2] The most recent version was issued in 1997 replacing the previous 1977 version.
[3] See *Lock v Cardiff Rly Co Ltd* [1998] IRLR 358, EAT.

7.2 Developments in the common law have also had an impact in this area. In *W A Goold (Pearmak) Ltd v McConnell*,[1] for instance, the Employment Appeal Tribunal (EAT) placed considerable emphasis on the provision of adequate grievance procedures in the context of discrimination cases and indicated that it was an implied term of the contract of employment that the employer would take steps to ensure the prompt and adequate redress of grievances.

[1] [1995] IRLR 516.

7.3 Previously there was no statutory right to be accompanied at disciplinary and grievance hearings, although some statutory support for this right exists indirectly through the requirement on the employer to provide an employee with relevant details of his terms and conditions of employment. When complying with this duty the employer is required to include details of any relevant grievance and disciplinary procedures.[1]

[1] Employment Rights Act 1996, Pt I.

THE WHITE PAPER

7.4 The White Paper 'Fairness at Work' stressed the government's intention that the law should protect workers from intimidation and assist those who may have difficulties in representing themselves. A statutory right to be accompanied at both disciplinary and grievance hearings was proposed. Such a right would not create a concomitant obligation on the trade union, or other worker, to accompany their

7.4 Disciplinary matters

colleague unless they wished to do so. The White Paper also indicated the government's intention to introduce protection for those individuals who accompany the worker on such occasions.[1]

[1] Cm 3968, para 4.29.

7.5 These proposals were uncontroversial, all parties recognised the benefits for both sides of industry to be represented by competent assistance at such hearings. However concerns were expressed regarding the precise detail of the provisions and, in particular, the risk of unwarranted interference from outside individuals in an employer's business.

THE RIGHT TO BE ACCOMPANIED

7.6 The relevant provisions regarding the right to be accompanied are contained in the 1999 Act, ss 10–15. The general right to be accompanied is set out in the 1999 Act, s 10, and relates to both disciplinary and grievance hearings, which are defined in ss 13(4), (5). A disciplinary hearing is defined in s 13(4) as one which could result in the administration of a formal warning or the taking of some other action in respect of the worker, or the confirmation of such warning or action. It can be seen that this broad definition covers a wide range of disciplinary procedures and internal appeal hearings. A grievance hearing is defined in s 13(5) as 'a hearing which concerns the performance of a duty by an employer in relation to a worker.' The breadth of these definitions raised concern during the passage of the Bill about workers deliberately seeking representation at hearings when it was inappropriate to do so. The government countered these concerns by pointing out that the 1999 Act requires the request to be accompanied to be a 'reasonable' one (s 10(1)(b)).[1]

[1] HC SC E, 25 February 1999, col 156.

The nature of the right

7.7 The 1999 Act, s 10, entitles a worker who reasonably requests that he be accompanied at a relevant hearing to be accompanied by a single companion. That individual must be chosen by the worker himself and must fall within a group of specified individuals. These include full-time officials of trade unions, lay officials with appropriate experience and training, or another of the employer's workers (s 10(3)). These provisions attempt to reduce the risk of outside interference in the affairs of the employer by inappropriate individuals and to ensure an adequate standard of representation.[1]

[1] See HL Official Report, 8 July 1999, col 1096 and HL 3R, 15 July 1999, col 560.

The role of the companion

7.8 It is important to consider the distinction between a right to be represented and a right to be accompanied. Concerns regarding the nature of the role to be performed by the individual are addressed in the 1999 Act, s 10(2), which specifically states that the single companion must be permitted to address the hearing and to confer with the worker during the hearing but is not entitled to answer questions on behalf of the worker. These provisions reflect the statements made by the Minister of State for Trade and Industry, Ian McCartney, to the effect that the individual companion is there to 'advise and support' but not 'to intervene' between the worker and the employer.[1]

[1] HC SC E, 25 February 1999, col 164.

Code of practice

7.9 During the passage of the Bill through Parliament various attempts were made to expand the role of the worker's companion, for example, by specifically incorporating a right to take a contemporaneous note of any relevant meetings.[1] These were rejected by the government on the basis that further provisions regarding the role of the companion were best left to be dealt with in an amended ACAS Code of Practice.[2]

[1] HL Committee, 16 June 1999, col 322.
[2] Ibid, col 331.

Time for preparation

7.10 Amendments were also incorporated into the Bill to ensure that the worker and his companion should have sufficient time to prepare for any such hearing.[1] Accordingly s 10(4), (5) provides that the hearing should be postponed if the worker's chosen companion is not available, and he must be able to propose an alternative date and time which is reasonable. To be reasonable the date must fall before the end of the period of five working days beginning with the first working day after the day proposed by the employer.

[1] HC SC E, 25 February 1999, col 169.

Time off to accompany worker

7.11 Section 10(6) requires the employer to permit a worker to take time off during working hours for the purpose of accompanying another worker. The provisions relating to time off for carrying out trade union duties are also extended to apply to such circumstances (s 10(7)).

No obligation to accompany

7.12 It is important to note that Lord Simon of Highbury specifically reconfirmed the government's intention not to place an obligation on any body or individual to accompany a relevant worker if requested to do so.[1]

[1] HL Committee, 16 June 1999, col 330.

7.13   *Disciplinary matters*

Refusal to permit worker to be accompanied

7.13   If the employer fails, or threatens to refuse, to permit the worker to be accompanied at a disciplinary or grievance hearing the relevant worker may make a complaint to an employment tribunal in accordance with the 1999 Act, s 11. The complaint must be presented within the relevant three month time limit subject to the limited power of extension contained in the 1999 Act, s 11(2)(b). If the complaint is well founded the tribunal shall order the employer to pay compensation to the worker of an amount not exceeding two weeks' pay. This figure is to be calculated in accordance with the existing provisions contained in the Employment Rights Act 1996, Pt XIV, Ch II.

Detriment and dismissal

7.14   As stated at para 7.4 the government's concern was to ensure that workers who either request representation or who accompany their colleague to a relevant hearing are protected from intimidation. Such protection is now provided by the 1999 Act, s 12, which effectively mirrors the law on dismissals and detriment related to trade union membership and activities.[1]

---
[1]   See Ch 3 ibid.

SPECIAL PROVISIONS RELATING TO NATIONAL SECURITY

7.15   In view of the general extension of employment rights to workers in the national security services, specific concerns were raised regarding the right of such workers to be accompanied by trade union officials from outside the security services.[1] Accordingly the 1999 Act, s 15, excludes the right to be accompanied from individuals who are employed by the Security Service, the Secret Intelligence Service or Government Communications Headquarters. The reason behind these exclusions in the view of the government is that the subject matter of such hearings might be confidential and unsuitable for communication to outside individuals or other work colleagues.[2]

---
[1]   HL Official Report, 8 July 1999, col 1101.
[2]   Ibid.

8 Part-time worker protection and extension of employment status

INTRODUCTION

8.1 Entrenched within the larger 'fairness at work' agenda is the aim to protect workers from unfair forms of contracting, where employers have an economic advantage. Prior to and at the time of the 1997 election, some of the argument surrounding this centred on the increased use by employers of 'nil-hours contracts', where the employee is bound to be available for work but only paid when actually given work to do.[1] The White Paper 'Fairness at Work' questioned whether such contracts should be controlled or banned,[2] but in the event this seems to have been viewed as too difficult (given that employers might simply find other potential ways around the employment laws) and was as a result not enacted in the 1999 Act. Hopefully the National Minimum Wage Act 1998 and its implementing regulations counteract this particular abuse, particularly through the general inclusion of stand-by time in calculations to determine whether the legal minimum is being paid.[3] Instead of specific action on such forms of arguably unfair contracting, the 1999 Act concentrates on two other significant, but more indirect approaches. The first is the obligation in the UK to implement the Part-time Work Directive (97/81/EC); the second is the more radical idea to alter the whole basis on which existing employment law applies to individuals generally, by extending the definition of 'employment' itself to include more of those who are not at present covered.

---

[1] The highest profile example of this was provided by Burger King, in relation to an employee reported in the press as having received £1 for a five hour shift because of a lack of customers. They eventually discontinued the practice under media pressure and compensated the workers involved, paying out £160,000: Independent, 19 December 1995.

[2] Cm 3968, para 3.14. The Irish government approached the matter directly (due to a year-long dispute at Dublin's major department store, caused by a demand that staff transfer to nil-hours contracts), by adding complex provisions to the statute implementing the Working Time Directive (Organisation of Working Time Act 1997, s 18).

[3] National Minimum Wage Regulations 1999, SI 1999/584, reg 15; see also DTI Guide (URN 99/662) para 126.

DISCRIMINATION AGAINST PART-TIME WORKERS

8.2 The UK labour market has changed dramatically over the last two decades and what was considered to be typical employment is no longer so. However the term 'atypical employment' is now considered something of a misnomer. Part-time employment has become commonplace,[1] but has little recognition in standard employment law, so that there has until now been little to deter less favourable treatment of part-time workers. Any changes have come *indirectly*, through the application of sex discrimination law (national or EC). Since the majority of part-time workers are female, a case can usually be made out that to treat part-time workers less favourably is indirect sex discrimination, and thus illegal unless the treatment in question can be shown to be objectively justifiable. In early cases it was ruled that working part-time was not a 'genuine material difference' for the purposes of the

8.2   *Part-time worker protection and extension of employment status*

Equal Pay Act 1970. More recently such arguments have been instrumental in opening up occupational pension schemes to part-time workers and in requiring the removal of the statutory requirement (under both Labour and Conservative governments) that an employee had to work for 16 hours or more per week in order to qualify for employment rights. A strong framework has been in place for challenging unfair treatment of part-time workers, but this had to operate through discrimination law, under which the onus was heavily on the complainant. This position has been altered by the Part-time Work Directive, which the present government welcomed, and which will provide more direct channels for challenging unfair treatment.

[1] The 1998 Workplace Employee Relations Survey found that part-time workers (defined as those working less than 30 hours per week) accounted for a quarter of all jobs in workplaces with more than 25 employees (though with major variations between the various industrial sectors). While 16% of workplaces employed none, in 26% of workplaces they formed a majority of the workforce (up from 16% in the 1990 Survey).

THE PART-TIME WORK DIRECTIVE

8.3   The Part-time Work Directive (97/81/EC) was the result of a framework agreement reached by the social partners (UNICE, CEEP and ETUC), promulgated by the EU Council. The aims of the Directive are to remove discrimination against part-time work and to improve its quality, and to facilitate the development of part-time work on a voluntary basis thus contributing to the flexible organisation of working time, taking into account the needs of employers and workers.[1]

[1] Council Directive 97/81/EC, Annex (Framework Directive), clause 1.

Non-discrimination

8.4   The Directive applies to part-time workers[1] who have an employment contract or an employment relationship. There is a derogation allowing a member state (in consultation with the social partners) to exclude wholly or partly (for objective reasons) part-time workers 'who work on a casual basis' (clause 2(2)).[2] The Directive sets out the 'principle of non-discrimination' as follows—

'1. In respect of employment conditions, part-time workers shall not be treated in a less favourable manner than comparable full-time workers[3] solely because they work part-time unless different treatment is justified on objective grounds.

2. Where appropriate, the principle of *pro rata temporis* shall apply' (clause 4).[4]

Again there is a derogation (for objective reasons, having consulted the social partners) allowing a member state to make access to particular conditions of employment subject to a period of service, time worked or earnings qualification (clause 4(4)).

[1] Part-time worker means 'an employee whose normal hours of work, calculated on a weekly basis or on average over a period of employment of up to one year, are less than the normal hours of work of a comparable full-time worker' (see note 3, below) (clause 3). Note that this definition is comparative,

The part-time working directive 8.7

and not based on the sort of threshold of hours that an economist might use to denote 'real' part-time work (eg less than 30 hours per week).
2   'Casual basis' is not defined.
3   Comparable full-time worker means 'a full-time worker in the same establishment having the same type of employment contract or relationship, who is engaged in the same or a similar work/occupation, due regard being given to other considerations which may include seniority and qualification/skills' (clause 3(2)). The sub-clause then states that where there is no comparable full-time worker in the same establishment, the comparison is to be made by reference to 'the applicable collective agreement or, where there is no applicable collective agreement, in accordance with national law, collective agreements or practice'.
4   The use of the legal Latin is, of course, with apologies to Lord Woolf.

Opportunities for part-time work

8.5   The other major part of the Directive is entitled 'Opportunities for part-time work'. A general obligation is placed on member states and the social partners to identify and review obstacles which may limit opportunities for part-time work and, where appropriate, eliminate them (Council Directive 97/81/EC, annex (Framework Directive) (clause 5(1)).[1] In addition there are two substantive requirements. The first, potentially impacting on UK unfair dismissal law, is as follows—

'A worker's refusal to transfer from full-time to part-time work or vice-versa should not in itself constitute a valid reason for termination of employment, without prejudice to termination in accordance with national law, collective agreements and practice, for other reasons such as may arise from the operational requirements of the establishment concerned' (clause 5(2)).

8.6   The other substantive requirement is that, as far as possible, employers should give consideration to a number of factors. The first of these is 'requests by workers to transfer from full-time to part-time work that becomes available in the establishment' (clause 5(3)(a)). Previously, there has been no common law right to change from full-time to part-time, any such move being purely a question of agreement and contract, *except* in one case—where an employee returns from maternity leave and requests a transfer from her previous full-time work to a part-time basis it has been held that a refusal can constitute indirect sex discrimination, which then has to be objectively justified by the employer: see *Home Office v Holmes*.[1] However, this falls far short of a positive right, and it may be that justification by the employer will often be possible, as in *Greater Glasgow Health Board v Carey*.[2]

1   [1984] ICR 678, [1984] IRLR 299, EAT.
2   [1987] IRLR 484, EAT; see *Harvey on Industrial Relations and Employment Law* L[162].

8.7   The second factor for consideration is 'requests by workers to transfer from part-time to full-time work or to increase their working time should the opportunity arise' (clause 5(3)(b)). This interesting provision indirectly relates back to the 'purpose' clause in the Framework Agreement (clause 1, see para 8.3) which refers to facilitating 'the development of part-time work *on a voluntary basis*'. The question of how desireable part-time work is has been a controversial one for some time.[1]

1   Employment White Papers of the previous government used to stress its desirability for both parties, in promoting a flexible workforce and helping with family responsibilities, whilst a Labour Market Trends survey in 1996 showed that 37% of male part-time workers and 79% of female part-time workers did not want a full-time job.

45

8.8 Part-time worker protection and extension of employment status

8.8 The third factor for consideration is 'the provision of timely information on the availability of part-time and full-time positions in the establishment in order to facilitate transfers from full-time to part-time or vice versa' (clause 5(3)(c)). One important question is how far such a requirement will be interpreted as an obligation to offer available jobs on an internal basis first, before advertising outside the company. The possibility that such a practice could be considered indirectly discriminatory on grounds of race or sex[1] may cause problems—would this provision of the Directive amount to justification? Another problem may arise in an organisation with a policy of open competition for all posts, either as a matter of a choice or (as with a university) as a matter of legal obligation. In the public sector, there could be a conflict with the widely-applied 'Nolan' principles on openness in appointments, especially in the light of the reference in sub-clause 3(d) to 'skilled and managerial positions'.

[1] Through perpetuating the existing racial or sexual profile of the organisation.

8.9 Finally employers should consider 'measures to facilitate access to part-time work at all levels of the enterprise, including skilled and managerial positions. They should, where appropriate, facilitate access by part-time workers to vocational training to enhance career opportunities and occupational mobility' (clause 5(3)(d)) and provide for 'the provision of appropriate information to existing bodies representing workers about part-time working in the enterprise' (clause 5(3)(e)).

IMPLEMENTATION OF THE DIRECTIVE

8.10 The government have taken steps to implement the Directive in the 1999 Act, s 19. Although Directives are usually implemented by regulations made under the European Communities Act 1972, in this case primary legislation was considered necessary. The government wanted to go further than the Directive in one important matter and cover questions of pay as well as employment conditions.[1] Section 19(1) states that regulations are to be made to ensure that persons in part-time employment are treated, for specified purposes, no less favourably than persons in full-time employment. Section 19(2)–(5) sets out the specific purposes for which regulations may be made, namely to define part-time and full-time employees, to define less favourable treatment, to provide for civil and criminal enforcement and to provide for 'specified agreements to have effect in place of the provisions of the regulations to such extent and in such circumstances as may be specified'. The Directive contains a justification defence to discrimination against a part-time worker; this does not appear in the 1999 Act, but undertakings were given in committee in both the House of Commons and the House of Lords that the regulations are to contain provisions setting out such a defence.[2] In a general summary of the importance of the intended provisions, the Minister said that while surveys show little actual discrimination against part-time workers, it was advisable to have provisions in place to prevent it. He also pointed out that the law would be simplified; a part-time worker alleging discrimination would no longer have to go through the complicated process of trying to fit the complaint into the framework of sex discrimination law.[3]

[1] HC SC E, 2 March 1999, col 225; HL 2R, 10 May 1999, col 968.
[2] HC SC E, 2 March 1999, col 201; HL Committee, 16 June 1999, col 381.
[3] HC SC E, 2 March 1999, col 226.

Code of practice

8.11 In addition to regulations relating to part-time workers, the 1999 Act provides for the issuing of a code of practice by the Secretary of State 'for the purpose of—
  (a) eliminating discrimination in the field of employment against part-time workers;
  (b) facilitating the development of opportunities for part-time work;
  (c) facilitating the flexible organisation of working time taking into account the needs of workers and employers;
  (d) any matter dealt with in the framework agreement on part-time work annexed to Council Directive 97/81/EC' (s 20(1)).

The standard provisions are set out, stating that the code is not law in itself, but is admissible and to be considered in proceedings before an employment tribunal (s 20(3), (4)). The 1999 Act provides for consultation and the issuing of a draft code before eventual promulgation, which is to be by affirmative resolution of each House of Parliament (s 21). The Minister, in committee in the House of Commons, explained that the use of a Code of Practice would enable the government to implement the Directive without placing unnecessary restrictions on employers, especially as the advice and guidance to be given would not necessarily be restricted to matters required to be covered by the Directive.[1]

---
[1] HC SC E, 2 March 1999, col 231.

8.12 At the time of writing, the necessary regulations had not been drafted. The government did undertake, however, that there would be full consultation on both the regulations and the Code of Practice. When these are produced, readers will find them on the book's associated website.[1]

---
[1] See http://www.butterworths.co.uk/content/products/publications.

EXTENSION OF EMPLOYMENT STATUS

Definition of employment

8.13 As discussed at para 8.1, the government are trying to tackle unfair forms of contracting in the employment sphere through indirect measures such as the national minimum wage and limits on working time. In addition, they have taken powers under the 1999 Act to extend some or all of the existing employment legislation to classes of worker who at present fall, or may fall, outside the classic statutory definition of employment. The problem with this definition is that it has always been linked inextricably to the existence of a contract of employment,[1] which itself has *not* been statutorily defined, and remains a common law concept. The idea that an individual must fall neatly into the category either of either (a) an employee under a contract of employment or (b) an independent contractor in business on his own account, has been under severe strain for the last three decades. In reality there is a spectrum (from simple wage-earning employee to ambitious entrepreneur) with the courts or tribunals having to draw a line somewhere along it, where acceptable ideas of what constitutes a contract of employment run out.[2]

8.13 Part-time worker protection and extension of employment status

[1] The Employment Rights Act 1996, s 230(1) simply states that an employee is 'an individual who has entered into or works under . . . a contract of employment'. Section 230(2) only defines the latter as 'a contract of service or apprenticeship, whether express or implied, and (if it is express) whether oral or in writing'.
[2] See *Harvey on Industrial Relations and Employment Law* A (1)(A) and Smith & Wood, Industrial Law (6th edn), pp 8–21.

8.14 The steady rise of what used to be called 'atypical employment' has added to an already complicated situation. It is important that the law should stay abreast of economic developments in order to avoid a 'two tier workforce', with a shrinking proportion of male employees on full-time contracts with full employment and retirement rights, contrasted with a growing number of female employees on a variety of atypical contracts, but with no employment rights. While in most cases the courts have a good track record on this matter, final judgments are unpredictable.[1] One problem is that once a court or tribunal determines that an individual is not an 'employee', it does not then have to determine what their status actually *is*.[2] In other words, the definition is basically an exclusory one. It may be that the individual was an independent contractor, but might fall into the 'black hole' between employment and self-employment, and it is arguable that the scope for this has been increasing in recent years.

[1] From the recent case law on this subject, contrast *Clark v Oxfordshire Health Authority* [1998] IRLR 125, CA (bank nurse working for one authority at three different hospitals held not to be an employee) with *Carmichael v National Power plc* [1998] IRLR 301, CA (power station guides engaged on a 'casual, as required' basis held to be employees). There may also be problems with continuity of employment, as in *Booth v United States of America* [1999] IRLR 16, EAT where an employer was permitted to avoid statutory employment rights by deliberately and cynically breaking continuity in circumstances not actually covered by the anti-avoidance provisions in the legislation.
[2] For example, in *Clark v Oxfordshire Health Authority* (above), the bank nurse had been subject to PAYE and NI contributions, and yet was not an 'employee' for statutory purposes. She may have ended up as a curious hybrid, but for the purposes of her claim all that mattered was that she was held not to be an 'employee'.

Other definitions of employment

8.15 Discrimination legislation, designed to apply on the broadest possible front, has for long sought to avoid an over-technical approach by adopting for its purposes a wider definition of employment. The Sex Discrimination Act 1975, s 82 defines employment as—

'Employment under a contract of service or of apprenticeship *or a contract personally to execute any work or labour*' (emphasis added).

The Race Relations Act 1976, s 78, contains the same definition, and most of the trade union law provisions of the Trade Union and Labour Relations (Consolidation) Act 1992 adopt a similar (if slightly expanded) approach by using the term 'worker' (rather than 'employee'), defined as—

'an individual who works, or normally works or seeks to work—
(a) under a contract of employment, or
(b) under any other contract whereby he undertakes to do or perform personally any work or services for another party to the contract who is not a professional client of his . . .' (s 296).

Extension of employment status 8.16

When important new rights were introduced to prevent unauthorised deductions from wages by the Wages Act 1986, the term 'worker' was used, with a definition now incorporated in the Employment Rights Act 1996 (s 230(3)) (despite the fact that the rest of the 1996 Act only applies to 'employees'). The wording of the latter definition varies slightly, referring to the other party to the contract 'whose status is not by virtue of the contract that of a client or customer of any profession or business undertaking carried on by the individual'. All of these definitions include a reference to *personal* work, which, interestingly, the Court of Appeal recently stressed in relation to the existence of a contract of employment, in the negative sense that if there is no requirement that the work be done personally (eg if the individual can delegate freely to others, and only has the responsibility of ensuring that the work is done), that fact will be a powerful argument against the existence of a contract of employment.[1] Significantly, most of the government's recent employment legislation adopts similarly wide definitions of employment. The National Minimum Wage Act 1998 applies to 'workers' using a similar definition to that used in the Wages Act 1986 (now incorporated in the Employment Rights Act 1996, Pt II), as do the Working Time Regulations 1998, SI 1998/1833. The Public Interest Disclosure Act 1998 also uses the term 'worker' as defined in the Employment Rights Act 1996.[2]

---

[1] *Express and Echo Publications Ltd v Tanton* [1999] IRLR 367, CA.
[2] Public Interest Disclosure Act 1998 s 1, inserting the Employment Rights Act 1996, ss 43A–43L, which uses the definition of 'worker' as contained in s 230(3) of the 1996 Act, subject to further specific extensions in s 43K.

8.16 The adoption of an expanded definition of employment will not solve all problems; case law on these definitions is very underdeveloped[1] and lines will still have to be drawn somewhere along the spectrum. However, the important point is that the line is probably to be drawn towards the end of the spectrum labelled 'independent contractor', thus giving employment protection coverage to many more atypicals who are currently in danger of falling into a black hole in the middle. Significantly, the question 'Are you *genuinely* self-employed?' is used frequently throughout the DTI guidance on both the national minimum wage and the Working Time Regulations. The assumption is that only if someone is 'genuinely' self-employed will they *not* qualify for the right in question. This was echoed in the debates in Parliament on the 1999 Act. One could argue at this point that, at least from the standpoint of legal certainty, a new test based on the criteria of being 'genuinely self-employed' is just as vague as the classic test of whether there is or is not a contract of employment. However, the question of *emphasis* could be important, because arguably the wider definition used in the legislation (discussed at para 8.14) places a strong emphasis on including an individual in the statutory protection *unless* it is established (in many cases by the employer in practice) that the individual was genuinely self-employed. These definitions are therefore basically *inclusory*, with the benefit of any doubt being given to the individual claiming statutory protection.

---

[1] For the case law, such as it is (some going back to the Industrial Relations Act 1971) see *Harvey on Industrial Relations and Employment Law* Q [79], [156], [538] and [854]. A key case is *Mirror Group Newspapers Ltd v Gunning* [1986] ICR 145, [1986] IRLR 27, CA (under the Sex Discrimination Act 1975) where it was held that the test was whether the dominant purpose of the contract is that the party contracting to provide services is to perform personally the work or labour forming the substance of the contract; on the facts this was held not to be so in the case of a newspaper distributor whose function was to ensure the regular and efficient distribution of newspapers, not necessarily to be personally involved in that operation. This authority was applied recently by the EAT in *Sheehan v Post*

8.16 *Part-time worker protection and extension of employment status*

Office Counters Ltd [1999] ICR 734 in holding that a sub-postmaster was not an 'employee' under the Disability Discrimination Act 1995, s 68, which uses the same definition as that in the Sex Discrimination Act 1975, s 82.

STATUTORY POWERS TO MAKE REGULATIONS

8.17 The White Paper stated the government's intention to consult on the idea that 'some or all existing employment rights' should be extended by regulations, in the same way as the national minimum wage legislation and the Working Time Regulations.[1] Despite opposition from employers, worried about the potentially damaging effects on contractors and freelance workers,[2] the 1999 Act contains a wide-ranging enabling power in s 23. This permits the Secretary of State by order (subject to positive resolution of each House of Parliament)[3] to confer on individuals of a specified description any rights contained in the 1992 Act, the Employment Rights Act 1996, the 1999 Act itself or any instrument made under the European Communities Act 1972, s 2(2) (s 23(1), (2)). There are wide subsidiary powers to alter definitions or to modify any rights in question, and to make consequential, incidental or supplementary provisions (s 23(4)).[4] The breadth of this power was, not surprisingly, the subject of adverse comment at Committee stage in the House of Commons (though a surprising amount of discussion concerned the employment status of the clergy!), but the government were intent on keeping it broad (not even tying it to the present, wider definitions in the existing legislation), candidly accepting that they had not decided how they would exercise it. The Minister for Small Firms, Trade and Industry gave—

> 'an unqualified assurance that the Government have no intention of using the new power in [section 23] to extend employment rights to individuals who are genuinely self employed or who are excluded from their coverage for perfectly sound or logical reasons.'[5]

Moreover, a hint was given that the eventual approach may be differential and pragmatic—

> 'While the Government certainly want to rationalise the coverage of employment rights as far as possible, we also recognise that it may still sometimes be appropriate for different definitions of 'worker' to be used for different purposes, depending on the substance of the right in question.'[6]

There is clearly much more thought and consultation to be given to the eventual exercise of this power. At the time of writing, we seem to be some time from detailed regulations. When these are eventually passed, they will be available to readers on the book's associated website.[7]

---

1   Cm 3968, para 3.18.
2   House of Commons Research Paper 98/99, 17 November 1998 'Fairness at Work', at p 31.
3   Employment Relations Act 1999, s 42.
4   There is a wide power to amend existing Acts or instruments for these purposes (s 23(5)).
5   HC SC E, 2 March 1999, col 236.
6   Ibid, col 237.
7   See http://www.butterworths.co.uk/content/products/publications.

AMENDMENT OF THE NATIONAL MINIMUM WAGE ACT 1998

8.18 A miscellaneous amendment was included in the Bill at a late stage, in the House of Lords at Report stage, to exclude from the national minimum wage residential members of charitable religious establishments.[1] A wider amendment put forward by the Opposition to establish a general exemption for disabled people was opposed by the government and not proceeded with.[2]

---

[1] Employment Relations Act 1999, s 22, inserting the National Minimum Wage Act 1998, s 44A.
[2] HL Official Report, 8 July 1999, cols 1118–1119.

9 Reforms to statutory bodies

THE CENTRAL ARBITRATION COMMITTEE

9.1 The Central Arbitration Committee (CAC) was established by the Employment Protection Act 1975, as the successor to the Industrial Court and the subsequent Industrial Arbitration Board. It is a standing arbitration board which used to have a wide jurisdiction under the Labour government of the 1970s, in particular in enforcing certain forms of fair wages legislation. It was also intended to be used as a voluntary arbitration body and to enforce the law on the disclosure of bargaining information.[1] However, both statutory intervention in wage fixing and arbitration in general were viewed with deep disfavour during the Conservative governments of 1979–1997, and much of its jurisdiction was either repealed or fell into abeyance, leaving only its involvement with bargaining information and the occasional arbitration.[2] Now, however, it is facing at least a partial resurrection, not only because of its pivotal role in any case invoking the new statutory recognition procedure, but also because it is being suggested that it should have jurisdiction in the new laws necessary to enact the European Works Council Directive (94/45/EC) in the UK.[3] Attention has therefore been focused on this long-dormant body, and in particular on its composition (given the potentially sensitive nature of some of its decisions under the recognition procedure).

---

[1] Disclosure of bargaining information is governed by the Trade Union and Labour Relations (Consolidation) Act 1992, ss 181–185.

[2] At its busiest in 1978 the CAC received 1,065 references and issued 836 awards. In 1997 it received only 22 references (all on disclosure of bargaining information), resolving 19 of them informally and issuing no awards: CAC Report 1997.

[3] This suggestion was put forward by the government in their consultative document 'Implementation in the UK of the European Works Council Directive' (URN 99/926, July 1999).

Changes to composition

9.2 In the past, the chairman of the CAC and any deputy chairmen were appointed by the Secretary of State after consultation with ACAS, and members were appointed by him from persons nominated by ACAS. The 1999 Act, s 24, substitutes the Trade Union and Labour Relations (Consolidation) Act 1992 ('the 1992 Act'), s 260(1)–(3A), in order to leave the choice of appointments solely to the Secretary of State. The only provisos are that those appointed must have experience in industrial relations (some as representatives of employers and some as representatives of workers), and before making an appointment the Secretary of State must consult ACAS (and may consult other persons). The purpose of this change was explained by the Minister for Small Firms, Trade and Industry partly as being a means of widening the membership (the previous practice having been for ACAS to nominate from its own panel of arbitrators), and partly as being a way of adhering more closely to the now-pervasive 'Nolan' principles on public appointments.[1] Apart from being potentially more controversial than it has been for many years, the CAC may now have to be expanded and the Minister stated that any new positions would be advertised publicly and appointed on merit. At committee stage in the House of Commons an amendment was proposed to require members to register their interests (if any). This indicates a possible political controversy over the revamped body. This amendment was rejected, but the Minister stated that, in spite of its rather odd constitutional position (as a form of arbitral tribunal, but not subject to the Council on Tribunals), the CAC would (as a matter of policy by the DTI, its sponsoring department) be subject to Cabinet Office guidance on non-departmental public bodies (NDPBs) which includes matters such as members' interests.[2]

[1] HC SC E, 4 March 1999, col 247 (Michael Wills).
[2] Ibid, col 254.

Changes to proceedings

9.3 The normal provisions governing the proceedings of the CAC state that it is to consist of the chairman (or a deputy chairman) and 'such other members as the chairman may direct' (the 1992 Act, s 263(1)). However, in a recognition case the 1999 Act, s 25, inserts the 1992 Act, s 263A, containing a separate provision requiring the panel to consist of three people, the chairman or deputy chairman, a member of the Committee whose experience is as a representative of employers and a member of the Committee whose experience is as a representative of workers (new s 263A(1), (2)). Also, due again to the possibly controversial nature of its decisions, the method of decision-taking is altered. The existing procedure (when the CAC cannot reach a unanimous decision) is for the chairman to decide the matter with the full powers of an umpire or, in Scotland, an oversman (1992 Act, s 263(4)). However, in a recognition case a slightly more complex version of this now applies (s 263A(5), (6)). If a unanimous decision cannot be reached but a majority of the panel has the same opinion, that opinion decides the case. It is only when there is no majority in the panel (ie three different views) that the chairman is then to decide the matter as umpire or oversman. With regard to the ordinary members of the Committee, the Minister was keen to point out at Committee stage in the House of Commons that, although appointed because of previous experience with employers or workers, once appointed they are to act independently,[1] as in the case of employment tribunals.

[1] HC SC E, 4 March 1999, col 250.

THE ADVISORY, CONCILIATION AND ARBITRATION SERVICE (ACAS)

9.4 ACAS has been one of the major successes in modern employment law, and this view was strongly supported by all sides in the Commons debates. The 1999 Act makes a change to the statutory function of ACAS, the second this decade. The original statement of the function of ACAS was contained in the Employment Protection Act 1975, s 1(2) and was then consolidated in the 1992 Act, s 209 as follows—

> 'It is the general duty of ACAS to promote the improvement of industrial relations *and in particular to encourage the extension of collective bargaining and the development and, where necessary, reform of collective bargaining machinery*' (emphasis added).

9.4 Reforms to statutory bodies

After a decade of Conservative government in the 1980s, the second half of s 209 was not only unrealistic, but in fact contrary to government policy, and so the wording was amended by the Trade Union Reform and Employment Rights Act 1993, s 43(1), which substituted the words in italics by the subsequent words—

> '... in particular, by exercising its functions in relation to the settlement of trade disputes under sections 210–212.'

Sections 210–212 are those governing conciliation and arbitration, and thus the emphasis was shifted to resolving rather than preventing problems ('fire-fighting' rather than 'fire-prevention', to use the industrial relations jargon). This reflected reality in that the inexorable rise in tribunal actions (requiring individual conciliation) and the failure of the government to give ACAS significantly increased funding meant that wider-scale, more long-term work (such as diagnostic surveys or in-depth advice within a firm) was becoming less common than it had been.

9.5 While there was little likelihood of the present government going back to the 1970s formula for obvious political reasons, they did decide on another change to the functions clause to reflect the perception that ACAS may fit well into their 'partnership' approach with its *advice* function (not mentioned in the 1993 version). This is because in on important aspect ACAS differs from an ordinary management consultancy, namely that when it does give advice to an organisation its approach is to do so on a joint consultative basis with the workforce.[1] This clearly fits the partnership at work model and in at least a symbolic attempt to reflect this and to encourage the advice-giving role, the 1999 Act, s 26 repeals the wording substituted in 1993, leaving the statutory function of ACAS as simply 'to promote the improvement of industrial relations'. Explaining this in the House of Commons Committee, the Minister for Small Firms, Trade and Industry said—

> 'In addition, ACAS provides more intensive advisory services. For example, ACAS is able to provide in-depth advice to organisations with a history of poor labour relations or with a major problem in managing change in the workplace. Such work is undertaken by joint working parties in a non-adversarial atmosphere.
>
> Under ACAS's guidance, such organisations can identify and resolve their deep-seated problems, thereby establishing a new culture at work. The Bill is intended to assist with that. Such activity can represent very good value for public expenditure. It is far better to prevent disputes than to suffer the dislocations to an industrial sector or public service that strikes might create.
>
> [Section 26] makes a small yet important change to ACAS's statutory terms of reference. It has been welcomed by the ACAS council and signals an appreciation of ACAS's work in dispute prevention.'[2]

Whether ACAS is given the resources for this work is another matter, not the concern of this Act, and depends instead on the quinquennial review that ACAS are currently undergoing.[3]

---

[1] This has taken several forms over the years, and currently comes under the term 'advisory mediation'; see the ACAS Annual Report 1998 at p 52 and Kessler and Purcell 'Joint problem solving—does it work?' (ACAS Occasional Paper No 55).

[2] HC SC E, 4 March 1999, col 268 (Michael Wills).

[3] One other interesting speculation is whether ACAS might receive some of the 'partnership' funding under the 1999 Act, s 30.

9.6 The 1999 Act also amends the 1992 in relation to ACAS by changing the annual basis of its obligatory report (and its report on the CAC) from the calendar year to the financial year (s 27). This is a purely technical matter, intended to bring the report requirement into line with the organisation's accounting requirement.[1]

---

[1] HL Official Report, 8 July 1999, col 1119.

ABOLITION OF THE COMMISSIONERS

9.7 The previous Conservative governments instituted two offices causing considerable political controversy at the time. The Employment Act 1988 provided a Commissioner for the Rights of Trade Union Members (CRTUM) to give assistance to union members seeking to bring proceedings against their union to enforce certain statutory rights which that government had legislated for.[1] In 1993 Mr Major's administration brought in the right under the 'Citizen's Charter' for an individual affected by unlawful industrial action to bring legal proceedings to challenge it.[2] Following this model they provided for a Commissioner for Protection Against Unlawful Industrial Action (CPAUIA), to provide similar assistance to potential litigants.[3] The use of these two officers has, however, remained extremely low, with the CRTUM assisting on average only ten applicants a year and the CPAUIA with only one since 1993. Not surprisingly, the present government decided to abolish both offices, and this is effected by the 1999 Act, s 28.[4] However, to continue to 'enable trade union members to secure their rights more easily and effectively',[5] at least up to a point, the Certification Officer is given power to hear complaints (rather than, or as well as, a court) involving most aspects of law where the CRTUM could have provided assistance. The CPAUIA is, however, not to be replaced in any form (though the individual's cause of action under the 'Citizen's Charter' right itself remains in force).

> 'Protections will remain. We propose to extend and redefine the role of the Certification Officer to empower him to adjudicate disputes between individual trade unionists and their unions in relation to many of those areas where the CRTUM can currently provide assistance. The Certification Office is well respected and already provides an accessible alternative to the courts to resolve disputes involving trade unions. The extension of the Certification Officer's powers is in line with the Government's wish to encourage potential litigants—in any branch of the civil law—to use practical alternatives to court proceedings to resolve their disputes. That saves court time and often produces quicker, cheaper and more efficient remedies for the parties concerned.
>
> The right of individuals to obtain an injunction against a union organising unlawful industrial action—the so-called citizen's right—will remain. However, the abolition of the CPAUIA will remove the possibility of public funding for anyone seeking such an injunction—although since the right was introduced in 1993, nobody has applied to the courts for such an injunction'.[6]

---

[1] Now contained in the 1992 Act, ss 109–114.
[2] Ibid s 235A, added by the Trade Union Reform and Employment Rights Act 1993, s 22.
[3] Ibid ss 235B, 235C, as added by the 1993 Act. The offices of the Commissioners were established by the 1992 Act, ss 266–271, as substituted by the 1993 Act, Sch 8.

9.7 *Reforms to statutory bodies*

[4] Repealing the 1992 Act, ss 109–114, 235B, 235C, 266–271. In Committee in the House of Commons the Minister undertook that transitional provisions in regulations would ensure that any cases already pending could continue to receive assistance: HC SC E, 4 March 1999, col 273.
[5] White Paper, 'Fairness at Work', Cm 3968, para 4.31.
[6] HC SC E, 4 March 1999, col 276.

THE CERTIFICATION OFFICER

9.8 In relation to abolition of the two offices of Commissioner, as pointed out at para 9.7, the government stated that the *quid pro quo* for abolishing the CRTUM was a corresponding increase in the powers of the Certification Officer as an alternative to having to apply to the ordinary courts.[1] An aggrieved union member will no longer be able to seek assistance from the CRTUM for court proceedings, but will (in *most* cases where such assistance was previously available) be able to use the Certification Officer as a form of alternative dispute resolution. Areas where there are *no* corresponding increases or improvements in the Certification Officer's jurisdiction (where previously there would have been the possibility of assistance from the CRTUM) are as follows—

(1) the statutory power for an individual member to sue on behalf of the union (the 1992 Act, s 15),
(2) the right to restrain union trustees from unlawful use of trade union property (the 1992 Act, s 16),
(3) the right of a member to challenge industrial action which does not have the support of a ballot (the 1992 Act, s 62); and
(4) the ability of a member to bring a common law action in the courts to restrain breach of the union's rules relating to industrial action.[2]

[1] HC SC E, 4 March 1999, col 276. The other Commissioner, the CPAUIA, is being abolished altogether, with no compensating changes in the law elsewhere—ibid, col 277.
[2] This was contained in the 1992 Act, s 109(2) (having originally been added to the CRTUM's statutory jurisdiction by the Employment Act 1990). Section 109 is now repealed by the 1999 Act, s 28.

Changes to the Certification Officer's statutory jurisdiction

9.9 Schedule 6 to the 1999 Act contains a large number of detailed amendments to the 1992 Act relating to the Certification Officer's judicial (as opposed to administrative) functions. Traditionally, the Certification officer (CO) has had jurisdiction only over certain statutory rights in that Act. The principal changes in that sphere are summed up below.

(i) Adding to the CO's jurisdiction

9.10 The CO is given new jurisdiction to determine complaints relating to a breach of a union member's right to access to the union's accounts through the amendment of the 1992 Act, s 31 (Sch 6, para 6), and to a breach of the statutory rules on the use of funds for political objects (Sch 6, para 13, inserting the 1992 Act, s 72A). In each case this new jurisdiction is an alternative to court proceedings (the member cannot use both options) and the CO is empowered to make declarations and any necessary orders.

(ii) Increasing the CO's powers in existing jurisdictions

9.11 Although the amendments to the 1992 Act in this area are long and complex, the principal effect is to permit the CO to make binding and enforceable orders (where previously he was confined to granting a declaration). The alternative nature of these revamped jurisdictions is further emphasised by the addition of provisions preventing a person from applying both to the court and the CO. The jurisdictions subject to these changes are those relating to—
- (a) registers of members (Sch 6, paras 2–5),
- (b) the prohibition on certain offenders holding union office (Sch 6, para 7),
- (c) failure to comply with the statutory requirements for ballots for union office (Sch 6, paras 9–11), and
- (d) failure to comply with the statutory requirements for ballots on political resolutions (Sch 6, paras 15, 16).

In addition, the CO's powers of enquiry are strengthened in relation to complaints relating to breach of political fund rules (Sch 6, para 17) and failure to comply with the statutory rules on union amalgamations and transfers (Sch 6, para 18). In relation to the latter, the existing order-making power is strengthened.

(iii) Appeal to the EAT

9.12 Given the increased powers given to the CO, new rights of appeal to the EAT on points of law are given in relation to exercises of the CO's jurisdictions over registers of members, access to accounts and the prohibition on offenders holding office, (Sch 6, para 8, inserting the 1992 Act, s 45D) and also in relation to his jurisdiction over ballots for union office (Sch 6, para 12, inserting the 1992 Act, s 56A).

Jurisdiction over breaches of union rules

9.13 Perhaps the most fundamental change to the CO's functions is contained in the 1999 Act, Sch 6, para 19, which inserts the 1992 Act, Ch VIIA (ss 108A–108C), entitled 'Breach of Rules'. Hitherto, complaints about breaches of the union's own internal rules have required a common law action in the ordinary courts, but the new s 108A(1), (2) adds a right to apply to the CO instead. It states that such an application may be made by a person[1] who claims that there has been a breach of a trade union's rules[2] relating to—

'(a) the appointment or election of a person to, or the removal of a person from, any office;
(b) disciplinary proceedings by the union (including expulsion);
(c) the balloting of members on any issue other than industrial action;[3]
(d) the constitution or proceedings of any executive committee or any decision-making meeting;[4] or
(e) such other matters as may be specified in an order made by the Secretary of State. (s 108A(2))'.[5]

If a person applies under these provisions to the CO, he may not also apply to the court, and vice versa (s 108A(14), (15)). The CO may refuse an application unless he is satisfied that the applicant has taken all reasonable steps to resolve the claim through the union's internal complaints procedure (s 108B(1)). If he accepts the application, the CO has wide powers of enquiry, and can make a declaration that the complaint is

9.13   Reforms to statutory bodies

established, adding (if appropriate) an enforcement order requiring the union to rectify the breach in question (s 108B(2)–(5)). A declaration may be relied on as if it were a court declaration (s 108B(6)); an enforcement order may be enforced in the same way as a court order, at the suit of any member of the union (s 108B(7), (8)). An appeal on a point of law lies to the EAT in relation to this new jurisdiction for the CO (s 108C).

---

1   The applicant must be a member of the union (or have been a member at the time of the breach) (s 108A(3)).
2   This includes the rules of any branch or section of the union (s 108A(8)).
3   This means a strike or other industrial action by persons employed under contracts of employment (s 108A(9)).
4   Defined in s 108A(10)–(12).
5   No application may be made regarding the dismissal of, or disciplinary action against, an employee of the union (s 108A(5)). There is a six month time limit for an application, from either the date of breach, or the conclusion of an internal complaint procedure, or one year from the invoking of such a procedure (s 108A(6), (7)).

Procedure before the Certification Officer

9.14   Wherever the CO is given new or extended jurisdiction, the provisions of the 1999 Act, Sch 6, tend to add new general procedural requirements, in particular requiring parties to be heard. In addition to this, there is a specific change relating to disclosure of the identity of the applicant or complainant, with a slight change of emphasis so that disclosure will occur unless the CO thinks the circumstances are such that no disclosure should be made.[1] More controversially in Parliament,[2] a provision is added[3] giving the CO power to refuse to entertain an application or complaint from a person who has been declared to be a vexatious litigant.

---

1   The 1999 Act, Sch 6, para 22, amending the 1992 Act, s 256.
2   HL Committee, 16 June 1999, col 386.
3   The 1999 Act, Sch 6, para 23, inserting the 1992 Act, ss 256A, 256B.

10 Miscellaneous provisions

GENERAL

10.1 The Bill as originally published contained provisions dealing with a number of miscellaneous matters including the power to make regulations conferring rights on individuals and the regulation of employment agencies. In addition various substantial amendments were introduced at the Report Stage in the House of Lords covering the treatment of employees in the national security sector and the jurisdiction of employment tribunals. Most of these matters have been covered elsewhere in this book and the remainder are considered briefly in this chapter.

EMPLOYMENT AGENCIES

10.2 The 1999 Act grants wide-ranging powers to the Secretary of State to make regulations concerning the operation of employment agencies. These are contained in Sch 7, which amends the Employment Agencies Act 1973, and cover the levying of charges, powers of inspection, and offences under the 1973 Act.

10.3 The broad nature of these powers was criticised as pernicious by the opposition in the House of Commons.[1] However the government resisted attempts to reduce them and stated that that these reforms were necessary in order to bring the statutory regulation of employment agencies up to date. The existing system had not been changed substantially for 22 years despite the enormous increase in the number of individuals who are now working through employment agencies. The government considered many agency contracts unacceptable and examples were given of attempts to exclude liability for health and safety and the practice of imposing extortionate charges and fines.[2]

[1] HC 2R, 9 February 1999, col 140.
[2] Ibid.

NATIONAL SECURITY EMPLOYEES

10.4 Substantial amendments are made to the treatment of employees in the national security services. These reforms are contained in Sch 8. The purpose behind the amendments was to create a more liberal regime for such employees although substantial restrictions remain in place to protect national security.[1] In particular the right to be accompanied at grievance and disciplinary hearings has not been extended to such employees (s 15).[2]

[1] HL Official Report, 8 July 1999, at cols 1101, and 1133–1135.
[2] See further para 7.4.

10.5   *Miscellaneous provisions*

NATIONAL MINIMUM WAGE

10.5   Limited amendments are introduced to deal with enforcement of the national minimum wage. The provisions are contained in ss 22 and 39. Section 22 deals with communities and is of limited application.[1] Section 39 provides for the sharing of information relating to the minimum wage between various departments of the Inland Revenue.[2]

---

[1]   See para 8.18.
[2]   HL Official Report, 8 July 1999, cols 1138, 1139.

SCHOOL STAFF

10.6   Technical amendments are incorporated in s 40 to deal with the dismissal of school staff. These update the provisions relating to the dismissal of school staff on fixed term contracts under the School Standards and Framework Act 1998, Schs 16 and 17, and were necessitated by the reduction in the qualifying period for unfair dismissal rights.[1]

---

[1]   HL Official Report, 8 July 1999, cols 1141, 1142.

THE TRANSFER OF UNDERTAKINGS (PROTECTION OF EMPLOYMENT) REGULATIONS 1981

10.7   The 1999 Act, s 38 grants the Secretary of State the power to introduce regulations in order to amend the Transfer of Undertakings (Protection of Employment) Regulations 1981. The government justified the requirement for this additional power because of its intention to introduce amendments to the 1981 Regulations which go beyond the requirements of the Acquired Rights Directive.[1] These rights appear to relate to the extension of the 1981 Regulations to all forms of contracting out and the transfer of purely administrative functions. These powers are designed to eliminate uncertainties created by recent decisions of the ECJ in this area.[2]

---

[1]   Council Directive 77/187/EEC.
[2]   HL Official Report, 8 July 1999, cols 1137, 1138.

PARTNERSHIPS AT WORK

10.8   The 1999 Act, s 30 provides the Secretary of State with the power to spend money or provide money to other persons for the purposes of encouraging the social partners to 'improve the way they work together.'

Appendix 1

Employment Relations Act 1999

Employment Relations Act 1999

(1999 c 26)

ARRANGEMENT OF SECTIONS

Trade unions

Section
1 Collective bargaining: recognition
2 Detriment related to trade union membership
3 Blacklists
4 Ballots and notices
5 Training
6 Unfair dismissal connected with recognition: interim relief

Leave for family and domestic reasons

7 Maternity and parental leave
8 Time off for domestic incidents
9 Consequential amendments

Disciplinary and grievance hearings

10 Right to be accompanied
11 Complaint to employment tribunal
12 Detriment and dismissal
13 Interpretation
14 Contracting out and conciliation
15 National security employees

Other rights of individuals

16 Unfair dismissal of striking workers
17 Collective agreements: detriment and dismissal
18 Agreement to exclude dismissal rights
19 Part-time work: discrimination
20 Part-time work: code of practice
21 Code of practice: supplemental
22 National minimum wage: communities
23 Power to confer rights on individuals

CAC, ACAS, Commissioners and Certification Officer

24 CAC: members
25 CAC: proceedings
26 ACAS: general duty
27 ACAS: reports
28 Abolition of Commissioners
29 The Certification Officer

Miscellaneous

30 Partnerships at work
31 Employment agencies
32 Employment rights: employment outside Great Britain
33 Unfair dismissal: special and additional awards

Employment Relations Act 1999

  34 Indexation of amounts, &c
  35 Guarantee payments
  36 Sections 33 to 35: consequential
  37 Compensatory award etc: removal of limit in certain cases
  38 Transfer of undertakings
  39 Minimum wage: information
  40 Dismissal of school staff
  41 National security

General

  42 Orders and regulations
  43 Finance
  44 Repeals
  45 Commencement
  46 Extent
  47 Citation

SCHEDULES:

  Schedule 1—Collective Bargaining: Recognition
  Schedule 2—Union Membership: Detriment
  Schedule 3—Ballots and notices
  Schedule 4—Leave for Family Reasons Etc
    Part I—Maternity Leave and Parental Leave
    Part II—Time off for Dependants
    Part III—Consequential Amendments
  Schedule 5—Unfair Dismissal of Striking Workers
  Schedule 6—The Certification Officer
  Schedule 7—Employment Agencies
  Schedule 8—National Security
  Schedule 9—Repeals

An Act to amend the law relating to employment, to trade unions and to employment agencies and businesses

[27 July 1999]

Parliamentary debates.

House of Commons:

2nd Reading 9 February 1999: 325 HC Official Report (6th series) col 130.

Committee Stage 16 February 1999–23 March 1999: HC Official Report, SC E (Employment Relations Bill).

Report Stage 30, 31 March 1999: 328 HC Official Report (6th series) cols 875, 1110.

House of Lords:

2nd Reading 10 May 1999: 600 HL Official Report (5th series) col 1003.

Committee Stage 7 June 1999: 601 HL Official Report (5th series) col 1144; 16 June 1999: 602 HL Official Report (5th series) col 288.

Report Stage 8 July 1999: 603 HL Official Report (5th series) col 1037.

3rd Reading 15 July 1999: 604 HL Official Report (5th series) col 559.

Trade unions

1 Collective bargaining: recognition

(1) The Trade Union and Labour Relations (Consolidation) Act 1992 shall be amended as follows.

(2) After Chapter V of Part I (rights of trade union members) there shall be inserted—

Employment Relations Act 1999, s 3

"CHAPTER VA
COLLECTIVE BARGAINING: RECOGNITION

70A Recognition of trade unions

Schedule A1 shall have effect."

(3) Immediately before Schedule 1 there shall be inserted the Schedule set out in Schedule 1 to this Act.

References   See Chapter 2.

2 Detriment related to trade union membership

Schedule 2 shall have effect.

3 Blacklists

(1) The Secretary of State may make regulations prohibiting the compilation of lists which—
- (a) contain details of members of trade unions or persons who have taken part in the activities of trade unions, and
- (b) are compiled with a view to being used by employers or employment agencies for the purposes of discrimination in relation to recruitment or in relation to the treatment of workers.

(2) The Secretary of State may make regulations prohibiting—
- (a) the use of lists to which subsection (1) applies;
- (b) the sale or supply of lists to which subsection (1) applies.

(3) Regulations under this section may, in particular—
- (a) confer jurisdiction (including exclusive jurisdiction) on employment tribunals and on the Employment Appeal Tribunal;
- (b) include provision for or about the grant and enforcement of specified remedies by courts and tribunals;
- (c) include provision for the making of awards of compensation calculated in accordance with the regulations;
- (d) include provision permitting proceedings to be brought by trade unions on behalf of members in specified circumstances;
- (e) include provision about cases where an employee is dismissed by his employer and the reason or principal reason for the dismissal, or why the employee was selected for dismissal, relates to a list to which subsection (1) applies;
- (f) create criminal offences;
- (g) in specified cases or circumstances, extend liability for a criminal offence created under paragraph (f) to a person who aids the commission of the offence or to a person who is an agent, principal, employee, employer or officer of a person who commits the offence;
- (h) provide for specified obligations or offences not to apply in specified circumstances;
- (i) include supplemental, incidental, consequential and transitional provision, including provision amending an enactment;
- (j) make different provision for different cases or circumstances.

(4) Regulations under this section creating an offence may not provide for it to be punishable—
- (a) by imprisonment,

(b) by a fine in excess of level 5 on the standard scale in the case of an offence triable only summarily, or

(c) by a fine in excess of the statutory maximum in the case of summary conviction for an offence triable either way.

(5) In this section—
"list" includes any index or other set of items whether recorded electronically or by any other means, and
"worker" has the meaning given by section 13.

(6) Subject to subsection (5), expressions used in this section and in the Trade Union and Labour Relations (Consolidation) Act 1992 have the same meaning in this section as in that Act.

Definitions By virtue of sub-s (6) above, for "trade union", see the Trade Union and Labour Relations (Consolidation) Act 1992, s 1; for "employment agency", see s 143(1) thereof; for "employee", see ss 273(4)(a), 278(4)(a), 280, 295(1) thereof; for "dismissal", see ss 273(4)(b), 278(4)(b), 298 thereof; for "employer", see ss 279, 295, 296(2) thereof.
References See paras 4.12–4.14.

4 Ballots and notices

Schedule 3 shall have effect.

References See Chapter 3.

5 Training

In Chapter VA of Part I of the Trade Union and Labour Relations (Consolidation) Act 1992 (collective bargaining: recognition) as inserted by section 1 above, there shall be inserted after section 70A—

"70B Training

(1) This section applies where—
   (a) a trade union is recognised, in accordance with Schedule A1, as entitled to conduct collective bargaining on behalf of a bargaining unit (within the meaning of Part I of that Schedule), and
   (b) a method for the conduct of collective bargaining is specified by the Central Arbitration Committee under paragraph 31(3) of that Schedule (and is not the subject of an agreement under paragraph 31(5)(a) or (b)).

(2) The employer must from time to time invite the trade union to send representatives to a meeting for the purpose of—
   (a) consulting about the employer's policy on training for workers within the bargaining unit,
   (b) consulting about his plans for training for those workers during the period of six months starting with the day of the meeting, and
   (c) reporting about training provided for those workers since the previous meeting.

(3) The date set for a meeting under subsection (2) must not be later than—
   (a) in the case of a first meeting, the end of the period of six months starting with the day on which this section first applies in relation to a bargaining unit, and
   (b) in the case of each subsequent meeting, the end of the period of six months starting with the day of the previous meeting.

(4) The employer shall, before the period of two weeks ending with the date of a meeting, provide to the trade union any information—

(a) without which the union's representatives would be to a material extent impeded in participating in the meeting, and
(b) which it would be in accordance with good industrial relations practice to disclose for the purposes of the meeting.

(5) Section 182(1) shall apply in relation to the provision of information under subsection (4) as it applies in relation to the disclosure of information under section 181.

(6) The employer shall take account of any written representations about matters raised at a meeting which he receives from the trade union within the period of four weeks starting with the date of the meeting.

(7) Where more than one trade union is recognised as entitled to conduct collective bargaining on behalf of a bargaining unit, a reference in this section to "the trade union" is a reference to each trade union.

(8) Where at a meeting under this section (Meeting 1) an employer indicates his intention to convene a subsequent meeting (Meeting 2) before the expiry of the period of six months beginning with the date of Meeting 1, for the reference to a period of six months in subsection (2)(b) there shall be substituted a reference to the expected period between Meeting 1 and Meeting 2.

(9) The Secretary of State may by order made by statutory instrument amend any of subsections (2) to (6).

(10) No order shall be made under subsection (9) unless a draft has been laid before, and approved by resolution of, each House of Parliament.

70C Section 70B: complaint to employment tribunal

(1) A trade union may present a complaint to an employment tribunal that an employer has failed to comply with his obligations under section 70B in relation to a bargaining unit.

(2) An employment tribunal shall not consider a complaint under this section unless it is presented—
(a) before the end of the period of three months beginning with the date of the alleged failure, or
(b) within such further period as the tribunal considers reasonable in a case where it is satisfied that it was not reasonably practicable for the complaint to be presented before the end of that period of three months.

(3) Where an employment tribunal finds a complaint under this section well-founded it—
(a) shall make a declaration to that effect, and
(b) may make an award of compensation to be paid by the employer to each person who was, at the time when the failure occurred, a member of the bargaining unit.

(4) The amount of the award shall not, in relation to each person, exceed two weeks' pay.

(5) For the purpose of subsection (4) a week's pay—
(a) shall be calculated in accordance with Chapter II of Part XIV of the Employment Rights Act 1996 (taking the date of the employer's failure as the calculation date), and
(b) shall be subject to the limit in section 227(1) of that Act.

(6) Proceedings for enforcement of an award of compensation under this section—

Employment Relations Act 1999, s 5

      (a)   may, in relation to each person to whom compensation is payable, be commenced by that person, and
      (b)   may not be commenced by a trade union."

Definitions   For "trade union", see the Trade Union and Labour Relations (Consolidation) Act 1992, s 1, (and note s 70B(7) of that Act, as inserted by this section); for "collective bargaining", see s 178(1), (2) thereof, and Sch A1, Pt I, para 3 thereto, as inserted by s 1(1), (3), Sch 1; for "recognised", see s 178(3) thereof; for "worker", see ss 279, 280, 296(1) thereof; for "employer", see ss 279, 295, 296(2) thereof; for "bargaining unit", see Sch A1, Pt I, para 2(1), (2) thereof, as inserted by s 1 and Sch 1.
References   See para 2.31.

6 Unfair dismissal connected with recognition: interim relief

In sections 128(1)(b) and 129(1) of the Employment Rights Act 1996 (interim relief) after "103" there shall be inserted "or in paragraph 161(2) of Schedule A1 to the Trade Union and Labour Relations (Consolidation) Act 1992".

Leave for family and domestic reasons

References   See Chapter 6.

7 Maternity and parental leave

The provisions set out in Part I of Schedule 4 shall be substituted for Part VIII of the Employment Rights Act 1996.

References   See paras 6.2–6.20.

8 Time off for domestic incidents

The provisions set out in Part II of Schedule 4 shall be inserted after section 57 of that Act.

References   See paras 6.21–6.24.

9 Consequential amendments

Part III of Schedule 4 (which makes amendments consequential on sections 7 and 8) shall have effect.

References   See para 6.25.

Disciplinary and grievance hearings

10 Right to be accompanied

    (1)   This section applies where a worker—
        (a)   is required or invited by his employer to attend a disciplinary or grievance hearing, and
        (b)   reasonably requests to be accompanied at the hearing.

    (2)   Where this section applies the employer must permit the worker to be accompanied at the hearing by a single companion who—
        (a)   is chosen by the worker and is within subsection (3),
        (b)   is to be permitted to address the hearing (but not to answer questions on behalf of the worker), and

(c) is to be permitted to confer with the worker during the hearing.

(3) A person is within this subsection if he is—
  (a) employed by a trade union of which he is an official within the meaning of sections 1 and 119 of the Trade Union and Labour Relations (Consolidation) Act 1992,
  (b) an official of a trade union (within that meaning) whom the union has reasonably certified in writing as having experience of, or as having received training in, acting as a worker's companion at disciplinary or grievance hearings, or
  (c) another of the employer's workers.

(4) If—
  (a) a worker has a right under this section to be accompanied at a hearing,
  (b) his chosen companion will not be available at the time proposed for the hearing by the employer, and
  (c) the worker proposes an alternative time which satisfies subsection (5),
the employer must postpone the hearing to the time proposed by the worker.

(5) An alternative time must—
  (a) be reasonable, and
  (b) fall before the end of the period of five working days beginning with the first working day after the day proposed by the employer.

(6) An employer shall permit a worker to take time off during working hours for the purpose of accompanying another of the employer's workers in accordance with a request under subsection (1)(b).

(7) Sections 168(3) and (4), 169 and 171 to 173 of the Trade Union and Labour Relations (Consolidation) Act 1992 (time off for carrying out trade union duties) shall apply in relation to subsection (6) above as they apply in relation to section 168(1) of that Act.

Definitions For "worker", see s 13(1)–(3); for "disciplinary hearing", see s 13(4); for "grievance hearing", see s 13(5); for "working day" in sub-s (5)(b) above, see s 13(6).
References See paras 7.6–7.14.

11 Complaint to employment tribunal

(1) A worker may present a complaint to an employment tribunal that his employer has failed, or threatened to fail, to comply with section 10(2) or (4).

(2) A tribunal shall not consider a complaint under this section in relation to a failure or threat unless the complaint is presented—
  (a) before the end of the period of three months beginning with the date of the failure or threat, or
  (b) within such further period as the tribunal considers reasonable in a case where it is satisfied that it was not reasonably practicable for the complaint to be presented before the end of that period of three months.

(3) Where a tribunal finds that a complaint under this section is well-founded it shall order the employer to pay compensation to the worker of an amount not exceeding two weeks' pay.

(4) Chapter II of Part XIV of the Employment Rights Act 1996 (calculation of a week's pay) shall apply for the purposes of subsection (3); and in applying that Chapter the calculation date shall be taken to be—

Employment Relations Act 1999, s 11

  (a) in the case of a claim which is made in the course of a claim for unfair dismissal, the date on which the employer's notice of dismissal was given or, if there was no notice, the effective date of termination, and

  (b) in any other case, the date on which the relevant hearing took place (or was to have taken place).

(5) The limit in section 227(1) of the Employment Rights Act 1996 (maximum amount of week's pay) shall apply for the purposes of subsection (3) above.

(6) No award shall be made under subsection (3) in respect of a claim which is made in the course of a claim for unfair dismissal if the tribunal makes a supplementary award under section 127A(2) of the Employment Rights Act 1996 (internal appeal procedures).

Definitions For "worker", see s 13(1)–(3).
References See para 7.13.

12 Detriment and dismissal

(1) A worker has the right not to be subjected to any detriment by any act, or any deliberate failure to act, by his employer done on the ground that he—

  (a) exercised or sought to exercise the right under section 10(2) or (4), or

  (b) accompanied or sought to accompany another worker (whether of the same employer or not) pursuant to a request under that section.

(2) Section 48 of the Employment Rights Act 1996 shall apply in relation to contraventions of subsection (1) above as it applies in relation to contraventions of certain sections of that Act.

(3) A worker who is dismissed shall be regarded for the purposes of Part X of the Employment Rights Act 1996 as unfairly dismissed if the reason (or, if more than one, the principal reason) for the dismissal is that he—

  (a) exercised or sought to exercise the right under section 10(2) or (4), or

  (b) accompanied or sought to accompany another worker (whether of the same employer or not) pursuant to a request under that section.

(4) Sections 108 and 109 of that Act (qualifying period of employment and upper age limit) shall not apply in relation to subsection (3) above.

(5) Sections 128 to 132 of that Act (interim relief) shall apply in relation to dismissal for the reason specified in subsection (3)(a) or (b) above as they apply in relation to dismissal for a reason specified in section 128(1)(b) of that Act.

(6) In the application of Chapter II of Part X of that Act in relation to subsection (3) above, a reference to an employee shall be taken as a reference to a worker.

Definitions For "worker", see s 13(1)–(3). In the Employment Rights Act 1996, for "employee", see s 230(1) thereof.
References See para 7.14.

13 Interpretation

(1) In sections 10 to 12 and this section "worker" means an individual who is—

  (a) a worker within the meaning of section 230(3) of the Employment Rights Act 1996,

  (b) an agency worker,

  (c) a home worker,

(d) a person in Crown employment within the meaning of section 191 of that Act, other than a member of the naval, military, air or reserve forces of the Crown, or
(e) employed as a relevant member of the House of Lords staff or the House of Commons staff within the meaning of section 194(6) or 195(5) of that Act.

(2) In subsection (1) "agency worker" means an individual who—
(a) is supplied by a person ("the agent") to do work for another ("the principal") by arrangement between the agent and the principal,
(b) is not a party to a worker's contract, within the meaning of section 230(3) of that Act, relating to that work, and
(c) is not a party to a contract relating to that work under which he undertakes to do the work for another party to the contract whose status is, by virtue of the contract, that of a client or customer of any professional or business undertaking carried on by the individual;

and, for the purposes of sections 10 to 12, both the agent and the principal are employers of an agency worker.

(3) In subsection (1) "home worker" means an individual who—
(a) contracts with a person, for the purposes of the person's business, for the execution of work to be done in a place not under the person's control or management, and
(b) is not a party to a contract relating to that work under which the work is to be executed for another party to the contract whose status is, by virtue of the contract, that of a client or customer of any professional or business undertaking carried on by the individual;

and, for the purposes of sections 10 to 12, the person mentioned in paragraph (a) is the home worker's employer.

(4) For the purposes of section 10 a disciplinary hearing is a hearing which could result in—
(a) the administration of a formal warning to a worker by his employer,
(b) the taking of some other action in respect of a worker by his employer, or
(c) the confirmation of a warning issued or some other action taken.

(5) For the purposes of section 10 a grievance hearing is a hearing which concerns the performance of a duty by an employer in relation to a worker.

(6) For the purposes of section 10(5)(b) in its application to a part of Great Britain a working day is a day other than—
(a) a Saturday or a Sunday,
(b) Christmas Day or Good Friday, or
(c) a day which is a bank holiday under the Banking and Financial ealings Act 1971 in that part of Great Britain.

References   See para 7.6.

14 Contracting out and conciliation

Sections 10 to 13 of this Act shall be treated as provisions of Part V of the Employment Rights Act 1996 for the purposes of—
(a) section 203(1), (2)(e) and (f), (3) and (4) of that Act (restrictions on contracting out), and
(b) section 18(1)(d) of the Employment Tribunals Act 1996 (conciliation).

References   See para 7.6.

15 National security employees

Sections 10 to 13 of this Act shall not apply in relation to a person employed for the purposes of—
- (a) the Security Service,
- (b) the Secret Intelligence Service, or
- (c) the Government Communications Headquarters.

References   See para 7.15.

Other rights of individuals

16 Unfair dismissal of striking workers

Schedule 5 shall have effect.

References   See Chapter 5.

17 Collective agreements: detriment and dismissal

(1) The Secretary of State may make regulations about cases where a worker—
- (a) is subjected to detriment by his employer, or
- (b) is dismissed,

on the grounds that he refuses to enter into a contract which includes terms which differ from the terms of a collective agreement which applies to him.

(2) The regulations may—
- (a) make provision which applies only in specified classes of case;
- (b) make different provision for different circumstances;
- (c) include supplementary, incidental and transitional provision.

(3) In this section—
"collective agreement" has the meaning given by section 178(1) of the Trade Union and Labour Relations (Consolidation) Act 1992; and
"employer" and "worker" have the same meaning as in section 296 of that Act.

(4) The payment of higher wages or higher rates of pay or overtime or the payment of any signing on or other bonuses or the provision of other benefits having a monetary value to other workers employed by the same employer shall not constitute a detriment to any worker not receiving the same or similar payments or benefits within the meaning of subsection (1)(a) of this section so long as—
- (a) there is no inhibition in the contract of employment of the worker receiving the same from being the member of any trade union, and
- (b) the said payments of higher wages or rates of pay or overtime or bonuses or the provision of other benefits are in accordance with the terms of a contract of employment and reasonably relate to services provided by the worker under that contract.

References   See para 4.10.

18 Agreement to exclude dismissal rights

(1) In section 197 of the Employment Rights Act 1996 (fixed-term contracts) subsections (1) and (2) (agreement to exclude unfair dismissal provisions) shall be omitted; and subsections (2) to (5) below shall have effect in consequence.

(2) In sections 44(4), 46(2), 47(2), 47A(2) and 47B(2) of that Act—
  (a) the words from the beginning to "the dismissal," shall be omitted, and
  (b) for "that Part" there shall be substituted "Part X".

(3) In section 45A(4) of that Act the words from ", unless" to the end shall be omitted.

(4) In section 23 of the National Minimum Wage Act 1998, for subsection (4) there shall be substituted—

"(4) This section does not apply where the detriment in question amounts to dismissal within the meaning of—
  (a) Part X of the Employment Rights Act 1996 (unfair dismissal), or
  (b) Part XI of the Employment Rights (Northern Ireland) Order 1996 (corresponding provision for Northern Ireland),
except where in relation to Northern Ireland the person in question is dismissed in circumstances in which, by virtue of Article 240 of that Order (fixed term contracts), Part XI does not apply to the dismissal."

(5) In paragraph 1 of Schedule 3 to the Tax Credits Act 1999, for sub-paragraph (3) there shall be substituted—

"(3) This paragraph does not apply where the detriment in question amounts to dismissal within the meaning of—
  (a) Part X of the Employment Rights Act 1996 (unfair dismissal), or
  (b) Part XI of the Employment Rights (Northern Ireland) Order 1996 (corresponding provision for Northern Ireland),
except where in relation to Northern Ireland the employee is dismissed in circumstances in which, by virtue of Article 240 of that Order (fixed term contracts), Part XI does not apply to the dismissal."

(6) Section 197(1) of the Employment Rights Act 1996 does not prevent Part X of that Act from applying to a dismissal which is regarded as unfair by virtue of section 99 or 104 of that Act (pregnancy and childbirth, and assertion of statutory right).

References   See para 5.12.

19 Part-time work: discrimination

(1) The Secretary of State shall make regulations for the purpose of securing that persons in part-time employment are treated, for such purposes and to such extent as the regulations may specify, no less favourably than persons in full-time employment.

(2) The regulations may—
  (a) specify classes of person who are to be taken to be, or not to be, in part-time employment;
  (b) specify classes of person who are to be taken to be, or not to be, in full-time employment;
  (c) specify circumstances in which persons in part-time employment are to be taken to be, or not to be, treated less favourably than persons in full-time employment;
  (d) make provision which has effect in relation to persons in part-time employment generally or provision which has effect only in relation to specified classes of persons in part-time employment.

(3) The regulations may—
  (a) confer jurisdiction (including exclusive jurisdiction) on employment tribunals and on the Employment Appeal Tribunal;

Employment Relations Act 1999, s 19

    (b)   create criminal offences in relation to specified acts or omissions by an employer, by an organisation of employers, by an organisation of workers or by an organisation existing for the purposes of a profession or trade carried on by the organisation's members;

    (c)   in specified cases or circumstances, extend liability for a criminal offence created under paragraph (b) to a person who aids the commission of the offence or to a person who is an agent, principal, employee, employer or officer of a person who commits the offence;

    (d)   provide for specified obligations or offences not to apply in specified circumstances;

    (e)   make provision about notices or information to be given, evidence to be produced and other procedures to be followed;

    (f)   amend, apply with or without modifications, or make provision similar to any provision of the Employment Rights Act 1996 (including, in particular, Parts V, X and XIII) or the Trade Union and Labour Relations (Consolidation) Act 1992;

    (g)   provide for the provisions of specified agreements to have effect in place of provisions of the regulations to such extent and in such circumstances as may be specified;

    (h)   include supplemental, incidental, consequential and transitional provision, including provision amending an enactment;

    (i)   make different provision for different cases or circumstances.

(4) Without prejudice to the generality of this section the regulations may make any provision which appears to the Secretary of State to be necessary or expedient—

    (a)   for the purpose of implementing Council Directive 97/81/EC on the framework agreement on part-time work in its application to terms and conditions of employment;

    (b)   for the purpose of dealing with any matter arising out of or related to the United Kingdom's obligations under that Directive;

    (c)   for the purpose of any matter dealt with by the framework agreement or for the purpose of applying the provisions of the framework agreement to any matter relating to part-time workers.

(5) Regulations under this section which create an offence—

    (a)   shall provide for it to be triable summarily only, and

    (b)   may not provide for it to be punishable by imprisonment or by a fine in excess of level 5 on the standard scale.

References   See para 8.10.

20 Part-time work: code of practice

(1) The Secretary of State may issue codes of practice containing guidance for the purpose of—

    (a)   eliminating discrimination in the field of employment against part-time workers;

    (b)   facilitating the development of opportunities for part-time work;

    (c)   facilitating the flexible organisation of working time taking into account the needs of workers and employers;

    (d)   any matter dealt with in the framework agreement on part-time work annexed to Council Directive 97/81/EC.

(2) The Secretary of State may revise a code and issue the whole or part of the revised code.

(3) A person's failure to observe a provision of a code does not make him liable to any proceedings.

(4) A code—
- (a) is admissible in evidence in proceedings before an employment tribunal, and
- (b) shall be taken into account by an employment tribunal in any case in which it appears to the tribunal to be relevant.

References See para 8.11.

21 Code of practice: supplemental

(1) Before issuing or revising a code of practice under section 20 the Secretary of State shall consult such persons as he considers appropriate.

(2) Before issuing a code the Secretary of State shall—
- (a) publish a draft code,
- (b) consider any representations made to him about the draft,
- (c) if he thinks it appropriate, modify the draft in the light of any representations made to him.

(3) If, having followed the procedure under subsection (2), the Secretary of State decides to issue a code, he shall lay a draft code before each House of Parliament.

(4) If the draft code is approved by resolution of each House of Parliament, the Secretary of State shall issue the code in the form of the draft.

(5) In this section and section 20(3) and (4)—
- (a) a reference to a code includes a reference to a revised code,
- (b) a reference to a draft code includes a reference to a draft revision, and
- (c) a reference to issuing a code includes a reference to issuing part of a revised code.

References See para 8.11.

22 National minimum wage: communities

The following shall be inserted after section 44 of the National Minimum Wage Act 1998 (exclusions: voluntary workers)—

"44A Religious and other communities: resident workers

(1) A residential member of a community to which this section applies does not qualify for the national minimum wage in respect of employment by the community.

(2) Subject to subsection (3), this section applies to a community if—
- (a) it is a charity or is established by a charity,
- (b) a purpose of the community is to practise or advance a belief of a religious or similar nature, and
- (c) all or some of its members live together for that purpose.

(3) This section does not apply to a community which—
- (a) is an independent school, or
- (b) provides a course of further or higher education.

(4) The residential members of a community are those who live together as mentioned in subsection (2)(c).

(5) In this section—
- (a) "charity" has the same meaning as in section 44, and

(b) "independent school" has the same meaning as in section 463 of the Education Act 1996 (in England and Wales), section 135 of the Education (Scotland) Act 1980 (in Scotland) and Article 2 of the Education and Libraries (Northern Ireland) Order 1986 (in Northern Ireland).

(6) In this section "course of further or higher education" means—
    (a) in England and Wales, a course of a description referred to in Schedule 6 to the Education Reform Act 1988 or Schedule 2 to the Further and Higher Education Act 1992;
    (b) in Scotland, a course or programme of a description mentioned in or falling within section 6(1) or 38 of the Further and Higher Education (Scotland) Act 1992;
    (c) in Northern Ireland, a course of a description referred to in Schedule 1 to the Further Education (Northern Ireland) Order 1997 or a course providing further education within the meaning of Article 3 of that Order."

Definitions For "employment", see the National Minimum Wage Act 1998, s 54(5).
References See para 8.18.

23 Power to confer rights on individuals

(1) This section applies to any right conferred on an individual against an employer (however defined) under or by virtue of any of the following—
    (a) the Trade Union and Labour Relations (Consolidation) Act 1992;
    (b) the Employment Rights Act 1996;
    (c) this Act;
    (d) any instrument made under section 2(2) of the European Communities Act 1972.

(2) The Secretary of State may by order make provision which has the effect of conferring any such right on individuals who are of a specified description.

(3) The reference in subsection (2) to individuals includes a reference to individuals expressly excluded from exercising the right.

(4) An order under this section may—
    (a) provide that individuals are to be treated as parties to workers' contracts or contracts of employment;
    (b) make provision as to who are to be regarded as the employers of individuals;
    (c) make provision which has the effect of modifying the operation of any right as conferred on individuals by the order;
    (d) include such consequential, incidental or supplementary provisions as the Secretary of State thinks fit.

(5) An order under this section may make provision in such way as the Secretary of State thinks fit, whether by amending Acts or instruments or otherwise.

(6) Section 209(7) of the Employment Rights Act 1996 (which is superseded by this section) shall be omitted.

(7) Any order made or having effect as if made under section 209(7), so far as effective immediately before the commencement of this section, shall have effect as if made under this section.

References See para 8.17.

CAC, ACAS, Commissioners and Certification Officer

24 CAC: members

In section 260 of the Trade Union and Labour Relations (Consolidation) Act 1992 (members of the Committee) these subsections shall be substituted for subsections (1) to (3)—

"(1) The Central Arbitration Committee shall consist of members appointed by the Secretary of State.

(2) The Secretary of State shall appoint a member as chairman, and may appoint a member as deputy chairman or members as deputy chairmen.

(3) The Secretary of State may appoint as members only persons experienced in industrial relations, and they shall include some persons whose experience is as representatives of employers and some whose experience is as representatives of workers.

(3A) Before making an appointment under subsection (1) or (2) the Secretary of State shall consult ACAS and may consult other persons.".

Definitions For "ACAS", see the Trade Union and Labour Relations (Consolidation) Act 1992, s 247(1); for "Central Arbitration Committee", see s 259 of that Act; for "employer", see ss 279, 295, 296(2) thereof; for "worker", see ss 279, 280, 296(1) thereof.
References See para 9.2.

25 CAC: proceedings

(1) The Trade Union and Labour Relations (Consolidation) Act 1992 shall be amended as follows.

(2) In section 263 (proceedings of the Committee) this subsection shall be inserted after subsection (6)—

"(7) In relation to the discharge of the Committee's functions under Schedule A1—
(a) section 263A and subsection (6) above shall apply, and
(b) subsections (1) to (5) above shall not apply."

(3) This section shall be inserted after section 263—

"263A Proceedings of the Committee under Schedule A1

(1) For the purpose of discharging its functions under Schedule A1 in any particular case, the Central Arbitration Committee shall consist of a panel established under this section.

(2) The chairman of the Committee shall establish a panel or panels, and a panel shall consist of these three persons appointed by him—
(a) the chairman or a deputy chairman of the Committee, who shall be chairman of the panel;
(b) a member of the Committee whose experience is as a representative of employers;
(c) a member of the Committee whose experience is as a representative of workers.

(3) The chairman of the Committee shall decide which panel is to deal with a particular case.

(4) A panel may at the discretion of its chairman sit in private where it appears expedient to do so.

(5) If—
(a) a panel cannot reach a unanimous decision on a question arising before it, and
(b) a majority of the panel have the same opinion,
the question shall be decided according to that opinion.

(6) If—
(a) a panel cannot reach a unanimous decision on a question arising before it, and
(b) a majority of the panel do not have the same opinion,
the chairman of the panel shall decide the question acting with the full powers of an umpire or, in Scotland, an oversman.

(7) Subject to the above provisions, a panel shall determine its own procedure."

(4) In section 264 (awards of the Committee)—
(a) in subsection (1) after "award" there shall be inserted ", or in any decision or declaration of the Committee under Schedule A1,";
(b) in subsection (2) after "of the Committee," there shall be inserted "or of a decision or declaration of the Committee under Schedule A1,".

Definitions For "worker", see the Trade Union and Labour Relations (Consolidation) Act 1992, ss 279, 280, 296(1); for "employer", see, ss 279, 295, 296(2) thereof.
References See para 9.3.

26 ACAS: general duty

In section 209 of the Trade Union and Labour Relations (Consolidation) Act 1992 (ACAS' general duty) the words from ", in particular" to the end shall be omitted.

References See para 9.5.

27 ACAS: reports

(1) In section 253(1) of the Trade Union and Labour Relations (Consolidation) Act 1992 (ACAS: annual report) for "calendar year" there shall be substituted "financial year".

(2) In section 265(1) of that Act (ACAS: report about CAC) for "calendar year" there shall be substituted "financial year".

Definitions For "financial year", see the Trade Union and Labour Relations (Consolidation) Act 1992, s 272.
References See para 9.6.

28 Abolition of Commissioners

(1) These offices shall cease to exist—
(a) the office of Commissioner for the Rights of Trade Union Members;
(b) the office of Commissioner for Protection Against Unlawful Industrial Action.

(2) In the Trade Union and Labour Relations (Consolidation) Act 1992 these provisions shall cease to have effect—
(a) Chapter VIII of Part I (provision by Commissioner for the Rights of Trade Union Members of assistance in relation to certain proceedings);

(b) sections 235B and 235C (provision of assistance by Commissioner for Protection Against Unlawful Industrial Action of assistance in relation to certain proceedings);
(c) section 266 (and the heading immediately preceding it) and sections 267 to 271 (Commissioners' appointment, remuneration, staff, reports, accounts, etc).

(3) In section 32A of that Act (statement to members of union following annual return) in the third paragraph of subsection (6)(a) (application for assistance from Commissioner for the Rights of Trade Union Members) for the words from "may" to "case," there shall be substituted "should".

29 The Certification Officer

Schedule 6 shall have effect.

References See paras 9.7, 9.8.

Miscellaneous

30 Partnerships at work

(1) The Secretary of State may spend money or provide money to other persons for the purpose of encouraging and helping employers (or their representatives) and employees (or their representatives) to improve the way they work together.

(2) Money may be provided in such way as the Secretary of State thinks fit (whether as grants or otherwise) and on such terms as he thinks fit (whether as to repayment or otherwise).

References See paras 9.5; 10.8.

31 Employment agencies

Schedule 7 shall have effect.

References See pars 10.2, 10.3.

32 Employment rights: employment outside Great Britain

(1) In section 285(1) of the Trade Union and Labour Relations (Consolidation) Act 1992 (employment outside Great Britain) for "Chapter II (procedure for handling redundancies)" there shall be substituted "sections 193 and 194 (duty to notify Secretary of State of certain redundancies)".

(2) After section 287(3) of that Act (offshore employment) there shall be inserted—

"(3A) An Order in Council under this section shall be subject to annulment in pursuance of a resolution of either House of Parliament.".

(3) Section 196 of the Employment Rights Act 1996 (employment outside Great Britain) shall cease to have effect; and in section 5(1) for "sections 196 and" there shall be substituted "section".

(4) After section 199(6) of that Act (mariners) there shall be inserted—

Employment Relations Act 1999, s 32

"(7) The provisions mentioned in subsection (8) apply to employment on board a ship registered in the register maintained under section 8 of the Merchant Shipping Act 1995 if and only if—
  (a) the ship's entry in the register specifies a port in Great Britain as the port to which the vessel is to be treated as belonging,
  (b) under his contract of employment the person employed does not work wholly outside Great Britain, and
  (c) the person employed is ordinarily resident in Great Britain.

(8) The provisions are—
  (a) sections 8 to 10,
  (b) Parts II, III and V,
  (c) Part VI, apart from sections 58 to 60,
  (d) Parts VII and VIII,
  (e) sections 92 and 93, and
  (f) Part X."

Definitions   In the Employment Rights Act 1996, for "contract of employment", see s 230(2) thereof; for "employment", see s 230(5) thereof.
References   See para 5.15.

33 Unfair dismissal: special and additional awards

(1) The following provisions (which require, or relate to, the making of special awards by employment tribunals in unfair dismissal cases) shall cease to have effect—
  (a) sections 117(4)(b), 118(2) and (3) and 125 of the Employment Rights Act 1996 (and the word "or" before section 117(4)(b));
  (b) sections 157 and 158 of the Trade Union and Labour Relations (Consolidation) Act 1992.

(2) In section 117(3)(b) of the Employment Rights Act 1996 (amount of additional award) for "the appropriate amount" there shall be substituted "an amount not less than twenty-six nor more than fifty-two weeks' pay"; and subsections (5) and (6) of section 117 shall cease to have effect.

(3) In section 14 of the Employment Rights (Dispute Resolution) Act 1998—
  (a) subsection (1) shall cease to have effect, and
  (b) in subsection (2) for "that Act" substitute "the Employment Rights Act 1996".

Definitions   For "week", see the Employment Rights Act 1996, s 235(1).
References   See para 5.8.

34 Indexation of amounts, &c

(1) This section applies to the sums specified in the following provisions—
  (a) section 31(1) of the Employment Rights Act 1996 (guarantee payments: limits);
  (b) section 120(1) of that Act (unfair dismissal: minimum amount of basic award);
  (c) section 124(1) of that Act (unfair dismissal: limit of compensatory award);
  (d) section 186(1)(a) and (b) of that Act (employee's rights on insolvency of employer: maximum amount payable);
  (e) section 227(1) of that Act (maximum amount of a week's pay for purposes of certain calculations);
  (f) section 156(1) of the Trade Union and Labour Relations (Consolidation) Act 1992 (unfair dismissal: minimum basic award);

(g) section 176(6) of that Act (right to membership of trade union: remedies).

(2) If the retail prices index for September of a year is higher or lower than the index for the previous September, the Secretary of State shall as soon as practicable make an order in relation to each sum mentioned in subsection (1)—
   (a) increasing each sum, if the new index is higher, or
   (b) decreasing each sum, if the new index is lower,
by the same percentage as the amount of the increase or decrease of the index.

(3) In making the calculation required by subsection (2) the Secretary of State shall—
   (a) in the case of the sum mentioned in subsection (1)(a), round the result up to the nearest 10 pence,
   (b) in the case of the sums mentioned in subsection (1)(b), (c), (f) and (g), round the result up to the nearest £100, and
   (c) in the case of the sums mentioned in subsection (1)(d) and (e), round the result up to the nearest £10.

(4) For the sum specified in section 124(1) of the Employment Rights Act 1996 (unfair dismissal: limit of compensatory award) there shall be substituted the sum of £50,000 (subject to subsection (2) above).

(5) In this section "the retail prices index" means—
   (a) the general index of retail prices (for all items) published by the Office for National Statistics, or
   (b) where that index is not published for a month, any substituted index or figures published by that Office.

(6) An order under this section—
   (a) shall be made by statutory instrument,
   (b) may include transitional provision, and
   (c) shall be laid before Parliament after being made.

References See para 5.9.

35 Guarantee payments

For section 31(7) of the Employment Rights Act 1996 (guarantee payments: limits) there shall be substituted—

   "(7) The Secretary of State may by order vary—
      (a) the length of the period specified in subsection (2);
      (b) a limit specified in subsection (3) or (4)."

References See para 5.9.

36 Sections 33 to 35: consequential

(1) The following provisions (which confer power to increase sums) shall cease to have effect—
   (a) sections 120(2), 124(2), 186(2) and 227(2) to (4) of the Employment Rights Act 1996;
   (b) sections 159 and 176(7) and (8) of the Trade Union and Labour Relations (Consolidation) Act 1992.

(2) Section 208 of the Employment Rights Act 1996 (review of limits) shall cease to have effect.

(3) An increase effected, before section 34 comes into force, by virtue of a provision repealed by this section shall continue to have effect notwithstanding this section (but subject to section 34(2) and (4)).

37 Compensatory award etc: removal of limit in certain cases

(1) After section 124(1) of the Employment Rights Act 1996 (limit of compensatory award etc) there shall be inserted—

"(1A) Subsection (1) shall not apply to compensation awarded, or a compensatory award made, to a person in a case where he is regarded as unfairly dismissed by virtue of section 100, 103A, 105(3) or 105(6A)."

(2) Section 127B of that Act (power to specify method of calculation of compensation where dismissal a result of protected disclosure) shall cease to have effect.

References   See para 5.7.

38 Transfer of undertakings

(1) This section applies where regulations under section 2(2) of the European Communities Act 1972 (general implementation of Treaties) make provision for the purpose of implementing, or for a purpose concerning, a Community obligation of the United Kingdom which relates to the treatment of employees on the transfer of an undertaking or business or part of an undertaking or business.

(2) The Secretary of State may by regulations make the same or similar provision in relation to the treatment of employees in circumstances other than those to which the Community obligation applies (including circumstances in which there is no transfer, or no transfer to which the Community obligation applies).

(3) Regulations under this section shall be subject to annulment in pursuance of a resolution of either House of Parliament.

References   See para 10.7.

39 Minimum wage: information

(1) Information obtained by a revenue official in the course of carrying out a function of the Commissioners of Inland Revenue may be—
- (a) supplied by the Commissioners of Inland Revenue to the Secretary of State for any purpose relating to the National Minimum Wage Act 1998;
- (b) supplied by the Secretary of State with the authority of the Commissioners of Inland Revenue to any person acting under section 13(1)(b) of that Act;
- (c) supplied by the Secretary of State with the authority of the Commissioners of Inland Revenue to an officer acting for the purposes of any of the agricultural wages legislation.

(2) In this section—
"revenue official" means an officer of the Commissioners of Inland Revenue appointed under section 4 of the Inland Revenue Regulation Act 1890 (appointment of collectors, officers and other persons), and
"the agricultural wages legislation" has the same meaning as in section 16 of the National Minimum Wage Act 1998 (agricultural wages officers).

References   See para 10.5.

40 Dismissal of school staff

(1) In paragraph 27(3)(b) of Schedule 16 to the School Standards and Framework Act 1998 (dismissal of staff: representations and appeal) for "for a period of two years or more (within the meaning of the Employment Rights Act 1996)" there shall be substituted ", within the meaning of the Employment Rights Act 1996, for a period at least as long as the period for the time being specified in section 108(1) of that Act (unfair dismissal: qualifying period)".

(2) In paragraph 24(4)(b) of Schedule 17 to the School Standards and Framework Act 1998 (dismissal of staff: representations and appeal) for "for a period of two years or more (within the meaning of the Employment Rights Act 1996)" there shall be substituted ", within the meaning of the Employment Rights Act 1996, for a period at least as long as the period for the time being specified in section 108(1) of that Act (unfair dismissal: qualifying period)".

References See para 10.6.

41 National security

Schedule 8 shall have effect.

References See para 10.4.

General

42 Orders and regulations

(1) Any power to make an order or regulations under this Act shall be exercised by statutory instrument.

(2) No order or regulations shall be made under section 3, 17, 19 or 23 unless a draft has been laid before, and approved by resolution of, each House of Parliament.

References See para 8.17.

43 Finance

There shall be paid out of money provided by Parliament—
- (a) any increase attributable to this Act in the sums so payable under any other enactment;
- (b) any other expenditure of the Secretary of State under this Act.

44 Repeals

The provisions mentioned in Schedule 9 are repealed (or revoked) to the extent specified in column 3.

45 Commencement

(1) The preceding provisions of this Act shall come into force in accordance with provision made by the Secretary of State by order made by statutory instrument.

(2) An order under this section—
- (a) may make different provision for different purposes;
- (b) may include supplementary, incidental, saving or transitional provisions.

46 Extent

(1) Any amendment or repeal in this Act has the same extent as the provision amended or repealed.

(2) An Order in Council under paragraph 1(1)(b) of Schedule 1 to the Northern Ireland Act 1974 (legislation for Northern Ireland in the interim period) which contains a statement that it is made only for purposes corresponding to any of the purposes of this Act—
- (a) shall not be subject to paragraph 1(4) and (5) of that Schedule (affirmative resolution of both Houses of Parliament), but
- (b) shall be subject to annulment in pursuance of a resolution of either House of Parliament.

(3) Apart from sections 39 and 45 and subject to subsection (1), the preceding sections of this Act shall not extend to Northern Ireland.

47 Citation

This Act may be cited as the Employment Relations Act 1999.

SCHEDULE 1

Section 1

COLLECTIVE BARGAINING: RECOGNITION

The Schedule to be inserted immediately before Schedule 1 to the Trade Union and Labour Relations (Consolidation) Act 1992 is as follows—

"SCHEDULE A1
COLLECTIVE BARGAINING: RECOGNITION

PART I
RECOGNITION

Introduction

1. A trade union (or trade unions) seeking recognition to be entitled to conduct collective bargaining on behalf of a group or groups of workers may make a request in accordance with this Part of this Schedule.

2.—(1) This paragraph applies for the purposes of this Part of this Schedule.

(2) References to the bargaining unit are to the group of workers concerned (or the groups taken together).

(3) References to the proposed bargaining unit are to the bargaining unit proposed in the request for recognition.

(4) References to the employer are to the employer of the workers constituting the bargaining unit concerned.

(5) References to the parties are to the union (or unions) and the employer.

3.—(1) This paragraph applies for the purposes of this Part of this Schedule.

(2) The meaning of collective bargaining given by section 178(1) shall not apply.

(3) References to collective bargaining are to negotiations relating to pay, hours and holidays; but this has effect subject to sub-paragraph (4).

(4) If the parties agree matters as the subject of collective bargaining, references to collective bargaining are to negotiations relating to the agreed matters; and this is the case whether the agreement is made before or after the time when the CAC issues a declaration, or the parties agree, that the union is (or unions are) entitled to conduct collective bargaining on behalf of a bargaining unit.

(5) Sub-paragraph (4) does not apply in construing paragraph 31(3).

(6) Sub-paragraphs (2) to (5) do not apply in construing paragraph 35 or 44.

Request for recognition

4.—(1) The union or unions seeking recognition must make a request for recognition to the employer.

(2) Paragraphs 5 to 9 apply to the request.

5. The request is not valid unless it is received by the employer.

6. The request is not valid unless the union (or each of the unions) has a certificate under section 6 that it is independent.

7.—(1) The request is not valid unless the employer, taken with any associated employer or employers, employs—
    (a) at least 21 workers on the day the employer receives the request, or
    (b) an average of at least 21 workers in the 13 weeks ending with that day.

(2) To find the average under sub-paragraph (1)(b)—
    (a) take the number of workers employed in each of the 13 weeks (including workers not employed for the whole of the week);
    (b) aggregate the 13 numbers;
    (c) divide the aggregate by 13.

(3) For the purposes of sub-paragraph (1)(a) any worker employed by an associated company incorporated outside Great Britain must be ignored unless the day the request was made fell within a period during which he ordinarily worked in Great Britain.

(4) For the purposes of sub-paragraph (1)(b) any worker employed by an associated company incorporated outside Great Britain must be ignored in relation to a week unless the whole or any part of that week fell within a period during which he ordinarily worked in Great Britain.

(5) For the purposes of sub-paragraphs (3) and (4) a worker who is employed on board a ship registered in the register maintained under section 8 of the Merchant Shipping Act 1995 shall be treated as ordinarily working in Great Britain unless—
    (a) the ship's entry in the register specifies a port outside Great Britain as the port to which the vessel is to be treated as belonging,
    (b) the employment is wholly outside Great Britain, or
    (c) the worker is not ordinarily resident in Great Britain.

(6) The Secretary of State may by order—
    (a) provide that sub-paragraphs (1) to (5) are not to apply, or are not to apply in specified circumstances, or
    (b) vary the number of workers for the time being specified in sub-paragraph (1);
and different provision may be made for different circumstances.

(7) An order under sub-paragraph (6)—
    (a) shall be made by statutory instrument, and
    (b) may include supplementary, incidental, saving or transitional provisions.

(8) No such order shall be made unless a draft of it has been laid before Parliament and approved by a resolution of each House of Parliament.

8. The request is not valid unless it—
    (a) is in writing,
    (b) identifies the union or unions and the bargaining unit, and
    (c) states that it is made under this Schedule.

9. The Secretary of State may by order made by statutory instrument prescribe the form of requests and the procedure for making them; and if he does so the request is not valid unless it complies with the order.

Parties agree

10.—(1) If before the end of the first period the parties agree a bargaining unit and that the union is (or unions are) to be recognised as entitled to conduct collective bargaining on behalf of the unit, no further steps are to be taken under this Part of this Schedule.

Employment Relations Act 1999, Sch 1

(2) If before the end of the first period the employer informs the union (or unions) that the employer does not accept the request but is willing to negotiate, sub-paragraph (3) applies.

(3) The parties may conduct negotiations with a view to agreeing a bargaining unit and that the union is (or unions are) to be recognised as entitled to conduct collective bargaining on behalf of the unit.

(4) If such an agreement is made before the end of the second period no further steps are to be taken under this Part of this Schedule.

(5) The employer and the union (or unions) may request ACAS to assist in conducting the negotiations.

(6) The first period is the period of 10 working days starting with the day after that on which the employer receives the request for recognition.

(7) The second period is—
   (a) the period of 20 working days starting with the day after that on which the first period ends, or
   (b) such longer period (so starting) as the parties may from time to time agree.

Employer rejects request

11.—(1) This paragraph applies if—
   (a) before the end of the first period the employer fails to respond to the request, or
   (b) before the end of the first period the employer informs the union (or unions) that the employer does not accept the request (without indicating a willingness to negotiate).

(2) The union (or unions) may apply to the CAC to decide both these questions—
   (a) whether the proposed bargaining unit is appropriate or some other bargaining unit is appropriate;
   (b) whether the union has (or unions have) the support of a majority of the workers constituting the appropriate bargaining unit.

Negotiations fail

12.—(1) Sub-paragraph (2) applies if—
   (a) the employer informs the union (or unions) under paragraph 10(2), and
   (b) no agreement is made before the end of the second period.

(2) The union (or unions) may apply to the CAC to decide both these questions—
   (a) whether the proposed bargaining unit is appropriate or some other bargaining unit is appropriate;
   (b) whether the union has (or unions have) the support of a majority of the workers constituting the appropriate bargaining unit.

(3) Sub-paragraph (4) applies if—
   (a) the employer informs the union (or unions) under paragraph 10(2), and
   (b) before the end of the second period the parties agree a bargaining unit but not that the union is (or unions are) to be recognised as entitled to conduct collective bargaining on behalf of the unit.

(4) The union (or unions) may apply to the CAC to decide the question whether the union has (or unions have) the support of a majority of the workers constituting the bargaining unit.

(5) But no application may be made under this paragraph if within the period of 10 working days starting with the day after that on which the employer informs the union (or unions) under paragraph 10(2) the employer proposes that ACAS be requested to assist in conducting the negotiations and—
   (a) the union rejects (or unions reject) the proposal, or
   (b) the union fails (or unions fail) to accept the proposal within the period of 10 working days starting with the day after that on which the employer makes the proposal.

Acceptance of applications

13. The CAC must give notice to the parties of receipt of an application under paragraph 11 or 12.

14.—(1) This paragraph applies if—
  (a) two or more relevant applications are made,
  (b) at least one worker falling within one of the relevant bargaining units also falls within the other relevant bargaining unit (or units), and
  (c) the CAC has not accepted any of the applications.

(2) A relevant application is an application under paragraph 11 or 12.

(3) In relation to a relevant application, the relevant bargaining unit is—
  (a) the proposed bargaining unit, where the application is under paragraph 11(2) or 12(2);
  (b) the agreed bargaining unit, where the application is under paragraph 12(4).

(4) Within the acceptance period the CAC must decide, with regard to each relevant application, whether the 10 per cent test is satisfied.

(5) The 10 per cent test is satisfied if members of the union (or unions) constitute at least 10 per cent of the workers constituting the relevant bargaining unit.

(6) The acceptance period is—
  (a) the period of 10 working days starting with the day after that on which the CAC receives the last relevant application, or
  (b) such longer period (so starting) as the CAC may specify to the parties by notice containing reasons for the extension.

(7) If the CAC decides that—
  (a) the 10 per cent test is satisfied with regard to more than one of the relevant applications, or
  (b) the 10 per cent test is satisfied with regard to none of the relevant applications,
the CAC must not accept any of the relevant applications.

(8) If the CAC decides that the 10 per cent test is satisfied with regard to one only of the relevant applications the CAC—
  (a) must proceed under paragraph 15 with regard to that application, and
  (b) must not accept any of the other relevant applications.

(9) The CAC must give notice of its decision to the parties.

(10) If by virtue of this paragraph the CAC does not accept an application, no further steps are to be taken under this Part of this Schedule in relation to that application.

15.—(1) This paragraph applies to these applications—
  (a) any application with regard to which no decision has to be made under paragraph 14;
  (b) any application with regard to which the CAC must proceed under this paragraph by virtue of paragraph 14.

(2) Within the acceptance period the CAC must decide whether—
  (a) the request for recognition to which the application relates is valid within the terms of paragraphs 5 to 9, and
  (b) the application is made in accordance with paragraph 11 or 12 and admissible within the terms of paragraphs 33 to 42.

(3) In deciding those questions the CAC must consider any evidence which it has been given by the employer or the union (or unions).

(4) If the CAC decides that the request is not valid or the application is not made in accordance with paragraph 11 or 12 or is not admissible—
  (a) the CAC must give notice of its decision to the parties,
  (b) the CAC must not accept the application, and
  (c) no further steps are to be taken under this Part of this Schedule.

Employment Relations Act 1999, Sch 1

(5) If the CAC decides that the request is valid and the application is made in accordance with paragraph 11 or 12 and is admissible it must—
 (a) accept the application, and
 (b) give notice of the acceptance to the parties.

(6) The acceptance period is—
 (a) the period of 10 working days starting with the day after that on which the CAC receives the application, or
 (b) such longer period (so starting) as the CAC may specify to the parties by notice containing reasons for the extension.

Withdrawal of application

16.—(1) If an application under paragraph 11 or 12 is accepted by the CAC, the union (or unions) may not withdraw the application—
 (a) after the CAC issues a declaration under paragraph 22(2), or
 (b) after the union (or the last of the unions) receives notice under paragraph 22(3) or 23(2).

(2) If an application is withdrawn by the union (or unions)—
 (a) the CAC must give notice of the withdrawal to the employer, and
 (b) no further steps are to be taken under this Part of this Schedule.

Notice to cease consideration of application

17.—(1) This paragraph applies if the CAC has received an application under paragraph 11 or 12 and—
 (a) it has not decided whether the application is admissible, or
 (b) it has decided that the application is admissible.

(2) No further steps are to be taken under this Part of this Schedule if, before the final event occurs, the parties give notice to the CAC that they want no further steps to be taken.

(3) The final event occurs when the first of the following occurs—
 (a) the CAC issues a declaration under paragraph 22(2) in consequence of the application;
 (b) the last day of the notification period ends;
and the notification period is that defined by paragraph 24(5) and arising from the application.

Appropriate bargaining unit

18.—(1) If the CAC accepts an application under paragraph 11(2) or 12(2) it must try to help the parties to reach within the appropriate period an agreement as to what the appropriate bargaining unit is.

(2) The appropriate period is—
 (a) the period of 20 working days starting with the day after that on which the CAC gives notice of acceptance of the application, or
 (b) such longer period (so starting) as the CAC may specify to the parties by notice containing reasons for the extension.

19.—(1) This paragraph applies if—
 (a) the CAC accepts an application under paragraph 11(2) or 12(2), and
 (b) the parties have not agreed an appropriate bargaining unit at the end of the appropriate period.

(2) The CAC must decide the appropriate bargaining unit within—
 (a) the period of 10 working days starting with the day after that on which the appropriate period ends, or
 (b) such longer period (so starting) as the CAC may specify to the parties by notice containing reasons for the extension.

(3) In deciding the appropriate bargaining unit the CAC must take these matters into account—
 (a) the need for the unit to be compatible with effective management;
 (b) the matters listed in sub-paragraph (4), so far as they do not conflict with that need.

Employment Relations Act 1999, Sch 1

(4) The matters are—
- (a) the views of the employer and of the union (or unions);
- (b) existing national and local bargaining arrangements;
- (c) the desirability of avoiding small fragmented bargaining units within an undertaking;
- (d) the characteristics of workers falling within the proposed bargaining unit and of any other employees of the employer whom the CAC considers relevant;
- (e) the location of workers.

(5) The CAC must give notice of its decision to the parties.

Union recognition

20.—(1) This paragraph applies if—
- (a) the CAC accepts an application under paragraph 11(2) or 12(2),
- (b) the parties have agreed an appropriate bargaining unit at the end of the appropriate period, or the CAC has decided an appropriate bargaining unit, and
- (c) that bargaining unit differs from the proposed bargaining unit.

(2) Within the decision period the CAC must decide whether the application is invalid within the terms of paragraphs 43 to 50.

(3) In deciding whether the application is invalid, the CAC must consider any evidence which it has been given by the employer or the union (or unions).

(4) If the CAC decides that the application is invalid—
- (a) the CAC must give notice of its decision to the parties,
- (b) the CAC must not proceed with the application, and
- (c) no further steps are to be taken under this Part of this Schedule.

(5) If the CAC decides that the application is not invalid it must—
- (a) proceed with the application, and
- (b) give notice to the parties that it is so proceeding.

(6) The decision period is—
- (a) the period of 10 working days starting with the day after that on which the parties agree an appropriate bargaining unit or the CAC decides an appropriate bargaining unit, or
- (b) such longer period (so starting) as the CAC may specify to the parties by notice containing reasons for the extension.

21.—(1) This paragraph applies if—
- (a) the CAC accepts an application under paragraph 11(2) or 12(2),
- (b) the parties have agreed an appropriate bargaining unit at the end of the appropriate period, or the CAC has decided an appropriate bargaining unit, and
- (c) that bargaining unit is the same as the proposed bargaining unit.

(2) This paragraph also applies if the CAC accepts an application under paragraph 12(4).

(3) The CAC must proceed with the application.

22.—(1) This paragraph applies if—
- (a) the CAC proceeds with an application in accordance with paragraph 20 or 21, and
- (b) the CAC is satisfied that a majority of the workers constituting the bargaining unit are members of the union (or unions).

(2) The CAC must issue a declaration that the union is (or unions are) recognised as entitled to conduct collective bargaining on behalf of the workers constituting the bargaining unit.

(3) But if any of the three qualifying conditions is fulfilled, instead of issuing a declaration under sub-paragraph (2) the CAC must give notice to the parties that it intends to arrange for the holding of a secret ballot in which the workers constituting the bargaining unit are asked whether they want the union (or unions) to conduct collective bargaining on their behalf.

Employment Relations Act 1999, Sch 1

(4) These are the three qualifying conditions—
  (a) the CAC is satisfied that a ballot should be held in the interests of good industrial relations;
  (b) a significant number of the union members within the bargaining unit inform the CAC that they do not want the union (or unions) to conduct collective bargaining on their behalf;
  (c) membership evidence is produced which leads the CAC to conclude that there are doubts whether a significant number of the union members within the bargaining unit want the union (or unions) to conduct collective bargaining on their behalf.

(5) For the purposes of sub-paragraph (4)(c) membership evidence is—
  (a) evidence about the circumstances in which union members became members;
  (b) evidence about the length of time for which union members have been members, in a case where the CAC is satisfied that such evidence should be taken into account.

23.—(1) This paragraph applies if—
  (a) the CAC proceeds with an application in accordance with paragraph 20 or 21, and
  (b) the CAC is not satisfied that a majority of the workers constituting the bargaining unit are members of the union (or unions).

(2) The CAC must give notice to the parties that it intends to arrange for the holding of a secret ballot in which the workers constituting the bargaining unit are asked whether they want the union (or unions) to conduct collective bargaining on their behalf.

24.—(1) This paragraph applies if the CAC gives notice under paragraph 22(3) or 23(2).

(2) Within the notification period—
  (a) the union (or unions), or
  (b) the union (or unions) and the employer,
may notify the CAC that the party making the notification does not (or the parties making the notification do not) want the CAC to arrange for the holding of the ballot.

(3) If the CAC is so notified—
  (a) it must not arrange for the holding of the ballot,
  (b) it must inform the parties that it will not arrange for the holding of the ballot, and why, and
  (c) no further steps are to be taken under this Part of this Schedule.

(4) If the CAC is not so notified it must arrange for the holding of the ballot.

(5) The notification period is the period of 10 working days starting—
  (a) for the purposes of sub-paragraph (2)(a), with the day on which the union (or last of the unions) receives the CAC's notice under paragraph 22(3) or 23(2), or
  (b) for the purposes of sub-paragraph (2)(b), with that day or (if later) the day on which the employer receives the CAC's notice under paragraph 22(3) or 23(2).

25.—(1) This paragraph applies if the CAC arranges under paragraph 24 for the holding of a ballot.

(2) The ballot must be conducted by a qualified independent person appointed by the CAC.

(3) The ballot must be conducted within—
  (a) the period of 20 working days starting with the day after that on which the qualified independent person is appointed, or
  (b) such longer period (so starting) as the CAC may decide.

(4) The ballot must be conducted—
  (a) at a workplace or workplaces decided by the CAC,
  (b) by post, or
  (c) by a combination of the methods described in sub-paragraphs (a) and (b),
depending on the CAC's preference.

(5) In deciding how the ballot is to be conducted the CAC must take into account—
- (a) the likelihood of the ballot being affected by unfairness or malpractice if it were conducted at a workplace or workplaces;
- (b) costs and practicality;
- (c) such other matters as the CAC considers appropriate.

(6) The CAC may not decide that the ballot is to be conducted as mentioned in sub-paragraph (4)(c) unless there are special factors making such a decision appropriate; and special factors include—
- (a) factors arising from the location of workers or the nature of their employment;
- (b) factors put to the CAC by the employer or the union (or unions).

(7) A person is a qualified independent person if—
- (a) he satisfies such conditions as may be specified for the purposes of this paragraph by order of the Secretary of State or is himself so specified, and
- (b) there are no grounds for believing either that he will carry out any functions conferred on him in relation to the ballot otherwise than competently or that his independence in relation to the ballot might reasonably be called into question.

(8) An order under sub-paragraph (7)(a) shall be made by statutory instrument subject to annulment in pursuance of a resolution of either House of Parliament.

(9) As soon as is reasonably practicable after the CAC is required under paragraph 24 to arrange for the holding of a ballot it must inform the parties—
- (a) that it is so required;
- (b) of the name of the person appointed to conduct the ballot and the date of his appointment;
- (c) of the period within which the ballot must be conducted;
- (d) whether the ballot is to be conducted by post or at a workplace or workplaces;
- (e) of the workplace or workplaces concerned (if the ballot is to be conducted at a workplace or workplaces).

26.—(1) An employer who is informed by the CAC under paragraph 25(9) must comply with the following three duties.

(2) The first duty is to co-operate generally, in connection with the ballot, with the union (or unions) and the person appointed to conduct the ballot; and the second and third duties are not to prejudice the generality of this.

(3) The second duty is to give to the union (or unions) such access to the workers constituting the bargaining unit as is reasonable to enable the union (or unions) to inform the workers of the object of the ballot and to seek their support and their opinions on the issues involved.

(4) The third duty is to do the following (so far as it is reasonable to expect the employer to do so)—
- (a) to give to the CAC, within the period of 10 working days starting with the day after that on which the employer is informed under paragraph 25(9), the names and home addresses of the workers constituting the bargaining unit;
- (b) to give to the CAC, as soon as is reasonably practicable, the name and home address of any worker who joins the unit after the employer has complied with paragraph (a);
- (c) to inform the CAC, as soon as is reasonably practicable, of any worker whose name has been given to the CAC under paragraph (a) or (b) but who ceases to be within the unit.

(5) As soon as is reasonably practicable after the CAC receives any information under sub-paragraph (4) it must pass it on to the person appointed to conduct the ballot.

(6) If asked to do so by the union (or unions) the person appointed to conduct the ballot must send to any worker—

Employment Relations Act 1999, Sch 1

      (a)   whose name and home address have been given under sub-paragraph (5), and
      (b)   who is still within the unit (so far as the person so appointed is aware),
any information supplied by the union (or unions) to the person so appointed.

(7)   The duty under sub-paragraph (6) does not apply unless the union bears (or unions bear) the cost of sending the information.

(8)   Each of the following powers shall be taken to include power to issue Codes of Practice about reasonable access for the purposes of sub-paragraph (3)—
      (a)   the power of ACAS under section 199(1);
      (b)   the power of the Secretary of State under section 203(1)(a).

27.—(1)   If the CAC is satisfied that the employer has failed to fulfil any of the three duties imposed by paragraph 26, and the ballot has not been held, the CAC may order the employer—
      (a)   to take such steps to remedy the failure as the CAC considers reasonable and specifies in the order, and
      (b)   to do so within such period as the CAC considers reasonable and specifies in the order.

(2)   If the CAC is satisfied that the employer has failed to comply with an order under sub-paragraph (1), and the ballot has not been held, the CAC may issue a declaration that the union is (or unions are) recognised as entitled to conduct collective bargaining on behalf of the bargaining unit.

(3)   If the CAC issues a declaration under sub-paragraph (2) it shall take steps to cancel the holding of the ballot; and if the ballot is held it shall have no effect.

28.—(1)   This paragraph applies if the holding of a ballot has been arranged under paragraph 24 whether or not it has been cancelled.

(2)   The gross costs of the ballot shall be borne—
      (a)   as to half, by the employer, and
      (b)   as to half, by the union (or unions).

(3)   If there is more than one union they shall bear their half of the gross costs—
      (a)   in such proportions as they jointly indicate to the person appointed to conduct the ballot, or
      (b)   in the absence of such an indication, in equal shares.

(4)   The person appointed to conduct the ballot may send to the employer and the union (or each of the unions) a demand stating—
      (a)   the gross costs of the ballot, and
      (b)   the amount of the gross costs to be borne by the recipient.

(5)   In such a case the recipient must pay the amount stated to the person sending the demand, and must do so within the period of 15 working days starting with the day after that on which the demand is received.

(6)   In England and Wales, if the amount stated is not paid in accordance with sub-paragraph (5) it shall, if a county court so orders, be recoverable by execution issued from that court or otherwise as if it were payable under an order of that court.

(7)   References to the costs of the ballot are to—
      (a)   the costs wholly, exclusively and necessarily incurred in connection with the ballot by the person appointed to conduct it,
      (b)   such reasonable amount as the person appointed to conduct the ballot charges for his services, and
      (c)   such other costs as the employer and the union (or unions) agree.

29.—(1)   As soon as is reasonably practicable after the CAC is informed of the result of a ballot by the person conducting it, the CAC must act under this paragraph.

(2)   The CAC must inform the employer and the union (or unions) of the result of the ballot.

(3)   If the result is that the union is (or unions are) supported by—
      (a)   a majority of the workers voting, and
      (b)   at least 40 per cent of the workers constituting the bargaining unit,

the CAC must issue a declaration that the union is (or unions are) recognised as entitled to conduct collective bargaining on behalf of the bargaining unit.

(4) If the result is otherwise the CAC must issue a declaration that the union is (or unions are) not entitled to be so recognised.

(5) The Secretary of State may by order amend sub-paragraph (3) so as to specify a different degree of support; and different provision may be made for different circumstances.

(6) An order under sub-paragraph (5) shall be made by statutory instrument.

(7) No such order shall be made unless a draft of it has been laid before Parliament and approved by a resolution of each House of Parliament.

Consequences of recognition

30.—(1) This paragraph applies if the CAC issues a declaration under this Part of this Schedule that the union is (or unions are) recognised as entitled to conduct collective bargaining on behalf of a bargaining unit.

(2) The parties may in the negotiation period conduct negotiations with a view to agreeing a method by which they will conduct collective bargaining.

(3) If no agreement is made in the negotiation period the employer or the union (or unions) may apply to the CAC for assistance.

(4) The negotiation period is—
    (a) the period of 30 working days starting with the start day, or
    (b) such longer period (so starting) as the parties may from time to time agree.

(5) The start day is the day after that on which the parties are notified of the declaration.

31.—(1) This paragraph applies if an application for assistance is made to the CAC under paragraph 30.

(2) The CAC must try to help the parties to reach in the agreement period an agreement on a method by which they will conduct collective bargaining.

(3) If at the end of the agreement period the parties have not made such an agreement the CAC must specify to the parties the method by which they are to conduct collective bargaining.

(4) Any method specified under sub-paragraph (3) is to have effect as if it were contained in a legally enforceable contract made by the parties.

(5) But if the parties agree in writing—
    (a) that sub-paragraph (4) shall not apply, or shall not apply to particular parts of the method specified by the CAC, or
    (b) to vary or replace the method specified by the CAC,
the written agreement shall have effect as a legally enforceable contract made by the parties.

(6) Specific performance shall be the only remedy available for breach of anything which is a legally enforceable contract by virtue of this paragraph.

(7) If at any time before a specification is made under sub-paragraph (3) the parties jointly apply to the CAC requesting it to stop taking steps under this paragraph, the CAC must comply with the request.

(8) The agreement period is—
    (a) the period of 20 working days starting with the day after that on which the CAC receives the application under paragraph 30, or
    (b) such longer period (so starting) as the CAC may decide with the consent of the parties.

Method not carried out

32.—(1) This paragraph applies if—

Employment Relations Act 1999, Sch 1

    (a) the CAC issues a declaration under this Part of this Schedule that the union is (or unions are) recognised as entitled to conduct collective bargaining on behalf of a bargaining unit,

    (b) the parties agree a method by which they will conduct collective bargaining, and

    (c) one or more of the parties fails to carry out the agreement.

(2) The parties may apply to the CAC for assistance.

(3) Paragraph 31 applies as if "paragraph 30" (in each place) read "paragraph 30 or paragraph 32".

General provisions about admissibility

33. An application under paragraph 11 or 12 is not admissible unless—

    (a) it is made in such form as the CAC specifies, and

    (b) it is supported by such documents as the CAC specifies.

34. An application under paragraph 11 or 12 is not admissible unless the union gives (or unions give) to the employer—

    (a) notice of the application, and

    (b) a copy of the application and any documents supporting it.

35.—(1) An application under paragraph 11 or 12 is not admissible if the CAC is satisfied that there is already in force a collective agreement under which a union is (or unions are) recognised as entitled to conduct collective bargaining on behalf of any workers falling within the relevant bargaining unit.

(2) But sub-paragraph (1) does not apply to an application under paragraph 11 or 12 if—

    (a) the union (or unions) recognised under the collective agreement and the union (or unions) making the application under paragraph 11 or 12 are the same, and

    (b) the matters in respect of which the union is (or unions are) entitled to conduct collective bargaining do not include pay, hours or holidays.

(3) A declaration of recognition which is the subject of a declaration under paragraph 83(2) must for the purposes of sub-paragraph (1) be treated as ceasing to have effect to the extent specified in paragraph 83(2) on the making of the declaration under paragraph 83(2).

(4) In applying sub-paragraph (1) an agreement for recognition (the agreement in question) must be ignored if—

    (a) the union does not have (or none of the unions has) a certificate under section 6 that it is independent,

    (b) at some time there was an agreement (the old agreement) between the employer and the union under which the union (whether alone or with other unions) was recognised as entitled to conduct collective bargaining on behalf of a group of workers which was the same or substantially the same as the group covered by the agreement in question, and

    (c) the old agreement ceased to have effect in the period of three years ending with the date of the agreement in question.

(5) It is for the CAC to decide whether one group of workers is the same or substantially the same as another, but in deciding the CAC may take account of the views of any person it believes has an interest in the matter.

(6) The relevant bargaining unit is—

    (a) the proposed bargaining unit, where the application is under paragraph 11(2) or 12(2);

    (b) the agreed bargaining unit, where the application is under paragraph 12(4).

36.—(1) An application under paragraph 11 or 12 is not admissible unless the CAC decides that—

    (a) members of the union (or unions) constitute at least 10 per cent of the workers constituting the relevant bargaining unit, and

(b) a majority of the workers constituting the relevant bargaining unit would be likely to favour recognition of the union (or unions) as entitled to conduct collective bargaining on behalf of the bargaining unit.

(2) The relevant bargaining unit is—
  (a) the proposed bargaining unit, where the application is under paragraph 11(2) or 12(2);
  (b) the agreed bargaining unit, where the application is under paragraph 12(4).

(3) The CAC must give reasons for the decision.

37.—(1) This paragraph applies to an application made by more than one union under paragraph 11 or 12.

(2) The application is not admissible unless—
  (a) the unions show that they will co-operate with each other in a manner likely to secure and maintain stable and effective collective bargaining arrangements, and
  (b) the unions show that, if the employer wishes, they will enter into arrangements under which collective bargaining is conducted by the unions acting together on behalf of the workers constituting the relevant bargaining unit.

(3) The relevant bargaining unit is—
  (a) the proposed bargaining unit, where the application is under paragraph 11(2) or 12(2);
  (b) the agreed bargaining unit, where the application is under paragraph 11(4).

38.—(1) This paragraph applies if—
  (a) the CAC accepts a relevant application relating to a bargaining unit or proceeds under paragraph 20 with an application relating to a bargaining unit,
  (b) the application has not been withdrawn,
  (c) no notice has been given under paragraph 17(2),
  (d) the CAC has not issued a declaration under paragraph 22(2), 27(2), 29(3) or 29(4) in relation to that bargaining unit, and
  (e) no notification has been made under paragraph 24(2).

(2) Another relevant application is not admissible if—
  (a) at least one worker falling within the relevant bargaining unit also falls within the bargaining unit referred to in sub-paragraph (1), and
  (b) the application is made by a union (or unions) other than the union (or unions) which made the application referred to in sub-paragraph (1).

(3) A relevant application is an application under paragraph 11 or 12.

(4) The relevant bargaining unit is—
  (a) the proposed bargaining unit, where the application is under paragraph 11(2) or 12(2);
  (b) the agreed bargaining unit, where the application is under paragraph 12(4).

39.—(1) This paragraph applies if the CAC accepts a relevant application relating to a bargaining unit or proceeds under paragraph 20 with an application relating to a bargaining unit.

(2) Another relevant application is not admissible if—
  (a) the application is made within the period of 3 years starting with the day after that on which the CAC gave notice of acceptance of the application mentioned in sub-paragraph (1),
  (b) the relevant bargaining unit is the same or substantially the same as the bargaining unit mentioned in sub-paragraph (1), and
  (c) the application is made by the union (or unions) which made the application mentioned in sub-paragraph (1).

(3) A relevant application is an application under paragraph 11 or 12.

(4) The relevant bargaining unit is—
  (a) the proposed bargaining unit, where the application is under paragraph 11(2) or 12(2);

Employment Relations Act 1999, Sch 1

      (b) the agreed bargaining unit, where the application is under paragraph 12(4).

  (5) This paragraph does not apply if paragraph 40 or 41 applies.

  40.—(1) This paragraph applies if the CAC issues a declaration under paragraph 29(4) that a union is (or unions are) not entitled to be recognised as entitled to conduct collective bargaining on behalf of a bargaining unit; and this is so whether the ballot concerned is held under this Part or Part III of this Schedule.

  (2) An application under paragraph 11 or 12 is not admissible if—
- (a) the application is made within the period of 3 years starting with the day after that on which the declaration was issued,
- (b) the relevant bargaining unit is the same or substantially the same as the bargaining unit mentioned in sub-paragraph (1), and
- (c) the application is made by the union (or unions) which made the application leading to the declaration.

  (3) The relevant bargaining unit is—
- (a) the proposed bargaining unit, where the application is under paragraph 11(2) or 12(2);
- (b) the agreed bargaining unit, where the application is under paragraph 12(4).

  41.—(1) This paragraph applies if the CAC issues a declaration under paragraph 121(3) that bargaining arrangements are to cease to have effect; and this is so whether the ballot concerned is held under Part IV or Part V of this Schedule.

  (2) An application under paragraph 11 or 12 is not admissible if—
- (a) the application is made within the period of 3 years starting with the day after that on which the declaration was issued,
- (b) the relevant bargaining unit is the same or substantially the same as the bargaining unit to which the bargaining arrangements mentioned in sub-paragraph (1) relate, and
- (c) the application is made by the union which was a party (or unions which were parties) to the proceedings leading to the declaration.

  (3) The relevant bargaining unit is—
- (a) the proposed bargaining unit, where the application is under paragraph 11(2) or 12(2);
- (b) the agreed bargaining unit, where the application is under paragraph 12(4).

  42.—(1) This paragraph applies for the purposes of paragraphs 39 to 41.

  (2) It is for the CAC to decide whether one bargaining unit is the same or substantially the same as another, but in deciding the CAC may take account of the views of any person it believes has an interest in the matter.

General provisions about validity

  43.—(1) Paragraphs 44 to 50 apply if the CAC has to decide under paragraph 20 whether an application is valid.

  (2) In those paragraphs—
- (a) references to the application in question are to that application, and
- (b) references to the relevant bargaining unit are to the bargaining unit agreed by the parties or decided by the CAC.

  44.—(1) The application in question is invalid if the CAC is satisfied that there is already in force a collective agreement under which a union is (or unions are) recognised as entitled to conduct collective bargaining on behalf of any workers falling within the relevant bargaining unit.

  (2) But sub-paragraph (1) does not apply to the application in question if—
- (a) the union (or unions) recognised under the collective agreement and the union (or unions) making the application in question are the same, and
- (b) the matters in respect of which the union is (or unions are) entitled to conduct collective bargaining do not include pay, hours or holidays.

  (3) A declaration of recognition which is the subject of a declaration under paragraph 83(2) must for the purposes of sub-paragraph (1) be treated as ceasing to have effect to the extent specified in paragraph 83(2) on the making of the declaration under paragraph 83(2).

Employment Relations Act 1999, Sch 1

(4) In applying sub-paragraph (1) an agreement for recognition (the agreement in question) must be ignored if—
- (a) the union does not have (or none of the unions has) a certificate under section 6 that it is independent,
- (b) at some time there was an agreement (the old agreement) between the employer and the union under which the union (whether alone or with other unions) was recognised as entitled to conduct collective bargaining on behalf of a group of workers which was the same or substantially the same as the group covered by the agreement in question, and
- (c) the old agreement ceased to have effect in the period of three years ending with the date of the agreement in question.

(5) It is for the CAC to decide whether one group of workers is the same or substantially the same an another, but in deciding the CAC may take account of the views of any person it believes has an interest in the matter.

45. The application in question is invalid unless the CAC decides that—
- (a) members of the union (or unions) constitute at least 10 per cent of the workers constituting the relevant bargaining unit, and
- (b) a majority of the workers constituting the relevant bargaining unit would be likely to favour recognition of the union (or unions) as entitled to conduct collective bargaining on behalf of the bargaining unit.

46.—(1) This paragraph applies if—
- (a) the CAC accepts an application under paragraph 11 or 12 relating to a bargaining unit or proceeds under paragraph 20 with an application relating to a bargaining unit,
- (b) the application has not been withdrawn,
- (c) no notice has been given under paragraph 17(2),
- (d) the CAC has not issued a declaration under paragraph 22(2), 27(2), 29(3) or 29(4) in relation to that bargaining unit, and
- (e) no notification has been made under paragraph 24(2).

(2) The application in question is invalid if—
- (a) at least one worker falling within the relevant bargaining unit also falls within the bargaining unit referred to in sub-paragraph (1), and
- (b) the application in question is made by a union (or unions) other than the union (or unions) which made the application referred to in sub-paragraph (1).

47.—(1) This paragraph applies if the CAC accepts an application under paragraph 11 or 12 relating to a bargaining unit or proceeds under paragraph 20 with an application relating to a bargaining unit.

(2) The application in question is invalid if—
- (a) the application is made within the period of 3 years starting with the day after that on which the CAC gave notice of acceptance of the application mentioned in sub-paragraph (1),
- (b) the relevant bargaining unit is the same or substantially the same as the bargaining unit mentioned in sub-paragraph (1), and
- (c) the application is made by the union (or unions) which made the application mentioned in sub-paragraph (1).

(3) This paragraph does not apply if paragraph 48 or 49 applies.

48.—(1) This paragraph applies if the CAC issues a declaration under paragraph 29(4) that a union is (or unions are) not entitled to be recognised as entitled to conduct collective bargaining on behalf of a bargaining unit; and this is so whether the ballot concerned is held under this Part or Part III of this Schedule.

(2) The application in question is invalid if—
- (a) the application is made within the period of 3 years starting with the date of the declaration,
- (b) the relevant bargaining unit is the same or substantially the same as the bargaining unit mentioned in sub-paragraph (1), and
- (c) the application is made by the union (or unions) which made the application leading to the declaration.

Employment Relations Act 1999, Sch 1

49.—(1) This paragraph applies if the CAC issues a declaration under paragraph 121(3) that bargaining arrangements are to cease to have effect; and this is so whether the ballot concerned is held under Part IV or Part V of this Schedule.

(2) The application in question is invalid if—
   (a) the application is made within the period of 3 years starting with the day after that on which the declaration was issued,
   (b) the relevant bargaining unit is the same or substantially the same as the bargaining unit to which the bargaining arrangements mentioned in sub-paragraph (1) relate, and
   (c) the application is made by the union which was a party (or unions which were parties) to the proceedings leading to the declaration.

50.—(1) This paragraph applies for the purposes of paragraphs 47 to 49.

(2) It is for the CAC to decide whether one bargaining unit is the same or substantially the same as another, but in deciding the CAC may take account of the views of any person it believes has an interest in the matter.

Competing applications

51.—(1) For the purposes of this paragraph—
   (a) the original application is the application referred to in paragraph 38(1) or 46(1), and
   (b) the competing application is the other application referred to in paragraph 38(2) or the application in question referred to in paragraph 46(2);

but an application cannot be an original application unless it was made under paragraph 11(2) or 12(2).

(2) This paragraph applies if—
   (a) the CAC decides that the competing application is not admissible by reason of paragraph 38 or is invalid by reason of paragraph 46,
   (b) at the time the decision is made the parties to the original application have not agreed the appropriate bargaining unit under paragraph 18, and the CAC has not decided the appropriate bargaining unit under paragraph 19, in relation to the application, and
   (c) the 10 per cent test (within the meaning given by paragraph 14) is satisfied with regard to the competing application.

(3) In such a case—
   (a) the CAC must cancel the original application,
   (b) the CAC must give notice to the parties to the application that it has been cancelled,
   (c) no further steps are to be taken under this Part of this Schedule in relation to the application, and
   (d) the application shall be treated as if it had never been admissible.

Definitions In the Trade Union and Labour Relations (Consolidation) Act 1992, for "trade union", see s 1 thereof; for "collective agreement" and "collective bargaining", see s 178(1), (2) of that Act (and note Sch A1, Pt I, para 3 thereto, as inserted by this Schedule); for "recognition" and "recognised", see s 178(3) thereof; for "ACAS", see s 247(1) thereof; for "employee", see ss 273(4)(a), 278(4)(a), 280, 295(1) thereof; for "undertaking", see ss 273(4)(e), 278(4)(c), (d) thereof; for "worker", see ss 279, 280, 296(1) thereof; for "employer", see ss 279, 295, 296(2) thereof (and note Sch A1, Pt I, para 2(1), (4) thereto, as inserted by this Schedule); for "associated employer", see s 297 thereof; for "post", see s 298 thereof; for "the CAC", see Sch A1, Pt IX, para 172(1) thereof, as inserted by this Schedule; for "working day", see Sch A1, Pt IX, para 172(2) thereof, as so inserted.
References See paras 2.1, 2.11–2.22.

PART II
VOLUNTARY RECOGNITION

Agreements for recognition

52.—(1) This paragraph applies for the purposes of this Part of this Schedule.

Employment Relations Act 1999, Sch 1

(2) An agreement is an agreement for recognition if the following conditions are fulfilled in relation to it—
   (a) the agreement is made in the permitted period between a union (or unions) and an employer in consequence of a request made under paragraph 4 and valid within the terms of paragraphs 5 to 9;
   (b) under the agreement the union is (or unions are) recognised as entitled to conduct collective bargaining on behalf of a group or groups of workers employed by the employer;
   (c) if sub-paragraph (5) applies to the agreement, it is satisfied.

(3) The permitted period is the period which begins with the day on which the employer receives the request and ends when the first of the following occurs—
   (a) the union withdraws (or unions withdraw) the request;
   (b) the union withdraws (or unions withdraw) any application under paragraph 11 or 12 made in consequence of the request;
   (c) the CAC gives notice of a decision under paragraph 14(7) which precludes it from accepting such an application under paragraph 11 or 12;
   (d) the CAC gives notice under paragraph 15(4)(a) or 20(4)(a) in relation to such an application under paragraph 11 or 12;
   (e) the parties give notice to the CAC under paragraph 17(2) in relation to such an application under paragraph 11 or 12;
   (f) the CAC issues a declaration under paragraph 22(2) in consequence of such an application under paragraph 11 or 12;
   (g) the CAC is notified under paragraph 24(2) in relation to such an application under paragraph 11 or 12;
   (h) the last day of the notification period ends (the notification period being that defined by paragraph 24(5) and arising from such an application under paragraph 11 or 12);
   (i) the CAC is required under paragraph 51(3) to cancel such an application under paragraph 11 or 12.

(4) Sub-paragraph (5) applies to an agreement if—
   (a) at the time it is made the CAC has received an application under paragraph 11 or 12 in consequence of the request mentioned in sub-paragraph (2), and
   (b) the CAC has not decided whether the application is admissible or it has decided that it is admissible.

(5) This sub-paragraph is satisfied if, in relation to the application under paragraph 11 or 12, the parties give notice to the CAC under paragraph 17 before the final event (as defined in paragraph 17) occurs.

Other interpretation

53.—(1) This paragraph applies for the purposes of this Part of this Schedule.

(2) In relation to an agreement for recognition, references to the bargaining unit are to the group of workers (or the groups taken together) to which the agreement for recognition relates.

(3) In relation to an agreement for recognition, references to the parties are to the union (or unions) and the employer who are parties to the agreement.

54.—(1) This paragraph applies for the purposes of this Part of this Schedule.

(2) The meaning of collective bargaining given by section 178(1) shall not apply Except in paragraph 63(2), in relation to an agreement for recognition references to collective bargaining are to negotiations relating to the matters in respect of which the union is (or unions are) recognised as entitled to conduct negotiations under the agreement for recognition.

(4) In paragraph 63(2) the reference to collective bargaining is to negotiations relating to pay, hours and holidays.

Determination of type of agreement

55.—(1) This paragraph applies if one or more of the parties to an agreement applies to the CAC for a decision whether or not the agreement is an agreement for recognition.

Employment Relations Act 1999, Sch 1

(2) The CAC must give notice of receipt of an application under sub-paragraph (1) to any parties to the agreement who are not parties to the application.

(3) The CAC must within the decision period decide whether the agreement is an agreement for recognition.

(4) If the CAC decides that the agreement is an agreement for recognition it must issue a declaration to that effect.

(5) If the CAC decides that the agreement is not an agreement for recognition it must issue a declaration to that effect.

(6) The decision period is—
 (a) the period of 10 working days starting with the day after that on which the CAC receives the application under sub-paragraph (1), or
 (b) such longer period (so starting) as the CAC may specify to the parties to the agreement by notice containing reasons for the extension.

Termination of agreement for recognition

56.—(1) The employer may not terminate an agreement for recognition before the relevant period ends.

(2) After that period ends the employer may terminate the agreement, with or without the consent of the union (or unions).

(3) The union (or unions) may terminate an agreement for recognition at any time, with or without the consent of the employer.

(4) Sub-paragraphs (1) to (3) have effect subject to the terms of the agreement or any other agreement of the parties.

(5) The relevant period is the period of three years starting with the day after the date of the agreement.

57.—(1) If an agreement for recognition is terminated, as from the termination the agreement and any provisions relating to the collective bargaining method shall cease to have effect.

(2) For this purpose provisions relating to the collective bargaining method are—
 (a) any agreement between the parties as to the method by which collective bargaining is to be conducted with regard to the bargaining unit, or
 (b) anything effective as, or as if contained in, a legally enforceable contract and relating to the method by which collective bargaining is to be conducted with regard to the bargaining unit.

Application to CAC to specify method

58.—(1) This paragraph applies if the parties make an agreement for recognition.

(2) The parties may in the negotiation period conduct negotiations with a view to agreeing a method by which they will conduct collective bargaining.

(3) If no agreement is made in the negotiation period the employer or the union (or unions) may apply to the CAC for assistance.

(4) The negotiation period is—
 (a) the period of 30 working days starting with the start day, or
 (b) such longer period (so starting) as the parties may from time to time agree.

(5) The start day is the day after that on which the agreement is made.

59.—(1) This paragraph applies if—
 (a) the parties to an agreement for recognition agree a method by which they will conduct collective bargaining, and
 (b) one or more of the parties fails to carry out the agreement as to a method.

(2) The employer or the union (or unions) may apply to the CAC for assistance.

60.—(1) This paragraph applies if an application for assistance is made to the CAC under paragraph 58 or 59.

Employment Relations Act 1999, Sch 1

(2) The application is not admissible unless the conditions in sub-paragraphs (3) and (4) are satisfied.

(3) The condition is that the employer, taken with any associated employer or employers, must—
- (a) employ at least 21 workers on the day the application is made, or
- (b) employ an average of at least 21 workers in the 13 weeks ending with that day.

(4) The condition is that the union (or every union) has a certificate under section 6 that it is independent.

(5) To find the average under sub-paragraph (3)(b)—
- (a) take the number of workers employed in each of the 13 weeks (including workers not employed for the whole of the week);
- (b) aggregate the 13 numbers;
- (c) divide the aggregate by 13.

(6) For the purposes of sub-paragraph (3)(a) any worker employed by an associated company incorporated outside Great Britain must be ignored unless the day the application was made fell within a period during which he ordinarily worked in Great Britain.

(7) For the purposes of sub-paragraph (3)(b) any worker employed by an associated company incorporated outside Great Britain must be ignored in relation to a week unless the whole or any part of that week fell within a period during which he ordinarily worked in Great Britain.

(8) For the purposes of sub-paragraphs (6) and (7) a worker who is employed on board a ship registered in the register maintained under section 8 of the Merchant Shipping Act 1995 shall be treated as ordinarily working in Great Britain unless—
- (a) the ship's entry in the register specifies a port outside Great Britain as the port to which the vessel is to be treated as belonging,
- (b) the employment is wholly outside Great Britain, or
- (c) the worker is not ordinarily resident in Great Britain.

(9) An order made under paragraph 7(6) may also—
- (a) provide that sub-paragraphs (2), (3) and (5) to (8) of this paragraph are not to apply, or are not to apply in specified circumstances, or
- (b) vary the number of workers for the time being specified in sub-paragraph (3).

61.—(1) An application to the CAC is not admissible unless—
- (a) it is made in such form as the CAC specifies, and
- (b) it is supported by such documents as the CAC specifies.

(2) An application which is made by a union (or unions) to the CAC is not admissible unless the union gives (or unions give) to the employer—
- (a) notice of the application, and
- (b) a copy of the application and any documents supporting it.

(3) An application which is made by an employer to the CAC is not admissible unless the employer gives to the union (or each of the unions)—
- (a) notice of the application, and
- (b) a copy of the application and any documents supporting it.

CAC's response to application

62.—(1) The CAC must give notice to the parties of receipt of an application under paragraph 58 or 59.

(2) Within the acceptance period the CAC must decide whether the application is admissible within the terms of paragraphs 60 and 61.

(3) In deciding whether an application is admissible the CAC must consider any evidence which it has been given by the employer or the union (or unions).

(4) If the CAC decides that the application is not admissible—
- (a) the CAC must give notice of its decision to the parties,
- (b) the CAC must not accept the application, and

Employment Relations Act 1999, Sch 1

    (c)   no further steps are to be taken under this Part of this Schedule.

(5)   If the CAC decides that the application is admissible it must—
- (a) accept the application, and
- (b) give notice of the acceptance to the parties.

(6)   The acceptance period is—
- (a) the period of 10 working days starting with the day after that on which the CAC receives the application, or
- (b) such longer period (so starting) as the CAC may specify to the parties by notice containing reasons for the extension.

63.—(1)   If the CAC accepts an application it must try to help the parties to reach in the agreement period an agreement on a method by which they will conduct collective bargaining.

(2)   If at the end of the agreement period the parties have not made such an agreement the CAC must specify to the parties the method by which they are to conduct collective bargaining.

(3)   Any method specified under sub-paragraph (2) is to have effect as if it were contained in a legally enforceable contract made by the parties.

(4)   But if the parties agree in writing—
- (a) that sub-paragraph (3) shall not apply, or shall not apply to particular parts of the method specified by the CAC, or
- (b) to vary or replace the method specified by the CAC,

the written agreement shall have effect as a legally enforceable contract made by the parties.

(5)   Specific performance shall be the only remedy available for breach of anything which is a legally enforceable contract by virtue of this paragraph.

(6)   If the CAC accepts an application, the applicant may not withdraw it after the end of the agreement period.

(7)   If at any time before a specification is made under sub-paragraph (2) the parties jointly apply to the CAC requesting it to stop taking steps under this paragraph, the CAC must comply with the request.

(8)   The agreement period is—
- (a) the period of 20 working days starting with the day after that on which the CAC gives notice of acceptance of the application, or
- (b) such longer period (so starting) as the parties may from time to time agree.

Definitions   In the Trade Union and Labour Relations (Consolidation) Act 1992, for "recognition" and "recognised", see s 178(3) thereof; for "worker", see ss 279, 280, 296(1) thereof; for "employer", see ss 279, 295, 296(2) thereof; as to "associated company", see s 297 thereof; for "the CAC", see Sch A1, Pt IX, para 172(1) thereof, as inserted by this Schedule; for "working day", see Sch A1, Pt IX, para 172(2) thereof, as so inserted.

References   See paras 2.23–2.25.

PART III
CHANGES AFFECTING BARGAINING UNIT

Introduction

64.—(1)   This Part of this Schedule applies if—
- (a) the CAC has issued a declaration that a union is (or unions are) recognised as entitled to conduct collective bargaining on behalf of a bargaining unit, and
- (b) provisions relating to the collective bargaining method apply in relation to the unit.

(2)   In such a case, in this Part of this Schedule—
- (a) references to the original unit are to the bargaining unit on whose behalf the union is (or unions are) recognised as entitled to conduct collective bargaining, and

(b) references to the bargaining arrangements are to the declaration and to the provisions relating to the collective bargaining method which apply in relation to the original unit.

(3) For this purpose provisions relating to the collective bargaining method are—
  (a) the parties' agreement as to the method by which collective bargaining is to be conducted with regard to the original unit,
  (b) anything effective as, or as if contained in, a legally enforceable contract and relating to the method by which collective bargaining is to be conducted with regard to the original unit, or
  (c) any provision of this Part of this Schedule that a method of collective bargaining is to have effect with regard to the original unit.

65. References in this Part of this Schedule to the parties are to the employer and the union (or unions) concerned.

Either party believes unit no longer appropriate

66.—(1) This paragraph applies if the employer believes or the union believes (or unions believe) that the original unit is no longer an appropriate bargaining unit.

(2) The employer or union (or unions) may apply to the CAC to make a decision as to what is an appropriate bargaining unit.

67.—(1) An application under paragraph 66 is not admissible unless the CAC decides that it is likely that the original unit is no longer appropriate by reason of any of the matters specified in sub-paragraph (2).

(2) The matters are—
  (a) a change in the organisation or structure of the business carried on by the employer;
  (b) a change in the activities pursued by the employer in the course of the business carried on by him;
  (c) a substantial change in the number of workers employed in the original unit.

68.—(1) The CAC must give notice to the parties of receipt of an application under paragraph 66.

(2) Within the acceptance period the CAC must decide whether the application is admissible within the terms of paragraphs 67 and 92.

(3) In deciding whether the application is admissible the CAC must consider any evidence which it has been given by the employer or the union (or unions).

(4) If the CAC decides that the application is not admissible—
  (a) the CAC must give notice of its decision to the parties,
  (b) the CAC must not accept the application, and
  (c) no further steps are to be taken under this Part of this Schedule.

(5) If the CAC decides that the application is admissible it must—
  (a) accept the application, and
  (b) give notice of the acceptance to the parties.

(6) The acceptance period is—
  (a) the period of 10 working days starting with the day after that on which the CAC receives the application, or
  (b) such longer period (so starting) as the CAC may specify to the parties by notice containing reasons for the extension.

69.—(1) This paragraph applies if—
  (a) the CAC gives notice of acceptance of the application, and
  (b) before the end of the first period the parties agree a bargaining unit or units (the new unit or units) differing from the original unit and inform the CAC of their agreement.

(2) If in the CAC's opinion the new unit (or any of the new units) contains at least one worker falling within an outside bargaining unit no further steps are to be taken under this Part of this Schedule.

Employment Relations Act 1999, Sch 1

(3) If sub-paragraph (2) does not apply—
- (a) the CAC must issue a declaration that the union is (or unions are) recognised as entitled to conduct collective bargaining on behalf of the new unit or units;
- (b) so far as it affects workers in the new unit (or units) who fall within the original unit, the declaration shall have effect in place of any declaration that the union is (or unions are) recognised as entitled to conduct collective bargaining on behalf of the original unit;
- (c) the method of collective bargaining relating to the original unit shall have effect in relation to the new unit or units, with any modifications which the CAC considers necessary to take account of the change of bargaining unit and specifies in the declaration.

(4) The first period is—
- (a) the period of 10 working days starting with the day after that on which the CAC gives notice of acceptance of the application, or
- (b) such longer period (so starting) as the parties may from time to time agree and notify to the CAC.

(5) An outside bargaining unit is a bargaining unit which fulfils these conditions—
- (a) it is not the original unit;
- (b) a union is (or unions are) recognised as entitled to conduct collective bargaining on its behalf;
- (c) the union (or at least one of the unions) is not a party referred to in paragraph 64.

70.—(1) This paragraph applies if—
- (a) the CAC gives notice of acceptance of the application, and
- (b) the parties do not inform the CAC before the end of the first period that they have agreed a bargaining unit or units differing from the original unit.

(2) During the second period—
- (a) the CAC must decide whether or not the original unit continues to be an appropriate bargaining unit;
- (b) if the CAC decides that the original unit does not so continue, it must decide what other bargaining unit is or units are appropriate;
- (c) the CAC must give notice to the parties of its decision or decisions under paragraphs (a) and (b).

(3) In deciding whether or not the original unit continues to be an appropriate bargaining unit the CAC must take into account only these matters—
- (a) any change in the organisation or structure of the business carried on by the employer;
- (b) any change in the activities pursued by the employer in the course of the business carried on by him;
- (c) any substantial change in the number of workers employed in the original unit.

(4) In deciding what other bargaining unit is or units are appropriate the CAC must take these matters into account—
- (a) the need for the unit or units to be compatible with effective management;
- (b) the matters listed in sub-paragraph (5), so far as they do not conflict with that need.

(5) The matters are—
- (a) the views of the employer and of the union (or unions);
- (b) existing national and local bargaining arrangements;
- (c) the desirability of avoiding small fragmented bargaining units within an undertaking;
- (d) the characteristics of workers falling within the original unit and of any other employees of the employer whom the CAC considers relevant;
- (e) the location of workers.

(6) If the CAC decides that two or more bargaining units are appropriate its decision must be such that no worker falls within more than one of them.

(7) The second period is—

(a) the period of 10 working days starting with the day after that on which the first period ends, or
(b) such longer period (so starting) as the CAC may specify to the parties by notice containing reasons for the extension.

71. If the CAC gives notice under paragraph 70 of a decision that the original unit continues to be an appropriate bargaining unit no further steps are to be taken under this Part of this Schedule.

72. Paragraph 82 applies if the CAC gives notice under paragraph 70 of—
(a) a decision that the original unit is no longer an appropriate bargaining unit, and
(b) a decision as to the bargaining unit which is (or units which are) appropriate.

73.—(1) This paragraph applies if—
(a) the parties agree under paragraph 69 a bargaining unit or units differing from the original unit,
(b) paragraph 69(2) does not apply, and
(c) at least one worker falling within the original unit does not fall within the new unit (or any of the new units).

(2) In such a case—
(a) the CAC must issue a declaration that the bargaining arrangements, so far as relating to the worker or workers mentioned in sub-paragraph (1)(c), are to cease to have effect on a date specified by the CAC in the declaration, and
(b) the bargaining arrangements shall cease to have effect accordingly.

Employer believes unit has ceased to exist

74.—(1) If the employer—
(a) believes that the original unit has ceased to exist, and
(b) wishes the bargaining arrangements to cease to have effect,
he must give the union (or each of the unions) a notice complying with sub-paragraph (2) and must give a copy of the notice to the CAC.

(2) A notice complies with this sub-paragraph if it—
(a) identifies the unit and the bargaining arrangements,
(b) states the date on which the notice is given,
(c) states that the unit has ceased to exist, and
(d) states that the bargaining arrangements are to cease to have effect on a date which is specified in the notice and which falls after the end of the period of 35 working days starting with the day after that on which the notice is given.

(3) Within the validation period the CAC must decide whether the notice complies with sub-paragraph (2).

(4) If the CAC decides that the notice does not comply with sub-paragraph (2)—
(a) the CAC must give the parties notice of its decision, and
(b) the employer's notice shall be treated as not having been given.

(5) If the CAC decides that the notice complies with sub-paragraph (2) it must give the parties notice of the decision.

(6) The bargaining arrangements shall cease to have effect on the date specified under sub-paragraph (2)(d) if—
(a) the CAC gives notice under sub-paragraph (5), and
(b) the union does not (or unions do not) apply to the CAC under paragraph 75.

(7) The validation period is—
(a) the period of 10 working days starting with the day after that on which the CAC receives the copy of the notice, or
(b) such longer period (so starting) as the CAC may specify to the parties by notice containing reasons for the extension.

75.—(1) Paragraph 76 applies if—
(a) the CAC gives notice under paragraph 74(5), and

(b) within the period of 10 working days starting with the day after that on which the notice is given the union makes (or unions make) an application to the CAC for a decision on the questions specified in sub-paragraph (2).

(2) The questions are—
   (a) whether the original unit has ceased to exist;
   (b) whether the original unit is no longer appropriate by reason of any of the matters specified in sub-paragraph (3).

(3) The matters are—
   (a) a change in the organisation or structure of the business carried on by the employer;
   (b) a change in the activities pursued by the employer in the course of the business carried on by him;
   (c) a substantial change in the number of workers employed in the original unit.

76.—(1) The CAC must give notice to the parties of receipt of an application under paragraph 75.

(2) Within the acceptance period the CAC must decide whether the application is admissible within the terms of paragraph 92.

(3) In deciding whether the application is admissible the CAC must consider any evidence which it has been given by the employer or the union (or unions).

(4) If the CAC decides that the application is not admissible—
   (a) the CAC must give notice of its decision to the parties,
   (b) the CAC must not accept the application, and
   (c) no further steps are to be taken under this Part of this Schedule.

(5) If the CAC decides that the application is admissible it must—
   (a) accept the application, and
   (b) give notice of the acceptance to the parties.

(6) The acceptance period is—
   (a) the period of 10 working days starting with the day after that on which the CAC receives the application, or
   (b) such longer period (so starting) as the CAC may specify to the parties by notice containing reasons for the extension.

77.—(1) If the CAC accepts an application it—
   (a) must give the employer and the union (or unions) an opportunity to put their views on the questions in relation to which the application was made;
   (b) must decide the questions before the end of the decision period.

(2) If the CAC decides that the original unit has ceased to exist—
   (a) the CAC must give the parties notice of its decision, and
   (b) the bargaining arrangements shall cease to have effect on the termination date.

(3) If the CAC decides that the original unit has not ceased to exist, and that it is not the case that the original unit is no longer appropriate by reason of any of the matters specified in paragraph 75(3)—
   (a) the CAC must give the parties notice of its decision, and
   (b) the employer's notice shall be treated as not having been given.

(4) If the CAC decides that the original unit has not ceased to exist, and that the original unit is no longer appropriate by reason of any of the matters specified in paragraph 75(3), the CAC must give the parties notice of its decision.

(5) The decision period is—
   (a) the period of 10 working days starting with the day after that on which the CAC gives notice of acceptance of the application, or
   (b) such longer period (so starting) as the CAC may specify to the parties by notice containing reasons for the extension.

(6) The termination date is the later of—
   (a) the date specified under paragraph 74(2)(d), and

Employment Relations Act 1999, Sch 1

    (b)   the day after the last day of the decision period.

78.—(1)   This paragraph applies if—
- (a) the CAC gives notice under paragraph 77(4), and
- (b) before the end of the first period the parties agree a bargaining unit or units (the new unit or units) differing from the original unit and inform the CAC of their agreement.

(2)   If in the CAC's opinion the new unit (or any of the new units) contains at least one worker falling within an outside bargaining unit no further steps are to be taken under this Part of this Schedule.

(3)   If sub-paragraph (2) does not apply—
- (a) the CAC must issue a declaration that the union is (or unions are) recognised as entitled to conduct collective bargaining on behalf of the new unit or units;
- (b) so far as it affects workers in the new unit (or units) who fall within the original unit, the declaration shall have effect in place of any declaration that the union is (or unions are) recognised as entitled to conduct collective bargaining on behalf of the original unit;
- (c) the method of collective bargaining relating to the original unit shall have effect in relation to the new unit or units, with any modifications which the CAC considers necessary to take account of the change of bargaining unit and specifies in the declaration.

(4)   The first period is—
- (a) the period of 10 working days starting with the day after that on which the CAC gives notice under paragraph 77(4), or
- (b) such longer period (so starting) as the parties may from time to time agree and notify to the CAC.

(5)   An outside bargaining unit is a bargaining unit which fulfils these conditions—
- (a) it is not the original unit;
- (b) a union is (or unions are) recognised as entitled to conduct collective bargaining on its behalf;
- (c) the union (or at least one of the unions) is not a party referred to in paragraph 64.

79.—(1)   This paragraph applies if—
- (a) the CAC gives notice under paragraph 77(4), and
- (b) the parties do not inform the CAC before the end of the first period that they have agreed a bargaining unit or units differing from the original unit.

(2)   During the second period the CAC—
- (a) must decide what other bargaining unit is or units are appropriate;
- (b) must give notice of its decision to the parties.

(3)   In deciding what other bargaining unit is or units are appropriate, the CAC must take these matters into account—
- (a) the need for the unit or units to be compatible with effective management;
- (b) the matters listed in sub-paragraph (4), so far as they do not conflict with that need.

(4)   The matters are—
- (a) the views of the employer and of the union (or unions);
- (b) existing national and local bargaining arrangements;
- (c) the desirability of avoiding small fragmented bargaining units within an undertaking;
- (d) the characteristics of workers falling within the original unit and of any other employees of the employer whom the CAC considers relevant;
- (e) the location of workers.

(5)   If the CAC decides that two or more bargaining units are appropriate its decision must be such that no worker falls within more than one of them.

(6)   The second period is—
- (a) the period of 10 working days starting with the day after that on which the first period ends, or

Employment Relations Act 1999, Sch 1

     (b)   such longer period (so starting) as the CAC may specify to the parties by notice containing reasons for the extension.

80.   Paragraph 82 applies if the CAC gives notice under paragraph 79 of a decision as to the bargaining unit which is (or units which are) appropriate.

81.—(1)   This paragraph applies if—
   (a)   the parties agree under paragraph 78 a bargaining unit or units differing from the original unit,
   (b)   paragraph 78(2) does not apply, and
   (c)   at least one worker falling within the original unit does not fall within the new unit (or any of the new units).

(2)   In such a case—
   (a)   the CAC must issue a declaration that the bargaining arrangements, so far as relating to the worker or workers mentioned in sub-paragraph (1)(c), are to cease to have effect on a date specified by the CAC in the declaration, and
   (b)   the bargaining arrangements shall cease to have effect accordingly.

Position where CAC decides new unit

82.—(1)   This paragraph applies if the CAC gives notice under paragraph 70 of—
   (a)   a decision that the original unit is no longer an appropriate bargaining unit, and
   (b)   a decision as to the bargaining unit which is (or units which are) appropriate.

(2)   This paragraph also applies if the CAC gives notice under paragraph 79 of a decision as to the bargaining unit which is (or units which are) appropriate.

(3)   The CAC—
   (a)   must proceed as stated in paragraphs 83 to 89 with regard to the appropriate unit (if there is one only), or
   (b)   must proceed as stated in paragraphs 83 to 89 with regard to each appropriate unit separately (if there are two or more).

(4)   References in those paragraphs to the new unit are to the appropriate unit under consideration.

83.—(1)   This paragraph applies if in the CAC's opinion the new unit contains at least one worker falling within a statutory outside bargaining unit.

(2)   In such a case—
   (a)   the CAC must issue a declaration that the relevant bargaining arrangements, so far as relating to workers falling within the new unit, are to cease to have effect on a date specified by the CAC in the declaration, and
   (b)   the relevant bargaining arrangements shall cease to have effect accordingly.

(3)   The relevant bargaining arrangements are—
   (a)   the bargaining arrangements relating to the original unit, and
   (b)   the bargaining arrangements relating to each statutory outside bargaining unit containing workers who fall within the new unit.

(4)   The bargaining arrangements relating to the original unit are the bargaining arrangements as defined in paragraph 64.

(5)   The bargaining arrangements relating to an outside unit are—
   (a)   the declaration recognising a union (or unions) as entitled to conduct collective bargaining on behalf of the workers constituting the outside unit, and
   (b)   the provisions relating to the collective bargaining method.

(6)   For this purpose the provisions relating to the collective bargaining method are—
   (a)   any agreement by the employer and the union (or unions) as to the method by which collective bargaining is to be conducted with regard to the outside unit,

Employment Relations Act 1999, Sch 1

    (b) anything effective as, or as if contained in, a legally enforceable contract and relating to the method by which collective bargaining is to be conducted with regard to the outside unit, or

    (c) any provision of this Part of this Schedule that a method of collective bargaining is to have effect with regard to the outside unit.

(7) A statutory outside bargaining unit is a bargaining unit which fulfils these conditions—

    (a) it is not the original unit;

    (b) a union is (or unions are) recognised as entitled to conduct collective bargaining on its behalf by virtue of a declaration of the CAC;

    (c) the union (or at least one of the unions) is not a party referred to in paragraph 64.

(8) The date specified under sub-paragraph (1)(a) must be—

    (a) the date on which the relevant period expires, or

    (b) if the CAC believes that to maintain the relevant bargaining arrangements would be impracticable or contrary to the interests of good industrial relations, the date after the date on which the declaration is issued;

and the relevant period is the period of 65 working days starting with the day after that on which the declaration is issued.

84.—(1) This paragraph applies if in the CAC's opinion the new unit contains—

    (a) at least one worker falling within a voluntary outside bargaining unit, but

    (b) no worker falling within a statutory outside bargaining unit.

(2) In such a case—

    (a) the CAC must issue a declaration that the original bargaining arrangements, so far as relating to workers falling within the new unit, are to cease to have effect on a date specified by the CAC in the declaration, and

    (b) the original bargaining arrangements shall cease to have effect accordingly.

(3) The original bargaining arrangements are the bargaining arrangements as defined in paragraph 64.

(4) A voluntary outside bargaining unit is a bargaining unit which fulfils these conditions—

    (a) it is not the original unit;

    (b) a union is (or unions are) recognised as entitled to conduct collective bargaining on its behalf by virtue of an agreement with the employer;

    (c) the union (or at least one of the unions) is not a party referred to in paragraph 64.

(5) The date specified under sub-paragraph (2)(a) must be—

    (a) the date on which the relevant period expires, or

    (b) if the CAC believes that to maintain the original bargaining arrangements would be impracticable or contrary to the interests of good industrial relations, the date after the date on which the declaration is issued;

and the relevant period is the period of 65 working days starting with the day after that on which the declaration is issued.

85.—(1) If the CAC's opinion is not that mentioned in paragraph 83(1) or 84(1) it must—

    (a) decide whether the difference between the original unit and the new unit is such that the support of the union (or unions) within the new unit needs to be assessed, and

    (b) inform the parties of its decision.

(2) If the CAC's decision is that such support does not need to be assessed—

    (a) the CAC must issue a declaration that the union is (or unions are) recognised as entitled to conduct collective bargaining on behalf of the new unit;

    (b) so far as it affects workers in the new unit who fall within the original unit, the declaration shall have effect in place of any declaration that the union is (or unions are) recognised as entitled to conduct collective bargaining on behalf of the original unit;

Employment Relations Act 1999, Sch 1

    (c) the method of collective bargaining relating to the original unit shall have effect in relation to the new unit, with any modifications which the CAC considers necessary to take account of the change of bargaining unit and specifies in the declaration.

86.—(1) This paragraph applies if the CAC decides under paragraph 85(1) that the support of the union (or unions) within the new unit needs to be assessed.

(2) The CAC must decide these questions—
    (a) whether members of the union (or unions) constitute at least 10 per cent of the workers constituting the new unit;
    (b) whether a majority of the workers constituting the new unit would be likely to favour recognition of the union (or unions) as entitled to conduct collective bargaining on behalf of the new unit.

(3) If the CAC decides one or both of the questions in the negative—
    (a) the CAC must issue a declaration that the bargaining arrangements, so far as relating to workers falling within the new unit, are to cease to have effect on a date specified by the CAC in the declaration, and
    (b) the bargaining arrangements shall cease to have effect accordingly.

87.—(1) This paragraph applies if—
    (a) the CAC decides both the questions in paragraph 86(2) in the affirmative, and
    (b) the CAC is satisfied that a majority of the workers constituting the new unit are members of the union (or unions).

(2) The CAC must issue a declaration that the union is (or unions are) recognised as entitled to conduct collective bargaining on behalf of the workers constituting the new unit.

(3) But if any of the three qualifying conditions is fulfilled, instead of issuing a declaration under sub-paragraph (2) the CAC must give notice to the parties that it intends to arrange for the holding of a secret ballot in which the workers constituting the new unit are asked whether they want the union (or unions) to conduct collective bargaining on their behalf.

(4) These are the three qualifying conditions—
    (a) the CAC is satisfied that a ballot should be held in the interests of good industrial relations;
    (b) a significant number of the union members within the new unit inform the CAC that they do not want the union (or unions) to conduct collective bargaining on their behalf;
    (c) membership evidence is produced which leads the CAC to conclude that there are doubts whether a significant number of the union members within the new unit want the union (or unions) to conduct collective bargaining on their behalf.

(5) For the purposes of sub-paragraph (4)(c) membership evidence is—
    (a) evidence about the circumstances in which union members became members;
    (b) evidence about the length of time for which union members have been members, in a case where the CAC is satisfied that such evidence should be taken into account.

(6) If the CAC issues a declaration under sub-paragraph (2)—
    (a) so far as it affects workers in the new unit who fall within the original unit, the declaration shall have effect in place of any declaration that the union is (or unions are) recognised as entitled to conduct collective bargaining on behalf of the original unit;
    (b) the method of collective bargaining relating to the original unit shall have effect in relation to the new unit, with any modifications which the CAC considers necessary to take account of the change of bargaining unit and specifies in the declaration.

88.—(1) This paragraph applies if—

(a) the CAC decides both the questions in paragraph 86(2) in the affirmative, and
(b) the CAC is not satisfied that a majority of the workers constituting the new unit are members of the union (or unions).

(2) The CAC must give notice to the parties that it intends to arrange for the holding of a secret ballot in which the workers constituting the new unit are asked whether they want the union (or unions) to conduct collective bargaining on their behalf.

89.—(1) If the CAC gives notice under paragraph 87(3) or 88(2) the union (or unions) may within the notification period notify the CAC that the union does not (or unions do not) want the CAC to arrange for the holding of the ballot; and the notification period is the period of 10 working days starting with the day after that on which the union (or last of the unions) receives the CAC's notice.

(2) If the CAC is so notified—
  (a) it must not arrange for the holding of the ballot,
  (b) it must inform the parties that it will not arrange for the holding of the ballot, and why,
  (c) it must issue a declaration that the bargaining arrangements, so far as relating to workers falling within the new unit, are to cease to have effect on a date specified by it in the declaration, and
  (d) the bargaining arrangements shall cease to have effect accordingly.

(3) If the CAC is not so notified it must arrange for the holding of the ballot.

(4) Paragraph 25 applies if the CAC arranges under this paragraph for the holding of a ballot (as well as if the CAC arranges under paragraph 24 for the holding of a ballot).

(5) Paragraphs 26 to 29 apply accordingly, but as if references to the bargaining unit were references to the new unit.

(6) If as a result of the ballot the CAC issues a declaration that the union is (or unions are) recognised as entitled to conduct collective bargaining on behalf of the new unit—
  (a) so far as it affects workers in the new unit who fall within the original unit, the declaration shall have effect in place of any declaration that the union is (or unions are) recognised as entitled to conduct collective bargaining on behalf of the original unit;
  (b) the method of collective bargaining relating to the original unit shall have effect in relation to the new unit, with any modifications which the CAC considers necessary to take account of the change of bargaining unit and specifies in the declaration.

(7) If as a result of the ballot the CAC issues a declaration that the union is (or unions are) not entitled to be recognised as entitled to conduct collective bargaining on behalf of the new unit—
  (a) the CAC must state in the declaration the date on which the bargaining arrangements, so far as relating to workers falling within the new unit, are to cease to have effect, and
  (b) the bargaining arrangements shall cease to have effect accordingly.

(8) Paragraphs (a) and (b) of sub-paragraph (6) also apply if the CAC issues a declaration under paragraph 27(2).

Residual workers

90.—(1) This paragraph applies if—
  (a) the CAC decides an appropriate bargaining unit or units under paragraph 70 or 79, and
  (b) at least one worker falling within the original unit does not fall within the new unit (or any of the new units).

(2) In such a case—
  (a) the CAC must issue a declaration that the bargaining arrangements, so far as relating to the worker or workers mentioned in sub-paragraph (1)(b), are to cease to have effect on a date specified by the CAC in the declaration, and

(b) the bargaining arrangements shall cease to have effect accordingly.

91.—(1) This paragraph applies if—
  (a) the CAC has proceeded as stated in paragraphs 83 to 89 with regard to the new unit (if there is one only) or with regard to each new unit (if there are two or more), and
  (b) in so doing the CAC has issued one or more declarations under paragraph 83.

(2) The CAC must—
  (a) consider each declaration issued under paragraph 83, and
  (b) in relation to each declaration, identify each statutory outside bargaining unit which contains at least one worker who also falls within the new unit to which the declaration relates;
and in this paragraph each statutory outside bargaining unit so identified is referred to as a parent unit.

(3) The CAC must then—
  (a) consider each parent unit, and
  (b) in relation to each parent unit, identify any workers who fall within the parent unit but who do not fall within the new unit (or any of the new units);
and in this paragraph the workers so identified in relation to a parent unit are referred to as a residual unit.

(4) In relation to each residual unit, the CAC must issue a declaration that the outside union is (or outside unions are) recognised as entitled to conduct collective bargaining on its behalf.

(5) But no such declaration shall be issued in relation to a residual unit if the CAC has received an application under paragraph 66 or 75 in relation to its parent unit.

(6) In this paragraph references to the outside union (or to outside unions) in relation to a residual unit are to the union which is (or unions which are) recognised as entitled to conduct collective bargaining on behalf of its parent unit.

(7) If the CAC issues a declaration under sub-paragraph (4)—
  (a) the declaration shall have effect in place of the existing declaration that the outside union is (or outside unions are) recognised as entitled to conduct collective bargaining on behalf of the parent unit, so far as the existing declaration relates to the residual unit;
  (b) if there is a method of collective bargaining relating to the parent unit, it shall have effect in relation to the residual unit with any modifications which the CAC considers necessary to take account of the change of bargaining unit and specifies in the declaration.

Applications under this Part

92.—(1) An application to the CAC under this Part of this Schedule is not admissible unless—
  (a) it is made in such form as the CAC specifies, and
  (b) it is supported by such documents as the CAC specifies.

(2) An application which is made by a union (or unions) to the CAC under this Part of this Schedule is not admissible unless the union gives (or unions give) to the employer—
  (a) notice of the application, and
  (b) a copy of the application and any documents supporting it.

(3) An application which is made by an employer to the CAC under this Part of this Schedule is not admissible unless the employer gives to the union (or each of the unions)—
  (a) notice of the application, and
  (b) a copy of the application and any documents supporting it.

Withdrawal of application

93.—(1) If an application under paragraph 66 or 75 is accepted by the CAC, the applicant (or applicants) may not withdraw the application—
  (a) after the CAC issues a declaration under paragraph 69(3) or 78(3),

Employment Relations Act 1999, Sch 1

(b) after the CAC decides under paragraph 77(2) or 77(3),
(c) after the CAC issues a declaration under paragraph 83(1), 85(2), 86(3) or 87(2) in relation to the new unit (where there is only one) or a declaration under any of those paragraphs in relation to any of the new units (where there is more than one),
(d) after the union has (or unions have) notified the CAC under paragraph 89(1) in relation to the new unit (where there is only one) or any of the new units (where there is more than one), or
(e) after the end of the notification period referred to in paragraph 89(1) and relating to the new unit (where there is only one) or any of the new units (where there is more than one).

(2) If an application is withdrawn by the applicant (or applicants)—
(a) the CAC must give notice of the withdrawal to the other party (or parties), and
(b) no further steps are to be taken under this Part of this Schedule.

Meaning of collective bargaining

94.—(1) This paragraph applies for the purposes of this Part of this Schedule.

(2) Except in relation to paragraphs 69(5), 78(5) and 83(6), the meaning of collective bargaining given by section 178(1) shall not apply.

(3) In relation to a new unit references to collective bargaining are to negotiations relating to the matters which were the subject of collective bargaining in relation to the corresponding original unit; and the corresponding original unit is the unit which was the subject of an application under paragraph 66 or 75 in consequence of which the new unit was agreed by the parties or decided by the CAC.

(4) But if the parties agree matters as the subject of collective bargaining in relation to the new unit, references to collective bargaining in relation to that unit are to negotiations relating to the agreed matters; and this is the case whether the agreement is made before or after the time when the CAC issues a declaration that the union is (or unions are) recognised as entitled to conduct collective bargaining on behalf of the new unit.

(5) In relation to a residual unit in relation to which a declaration is issued under paragraph 91, references to collective bargaining are to negotiations relating to the matters which were the subject of collective bargaining in relation to the corresponding parent unit.

(6) In construing paragraphs 69(3)(c), 78(3)(c), 85(2)(c), 87(6)(b) and 89(6)(b)—
(a) sub-paragraphs (3) and (4) do not apply, and
(b) references to collective bargaining are to negotiations relating to pay, hours and holidays.

Method of collective bargaining

95.—(1) This paragraph applies for the purposes of this Part of this Schedule.

(2) Where a method of collective bargaining has effect in relation to a new unit, that method shall have effect as if it were contained in a legally enforceable contract made by the parties.

(3) But if the parties agree in writing—
(a) that sub-paragraph (2) shall not apply, or shall not apply to particular parts of the method, or
(b) to vary or replace the method,
the written agreement shall have effect as a legally enforceable contract made by the parties.

(4) Specific performance shall be the only remedy available for breach of anything which is a legally enforceable contract by virtue of this paragraph.

Definitions In the Trade Union and Labour Relations (Consolidation) Act 1992, for "collective bargaining", see s 178(1), (2) thereof (and note Sch A1, Pt III, para 94, as inserted by this Schedule); for "recognition" and "recognised", see s 178(3) thereof; for "employee", see ss 273(4)(a), 278(4)(a), 280, 295(1) thereof; for "undertaking", see ss 273(4)(e), 278(4)(c), (d) thereof; for "worker", see ss 279, 280,

Employment Relations Act 1999, Sch 1

296(1) thereof; for "employer", see ss 279, 295, 296(2) thereof; for "the CAC", see Sch A1, Pt IX, para 172(1) thereof, as inserted by this Schedule; for "working day", see Sch A1, Pt IX, para 172(2) thereof, as so inserted.
References See para 2.26.

PART IV
DERECOGNITION: GENERAL

Introduction

96.—(1) This Part of this Schedule applies if the CAC has issued a declaration that a union is (or unions are) recognised as entitled to conduct collective bargaining on behalf of a bargaining unit.

(2) In such a case references in this Part of this Schedule to the bargaining arrangements are to the declaration and to the provisions relating to the collective bargaining method.

(3) For this purpose the provisions relating to the collective bargaining method are—
   (a) the parties' agreement as to the method by which collective bargaining is to be conducted,
   (b) anything effective as, or as if contained in, a legally enforceable contract and relating to the method by which collective bargaining is to be conducted, or
   (c) any provision of Part III of this Schedule that a method of collective bargaining is to have effect.

97. For the purposes of this Part of this Schedule the relevant date is the date of the expiry of the period of 3 years starting with the date of the CAC's declaration.

98. References in this Part of this Schedule to the parties are to the employer and the union (or unions) concerned.

Employer employs fewer than 21 workers

99.—(1) This paragraph applies if—
   (a) the employer believes that he, taken with any associated employer or employers, employed an average of fewer than 21 workers in any period of 13 weeks, and
   (b) that period ends on or after the relevant date.

(2) If the employer wishes the bargaining arrangements to cease to have effect, he must give the union (or each of the unions) a notice complying with sub-paragraph (3) and must give a copy of the notice to the CAC.

(3) A notice complies with this sub-paragraph if it—
   (a) identifies the bargaining arrangements,
   (b) specifies the period of 13 weeks in question,
   (c) states the date on which the notice is given,
   (d) is given within the period of 5 working days starting with the day after the last day of the specified period of 13 weeks,
   (e) states that the employer, taken with any associated employer or employers, employed an average of fewer than 21 workers in the specified period of 13 weeks, and
   (f) states that the bargaining arrangements are to cease to have effect on a date which is specified in the notice and which falls after the end of the period of 35 working days starting with the day after that on which the notice is given.

(4) To find the average number of workers employed by the employer, taken with any associated employer or employers, in the specified period of 13 weeks—
   (a) take the number of workers employed in each of the 13 weeks (including workers not employed for the whole of the week);
   (b) aggregate the 13 numbers;
   (c) divide the aggregate by 13.

(5) For the purposes of sub-paragraph (1)(a) any worker employed by an associated company incorporated outside Great Britain must be ignored in relation to a week unless the whole or any part of that week fell within a period during which he ordinarily worked in Great Britain.

(6) For the purposes of sub-paragraph (5) a worker who is employed on board a ship registered in the register maintained under section 8 of the Merchant Shipping Act 1995 shall be treated as ordinarily working in Great Britain unless—
    (a) the ship's entry in the register specifies a port outside Great Britain as the port to which the vessel is to be treated as belonging,
    (b) the employment is wholly outside Great Britain, or
    (c) the worker is not ordinarily resident in Great Britain.

(7) An order made under paragraph 7(6) may also—
    (a) provide that sub-paragraphs (1) to (6) of this paragraph and paragraphs 100 to 103 are not to apply, or are not to apply in specified circumstances, or
    (b) vary the number of workers for the time being specified in sub-paragraphs (1)(a) and (3)(e).

100.—(1) Within the validation period the CAC must decide whether the notice complies with paragraph 99(3).

(2) If the CAC decides that the notice does not comply with paragraph 99(3)—
    (a) the CAC must give the parties notice of its decision, and
    (b) the employer's notice shall be treated as not having been given.

(3) If the CAC decides that the notice complies with paragraph 99(3) it must give the parties notice of the decision.

(4) The bargaining arrangements shall cease to have effect on the date specified under paragraph 99(3)(f) if—
    (a) the CAC gives notice under sub-paragraph (3), and
    (b) the union does not (or unions do not) apply to the CAC under paragraph 101.

(5) The validation period is—
    (a) the period of 10 working days starting with the day after that on which the CAC receives the copy of the notice, or
    (b) such longer period (so starting) as the CAC may specify to the parties by notice containing reasons for the extension.

101.—(1) This paragraph applies if—
    (a) the CAC gives notice under paragraph 100(3), and
    (b) within the period of 10 working days starting with the day after that on which the notice is given, the union makes (or unions make) an application to the CAC for a decision whether the period of 13 weeks specified under paragraph 99(3)(b) ends on or after the relevant date and whether the statement made under paragraph 99(3)(e) is correct.

(2) An application is not admissible unless—
    (a) it is made in such form as the CAC specifies, and
    (b) it is supported by such documents as the CAC specifies.

(3) An application is not admissible unless the union gives (or unions give) to the employer—
    (a) notice of the application, and
    (b) a copy of the application and any documents supporting it.

(4) An application is not admissible if—
    (a) a relevant application was made within the period of 3 years prior to the date of the application,
    (b) the relevant application and the application relate to the same bargaining unit, and
    (c) the CAC accepted the relevant application.

(5) A relevant application is an application made to the CAC—
    (a) by the union (or the unions) under this paragraph,
    (b) by the employer under paragraph 106, 107 or 128, or
    (c) by a worker (or workers) under paragraph 112.

Employment Relations Act 1999, Sch 1

102.—(1) The CAC must give notice to the parties of receipt of an application under paragraph 101.

(2) Within the acceptance period the CAC must decide whether the application is admissible within the terms of paragraph 101.

(3) In deciding whether an application is admissible the CAC must consider any evidence which it has been given by the employer or the union (or unions).

(4) If the CAC decides that the application is not admissible—
  (a) the CAC must give notice of its decision to the parties,
  (b) the CAC must not accept the application,
  (c) no further steps are to be taken under this Part of this Schedule, and
  (d) the bargaining arrangements shall cease to have effect on the date specified under paragraph 99(3)(f).

(5) If the CAC decides that the application is admissible it must—
  (a) accept the application, and
  (b) give notice of the acceptance to the parties.

(6) The acceptance period is—
  (a) the period of 10 working days starting with the day after that on which the CAC receives the application, or
  (b) such longer period (so starting) as the CAC may specify to the parties by notice containing reasons for the extension.

103.—(1) If the CAC accepts an application it—
  (a) must give the employer and the union (or unions) an opportunity to put their views on the questions whether the period of 13 weeks specified under paragraph 99(3)(b) ends on or after the relevant date and whether the statement made under paragraph 99(3)(e) is correct;
  (b) must decide the questions within the decision period and must give reasons for the decision.

(2) If the CAC decides that the period of 13 weeks specified under paragraph 99(3)(b) ends on or after the relevant date and that the statement made under paragraph 99(3)(e) is correct the bargaining arrangements shall cease to have effect on the termination date.

(3) If the CAC decides that the period of 13 weeks specified under paragraph 99(3)(b) does not end on or after the relevant date or that the statement made under paragraph 99(3)(e) is not correct, the notice under paragraph 99 shall be treated as not having been given.

(4) The decision period is—
  (a) the period of 10 working days starting with the day after that on which the CAC gives notice of acceptance of the application, or
  (b) such longer period (so starting) as the CAC may specify to the parties by notice containing reasons for the extension.

(5) The termination date is the later of—
  (a) the date specified under paragraph 99(3)(f), and
  (b) the day after the last day of the decision period.

Employer's request to end arrangements

104.—(1) This paragraph and paragraphs 105 to 111 apply if after the relevant date the employer requests the union (or each of the unions) to agree to end the bargaining arrangements.

(2) The request is not valid unless it—
  (a) is in writing,
  (b) is received by the union (or each of the unions),
  (c) identifies the bargaining arrangements, and
  (d) states that it is made under this Schedule.

105.—(1) If before the end of the first period the parties agree to end the bargaining arrangements no further steps are to be taken under this Part of this Schedule.

Employment Relations Act 1999, Sch 1

(2) Sub-paragraph (3) applies if before the end of the first period—
- (a) the union informs the employer that the union does not accept the request but is willing to negotiate, or
- (b) the unions inform the employer that the unions do not accept the request but are willing to negotiate.

(3) The parties may conduct negotiations with a view to agreeing to end the bargaining arrangements.

(4) If such an agreement is made before the end of the second period no further steps are to be taken under this Part of this Schedule.

(5) The employer and the union (or unions) may request ACAS to assist in conducting the negotiations.

(6) The first period is the period of 10 working days starting with the day after—
- (a) the day on which the union receives the request, or
- (b) the last day on which any of the unions receives the request.

(7) The second period is—
- (a) the period of 20 working days starting with the day after that on which the first period ends, or
- (b) such longer period (so starting) as the parties may from time to time agree.

106.—(1) This paragraph applies if—
- (a) before the end of the first period the union fails (or unions fail) to respond to the request, or
- (b) before the end of the first period the union informs the employer that it does not (or unions inform the employer that they do not) accept the request (without indicating a willingness to negotiate).

(2) The employer may apply to the CAC for the holding of a secret ballot to decide whether the bargaining arrangements should be ended.

107.—(1) This paragraph applies if—
- (a) the union informs (or unions inform) the employer under paragraph 105(2), and
- (b) no agreement is made before the end of the second period.

(2) The employer may apply to the CAC for the holding of a secret ballot to decide whether the bargaining arrangements should be ended.

(3) But no application may be made if within the period of 10 working days starting with the day after that on which the union informs (or unions inform) the employer under paragraph 105(2) the union proposes (or unions propose) that ACAS be requested to assist in conducting the negotiations and—
- (a) the employer rejects the proposal, or
- (b) the employer fails to accept the proposal within the period of 10 working days starting with the day after that on which the union makes (or unions make) the proposal.

108.—(1) An application under paragraph 106 or 107 is not admissible unless—
- (a) it is made in such form as the CAC specifies, and
- (b) it is supported by such documents as the CAC specifies.

(2) An application under paragraph 106 or 107 is not admissible unless the employer gives to the union (or each of the unions)—
- (a) notice of the application, and
- (b) a copy of the application and any documents supporting it.

109.—(1) An application under paragraph 106 or 107 is not admissible if—
- (a) a relevant application was made within the period of 3 years prior to the date of the application under paragraph 106 or 107,
- (b) the relevant application and the application under paragraph 106 or 107 relate to the same bargaining unit, and
- (c) the CAC accepted the relevant application.

(2) A relevant application is an application made to the CAC—
- (a) by the union (or the unions) under paragraph 101,

Employment Relations Act 1999, Sch 1

    (b)   by the employer under paragraph 106, 107 or 128, or
    (c)   by a worker (or workers) under paragraph 112.

110.—(1) An application under paragraph 106 or 107 is not admissible unless the CAC decides that—
    (a)   at least 10 per cent of the workers constituting the bargaining unit favour an end of the bargaining arrangements, and
    (b)   a majority of the workers constituting the bargaining unit would be likely to favour an end of the bargaining arrangements.

(2)   The CAC must give reasons for the decision.

111.—(1) The CAC must give notice to the parties of receipt of an application under paragraph 106 or 107.

(2)   Within the acceptance period the CAC must decide whether—
    (a)   the request is valid within the terms of paragraph 104, and
    (b)   the application is made in accordance with paragraph 106 or 107 and admissible within the terms of paragraphs 108 to 110.

(3)   In deciding those questions the CAC must consider any evidence which it has been given by the employer or the union (or unions).

(4)   If the CAC decides that the request is not valid or the application is not made in accordance with paragraph 106 or 107 or is not admissible—
    (a)   the CAC must give notice of its decision to the parties,
    (b)   the CAC must not accept the application, and
    (c)   no further steps are to be taken under this Part of this Schedule.

(5)   If the CAC decides that the request is valid and the application is made in accordance with paragraph 106 or 107 and is admissible it must—
    (a)   accept the application, and
    (b)   give notice of the acceptance to the parties.

(6)   The acceptance period is—
    (a)   the period of 10 working days starting with the day after that on which the CAC receives the application, or
    (b)   such longer period (so starting) as the CAC may specify to the parties by notice containing reasons for the extension.

Workers' application to end arrangements

112.—(1) A worker or workers falling within the bargaining unit may after the relevant date apply to the CAC to have the bargaining arrangements ended.

(2)   An application is not admissible unless—
    (a)   it is made in such form as the CAC specifies, and
    (b)   it is supported by such documents as the CAC specifies.

(3)   An application is not admissible unless the worker gives (or workers give) to the employer and to the union (or each of the unions)—
    (a)   notice of the application, and
    (b)   a copy of the application and any documents supporting it.

113.—(1) An application under paragraph 112 is not admissible if—
    (a)   a relevant application was made within the period of 3 years prior to the date of the application under paragraph 112,
    (b)   the relevant application and the application under paragraph 112 relate to the same bargaining unit, and
    (c)   the CAC accepted the relevant application.

(2)   A relevant application is an application made to the CAC—
    (a)   by the union (or the unions) under paragraph 101,
    (b)   by the employer under paragraph 106, 107 or 128, or
    (c)   by a worker (or workers) under paragraph 112.

114.—(1) An application under paragraph 112 is not admissible unless the CAC decides that—

Employment Relations Act 1999, Sch 1

     (a)   at least 10 per cent of the workers constituting the bargaining unit favour an end of the bargaining arrangements, and
     (b)   a majority of the workers constituting the bargaining unit would be likely to favour an end of the bargaining arrangements.

(2)   The CAC must give reasons for the decision.

115.—(1) The CAC must give notice to the worker (or workers), the employer and the union (or unions) of receipt of an application under paragraph 112.

(2)   Within the acceptance period the CAC must decide whether the application is admissible within the terms of paragraphs 112 to 114.

(3)   In deciding whether the application is admissible the CAC must consider any evidence which it has been given by the employer, the union (or unions) or any of the workers falling within the bargaining unit.

(4)   If the CAC decides that the application is not admissible—
     (a)   the CAC must give notice of its decision to the worker (or workers), the employer and the union (or unions),
     (b)   the CAC must not accept the application, and
     (c)   no further steps are to be taken under this Part of this Schedule.

(5)   If the CAC decides that the application is admissible it must—
     (a)   accept the application, and
     (b)   give notice of the acceptance to the worker (or workers), the employer and the union (or unions).

(6)   The acceptance period is—
     (a)   the period of 10 working days starting with the day after that on which the CAC receives the application, or
     (b)   such longer period (so starting) as the CAC may specify to the worker (or workers), the employer and the union (or unions) by notice containing reasons for the extension.

116.—(1) If the CAC accepts the application, in the negotiation period the CAC must help the employer, the union (or unions) and the worker (or workers) with a view to—
     (a)   the employer and the union (or unions) agreeing to end the bargaining arrangements, or
     (b)   the worker (or workers) withdrawing the application.

(2)   The negotiation period is—
     (a)   the period of 20 working days starting with the day after that on which the CAC gives notice of acceptance of the application, or
     (b)   such longer period (so starting) as the CAC may decide with the consent of the worker (or workers), the employer and the union (or unions).

Ballot on derecognition

117.—(1) This paragraph applies if the CAC accepts an application under paragraph 106 or 107.

(2)   This paragraph also applies if—
     (a)   the CAC accepts an application under paragraph 112, and
     (b)   in the period mentioned in paragraph 116(1) there is no agreement or withdrawal as there described.

(3)   The CAC must arrange for the holding of a secret ballot in which the workers constituting the bargaining unit are asked whether the bargaining arrangements should be ended.

(4)   The ballot must be conducted by a qualified independent person appointed by the CAC.

(5)   The ballot must be conducted within—
     (a)   the period of 20 working days starting with the day after that on which the qualified independent person is appointed, or
     (b)   such longer period (so starting) as the CAC may decide.

(6)   The ballot must be conducted—

(a) at a workplace or workplaces decided by the CAC,
(b) by post, or
(c) by a combination of the methods described in sub-paragraphs (a) and (b),
depending on the CAC's preference.

(7) In deciding how the ballot is to be conducted the CAC must take into account—
- (a) the likelihood of the ballot being affected by unfairness or malpractice if it were conducted at a workplace or workplaces;
- (b) costs and practicality;
- (c) such other matters as the CAC considers appropriate.

(8) The CAC may not decide that the ballot is to be conducted as mentioned in sub-paragraph (6)(c) unless there are special factors making such a decision appropriate; and special factors include—
- (a) factors arising from the location of workers or the nature of their employment;
- (b) factors put to the CAC by the employer or the union (or unions).

(9) A person is a qualified independent person if—
- (a) he satisfies such conditions as may be specified for the purposes of this paragraph by order of the Secretary of State or is himself so specified, and
- (b) there are no grounds for believing either that he will carry out any functions conferred on him in relation to the ballot otherwise than competently or that his independence in relation to the ballot might reasonably be called into question.

(10) An order under sub-paragraph (9)(a) shall be made by statutory instrument subject to annulment in pursuance of a resolution of either House of Parliament.

(11) As soon as is reasonably practicable after the CAC is required under sub-paragraph (3) to arrange for the holding of a ballot it must inform the employer and the union (or unions)—
- (a) that it is so required;
- (b) of the name of the person appointed to conduct the ballot and the date of his appointment;
- (c) of the period within which the ballot must be conducted;
- (d) whether the ballot is to be conducted by post or at a workplace or workplaces;
- (e) of the workplace or workplaces concerned (if the ballot is to be conducted at a workplace or workplaces).

118.—(1) An employer who is informed by the CAC under paragraph 117(11) must comply with the following three duties.

(2) The first duty is to co-operate generally, in connection with the ballot, with the union (or unions) and the person appointed to conduct the ballot; and the second and third duties are not to prejudice the generality of this.

(3) The second duty is to give to the union (or unions) such access to the workers constituting the bargaining unit as is reasonable to enable the union (or unions) to inform the workers of the object of the ballot and to seek their support and their opinions on the issues involved.

(4) The third duty is to do the following (so far as it is reasonable to expect the employer to do so)—
- (a) to give to the CAC, within the period of 10 working days starting with the day after that on which the employer is informed under paragraph 117(11), the names and home addresses of the workers constituting the bargaining unit;
- (b) to give to the CAC, as soon as is reasonably practicable, the name and home address of any worker who joins the unit after the employer has complied with paragraph (a);
- (c) to inform the CAC, as soon as is reasonably practicable, of any worker whose name has been given to the CAC under paragraph (a) or (b) but who ceases to be within the unit.

(5) As soon as is reasonably practicable after the CAC receives any information under sub-paragraph (4) it must pass it on to the person appointed to conduct the ballot.

(6) If asked to do so by the union (or unions) the person appointed to conduct the ballot must send to any worker—
- (a) whose name and home address have been given under sub-paragraph (5), and
- (b) who is still within the unit (so far as the person so appointed is aware),

any information supplied by the union (or unions) to the person so appointed.

(7) The duty under sub-paragraph (6) does not apply unless the union bears (or unions bear) the cost of sending the information.

(8) Each of the following powers shall be taken to include power to issue Codes of Practice about reasonable access for the purposes of sub-paragraph (3)—
- (a) the power of ACAS under section 199(1);
- (b) the power of the Secretary of State under section 203(1)(a).

119.—(1) If the CAC is satisfied that the employer has failed to fulfil any of the three duties imposed by paragraph 118, and the ballot has not been held, the CAC may order the employer—
- (a) to take such steps to remedy the failure as the CAC considers reasonable and specifies in the order, and
- (b) to do so within such period as the CAC considers reasonable and specifies in the order.

(2) If—
- (a) the ballot has been arranged in consequence of an application under paragraph 106 or 107,
- (b) the CAC is satisfied that the employer has failed to comply with an order under sub-paragraph (1), and
- (c) the ballot has not been held,

the CAC may refuse the application.

(3) If—
- (a) the ballot has been arranged in consequence of an application under paragraph 112, and
- (b) the ballot has not been held,

an order under sub-paragraph (1), on being recorded in the county court, may be enforced in the same way as an order of that court.

(4) If the CAC refuses an application under sub-paragraph (2) it shall take steps to cancel the holding of the ballot; and if the ballot is held it shall have no effect.

120.—(1) This paragraph applies if the holding of a ballot has been arranged under paragraph 117(3), whether or not it has been cancelled.

(2) The gross costs of the ballot shall be borne—
- (a) as to half, by the employer, and
- (b) as to half, by the union (or unions).

(3) If there is more than one union they shall bear their half of the gross costs—
- (a) in such proportions as they jointly indicate to the person appointed to conduct the ballot, or
- (b) in the absence of such an indication, in equal shares.

(4) The person appointed to conduct the ballot may send to the employer and the union (or each of the unions) a demand stating—
- (a) the gross costs of the ballot, and
- (b) the amount of the gross costs to be borne by the recipient.

(5) In such a case the recipient must pay the amount stated to the person sending the demand, and must do so within the period of 15 working days starting with the day after that on which the demand is received.

(6) In England and Wales, if the amount stated is not paid in accordance with sub-paragraph (5) it shall, if a county court so orders, be recoverable by execution issued from that court or otherwise as if it were payable under an order of that court.

Employment Relations Act 1999, Sch 1

(7) References to the costs of the ballot are to—
    (a) the costs wholly, exclusively and necessarily incurred in connection with the ballot by the person appointed to conduct it,
    (b) such reasonable amount as the person appointed to conduct the ballot charges for his services, and
    (c) such other costs as the employer and the union (or unions) agree.

121.—(1) As soon as is reasonably practicable after the CAC is informed of the result of a ballot by the person conducting it, the CAC must act under this paragraph.

(2) The CAC must inform the employer and the union (or unions) of the result of the ballot.

(3) If the result is that the proposition that the bargaining arrangements should be ended is supported by—
    (a) a majority of the workers voting, and
    (b) at least 40 per cent of the workers constituting the bargaining unit,
the CAC must issue a declaration that the bargaining arrangements are to cease to have effect on a date specified by the CAC in the declaration.

(4) If the result is otherwise the CAC must refuse the application under paragraph 106, 107 or 112.

(5) If a declaration is issued under sub-paragraph (3) the bargaining arrangements shall cease to have effect accordingly.

(6) The Secretary of State may by order amend sub-paragraph (3) so as to specify a different degree of support; and different provision may be made for different circumstances.

(7) An order under sub-paragraph (6) shall be made by statutory instrument.

(8) No such order shall be made unless a draft of it has been laid before Parliament and approved by a resolution of each House of Parliament.

Definitions In the Trade Union and Labour Relations (Consolidation) Act 1992, for "collective bargaining", see s 178(1), (?) thereof; for "recognised", see s 178(3) thereof; for "ACAS", see s 247(1) thereof; for "worker", see ss 279, 280, 296(1) thereof; for "employer", see ss 279, 295, 296(2) thereof; for "associated employer", see s 297 thereof; for "post", see s 298 thereof; for "the CAC", see Sch A1, Pt IX, para 172(1) thereof, as inserted by this Schedule; for "working day", see Sch A1, Pt IX, para 172(2) thereof, as so inserted.
References See para 2.27.

PART V
DERECOGNITION WHERE RECOGNITION AUTOMATIC

Introduction

122.—(1) This Part of this Schedule applies if—
    (a) the CAC has issued a declaration under paragraph 22(2) that a union is (or unions are) recognised as entitled to conduct collective bargaining on behalf of a bargaining unit, and
    (b) the parties have agreed under paragraph 30 or 31 a method by which they will conduct collective bargaining.

(2) In such a case references in this Part of this Schedule to the bargaining arrangements are to—
    (a) the declaration, and
    (b) the parties' agreement.

123.—(1) This Part of this Schedule also applies if—
    (a) the CAC has issued a declaration under paragraph 22(2) that a union is (or unions are) recognised as entitled to conduct collective bargaining on behalf of a bargaining unit, and
    (b) the CAC has specified to the parties under paragraph 31(3) the method by which they are to conduct collective bargaining.

(2) In such a case references in this Part of this Schedule to the bargaining arrangements are to—
- (a) the declaration, and
- (b) anything effective as, or as if contained in, a legally enforceable contract by virtue of paragraph 31.

124.—(1) This Part of this Schedule also applies if the CAC has issued a declaration under paragraph 87(2) that a union is (or unions are) recognised as entitled to conduct collective bargaining on behalf of a bargaining unit.

(2) In such a case references in this Part of this Schedule to the bargaining arrangements are to—
- (a) the declaration, and
- (b) paragraph 87(6)(b).

125. For the purposes of this Part of this Schedule the relevant date is the date of the expiry of the period of 3 years starting with the date of the CAC's declaration.

126. References in this Part of this Schedule to the parties are to the employer and the union (or unions) concerned.

Employer's request to end arrangements

127.—(1) The employer may after the relevant date request the union (or each of the unions) to agree to end the bargaining arrangements.

(2) The request is not valid unless it—
- (a) is in writing,
- (b) is received by the union (or each of the unions),
- (c) identifies the bargaining arrangements,
- (d) states that it is made under this Schedule, and
- (e) states that fewer than half of the workers constituting the bargaining unit are members of the union (or unions).

128.—(1) If before the end of the negotiation period the parties agree to end the bargaining arrangements no further steps are to be taken under this Part of this Schedule.

(2) If no such agreement is made before the end of the negotiation period, the employer may apply to the CAC for the holding of a secret ballot to decide whether the bargaining arrangements should be ended.

(3) The negotiation period is the period of 10 working days starting with the day after—
- (a) the day on which the union receives the request, or
- (b) the last day on which any of the unions receives the request;

or such longer period (so starting) as the parties may from time to time agree.

129.—(1) An application under paragraph 128 is not admissible unless—
- (a) it is made in such form as the CAC specifies, and
- (b) it is supported by such documents as the CAC specifies.

(2) An application under paragraph 128 is not admissible unless the employer gives to the union (or each of the unions)—
- (a) notice of the application, and
- (b) a copy of the application and any documents supporting it.

130.—(1) An application under paragraph 128 is not admissible if—
- (a) a relevant application was made within the period of 3 years prior to the date of the application under paragraph 128,
- (b) the relevant application and the application under paragraph 128 relate to the same bargaining unit, and
- (c) the CAC accepted the relevant application.

(2) A relevant application is an application made to the CAC—
- (a) by the union (or the unions) under paragraph 101,
- (b) by the employer under paragraph 106, 107 or 128, or
- (c) by a worker (or workers) under paragraph 112.

Employment Relations Act 1999, Sch 1

131.—(1) An application under paragraph 128 is not admissible unless the CAC is satisfied that fewer than half of the workers constituting the bargaining unit are members of the union (or unions).

(2) The CAC must give reasons for the decision.

132.—(1) The CAC must give notice to the parties of receipt of an application under paragraph 128.

(2) Within the acceptance period the CAC must decide whether—
   (a) the request is valid within the terms of paragraph 127, and
   (b) the application is admissible within the terms of paragraphs 129 to 131.

(3) In deciding those questions the CAC must consider any evidence which it has been given by the parties.

(4) If the CAC decides that the request is not valid or the application is not admissible—
   (a) the CAC must give notice of its decision to the parties,
   (b) the CAC must not accept the application, and
   (c) no further steps are to be taken under this Part of this Schedule.

(5) If the CAC decides that the request is valid and the application is admissible it must—
   (a) accept the application, and
   (b) give notice of the acceptance to the parties.

(6) The acceptance period is—
   (a) the period of 10 working days starting with the day after that on which the CAC receives the application, or
   (b) such longer period (so starting) as the CAC may specify to the parties by notice containing reasons for the extension.

Ballot on derecognition

133.—(1) Paragraph 117 applies if the CAC accepts an application under paragraph 128 (as well as in the cases mentioned in paragraph 117(1) and (2)).

(2) Paragraphs 118 to 121 apply accordingly, but as if—
   (a) the reference in paragraph 119(2)(a) to paragraph 106 or 107 were to paragraph 106, 107 or 128;
   (b) the reference in paragraph 121(4) to paragraph 106, 107 or 112 were to paragraph 106, 107, 112 or 128.

Definitions In the Trade Union and Labour Relations (Consolidation) Act 1992, for "collective bargaining", see s 178(1), (2) thereof; for "recognised", see s 178(3) thereof; for "worker", see ss 279, 280, 296(1) thereof; for "employer", see ss 279, 295, 296(2) thereof; for "the CAC", see Sch A1, Pt IX, para 172(1) thereof, as inserted by this Schedule; for "working day", see Sch A1, Pt IX, para 172(2) thereof, as so inserted.
References See para 2.28.

PART VI
DERECOGNITION WHERE UNION NOT INDEPENDENT

Introduction

134.—(1) This Part of this Schedule applies if—
   (a) an employer and a union (or unions) have agreed that the union is (or unions are) recognised as entitled to conduct collective bargaining on behalf of a group or groups of workers, and
   (b) the union does not have (or none of the unions has) a certificate under section 6 that it is independent.

(2) In such a case references in this Part of this Schedule to the bargaining arrangements are to—
   (a) the parties' agreement mentioned in sub-paragraph (1)(a), and
   (b) any agreement between the parties as to the method by which they will conduct collective bargaining.

135. In this Part of this Schedule—
  (a) references to the parties are to the employer and the union (or unions);
  (b) references to the bargaining unit are to the group of workers referred to in paragraph 134(1)(a) (or the groups taken together).

136. The meaning of collective bargaining given by section 178(1) shall not apply in relation to this Part of this Schedule.

Workers' application to end arrangements

137.—(1) A worker or workers falling within the bargaining unit may apply to the CAC to have the bargaining arrangements ended.

(2) An application is not admissible unless—
  (a) it is made in such form as the CAC specifies, and
  (b) it is supported by such documents as the CAC specifies.

(3) An application is not admissible unless the worker gives (or workers give) to the employer and to the union (or each of the unions)—
  (a) notice of the application, and
  (b) a copy of the application and any documents supporting it.

138. An application under paragraph 137 is not admissible if the CAC is satisfied that any of the unions has a certificate under section 6 that it is independent.

139.—(1) An application under paragraph 137 is not admissible unless the CAC decides that—
  (a) at least 10 per cent of the workers constituting the bargaining unit favour an end of the bargaining arrangements, and
  (b) a majority of the workers constituting the bargaining unit would be likely to favour an end of the bargaining arrangements.

(2) The CAC must give reasons for the decision.

140. An application under paragraph 137 is not admissible if the CAC is satisfied that—
  (a) the union (or any of the unions) has made an application to the Certification Officer under section 6 for a certificate that it is independent, and
  (b) the Certification Officer has not come to a decision on the application (or each of the applications).

141.—(1) The CAC must give notice to the worker (or workers), the employer and the union (or unions) of receipt of an application under paragraph 137.

(2) Within the acceptance period the CAC must decide whether the application is admissible within the terms of paragraphs 137 to 140.

(3) In deciding whether the application is admissible the CAC must consider any evidence which it has been given by the employer, the union (or unions) or any of the workers falling within the bargaining unit.

(4) If the CAC decides that the application is not admissible—
  (a) the CAC must give notice of its decision to the worker (or workers), the employer and the union (or unions),
  (b) the CAC must not accept the application, and
  (c) no further steps are to be taken under this Part of this Schedule.

(5) If the CAC decides that the application is admissible it must—
  (a) accept the application, and
  (b) give notice of the acceptance to the worker (or workers), the employer and the union (or unions).

(6) The acceptance period is—
  (a) the period of 10 working days starting with the day after that on which the CAC receives the application, or
  (b) such longer period (so starting) as the CAC may specify to the worker (or workers), the employer and the union (or unions) by notice containing reasons for the extension.

Employment Relations Act 1999, Sch 1

142.—(1) If the CAC accepts the application, in the negotiation period the CAC must help the employer, the union (or unions) and the worker (or workers) with a view to—
    (a) the employer and the union (or unions) agreeing to end the bargaining arrangements, or
    (b) the worker (or workers) withdrawing the application.

(2) The negotiation period is—
    (a) the period of 20 working days starting with the day after that on which the CAC gives notice of acceptance of the application, or
    (b) such longer period (so starting) as the CAC may decide with the consent of the worker (or workers), the employer and the union (or unions).

143.—(1) This paragraph applies if—
    (a) the CAC accepts an application under paragraph 137,
    (b) during the period mentioned in paragraph 142(1) or 145(3) the CAC is satisfied that the union (or each of the unions) has made an application to the Certification Officer under section 6 for a certificate that it is independent, that the application (or each of the applications) to the Certification Officer was made before the application under paragraph 137 and that the Certification Officer has not come to a decision on the application (or each of the applications), and
    (c) at the time the CAC is so satisfied there has been no agreement or withdrawal as described in paragraph 142(1) or 145(3).

(2) In such a case paragraph 142(1) or 145(3) shall cease to apply from the time when the CAC is satisfied as mentioned in sub-paragraph (1)(b).

144.—(1) This paragraph applies if the CAC is subsequently satisfied that—
    (a) the Certification Officer has come to a decision on the application (or each of the applications) mentioned in paragraph 143(1)(b), and
    (b) his decision is that the union (or any of the unions) which made an application under section 6 is independent.

(2) In such a case—
    (a) the CAC must give the worker (or workers), the employer and the union (or unions) notice that it is so satisfied, and
    (b) the application under paragraph 137 shall be treated as not having been made.

145.—(1) This paragraph applies if the CAC is subsequently satisfied that—
    (a) the Certification Officer has come to a decision on the application (or each of the applications) mentioned in paragraph 143(1)(b), and
    (b) his decision is that the union (or each of the unions) which made an application under section 6 is not independent.

(2) The CAC must give the worker (or workers), the employer and the union (or unions) notice that it is so satisfied.

(3) In the new negotiation period the CAC must help the employer, the union (or unions) and the worker (or workers) with a view to—
    (a) the employer and the union (or unions) agreeing to end the bargaining arrangements, or
    (b) the worker (or workers) withdrawing the application.

(4) The new negotiation period is—
    (a) the period of 20 working days starting with the day after that on which the CAC gives notice under sub-paragraph (2), or
    (b) such longer period (so starting) as the CAC may decide with the consent of the worker (or workers), the employer and the union (or unions).

146.—(1) This paragraph applies if—
    (a) the CAC accepts an application under paragraph 137,
    (b) paragraph 143 does not apply, and
    (c) during the relevant period the CAC is satisfied that a certificate of independence has been issued to the union (or any of the unions) under section 6.

Employment Relations Act 1999, Sch 1

(2) In such a case the relevant period is the period starting with the first day of the negotiation period (as defined in paragraph 142(2)) and ending with the first of the following to occur—
- (a) any agreement by the employer and the union (or unions) to end the bargaining arrangements;
- (b) any withdrawal of the application by the worker (or workers);
- (c) the CAC being informed of the result of a relevant ballot by the person conducting it;

and a relevant ballot is a ballot held by virtue of this Part of this Schedule.

(3) This paragraph also applies if—
- (a) the CAC gives notice under paragraph 145(2), and
- (b) during the relevant period the CAC is satisfied that a certificate of independence has been issued to the union (or any of the unions) under section 6.

(4) In such a case, the relevant period is the period starting with the first day of the new negotiation period (as defined in paragraph 145(4)) and ending with the first of the following to occur—
- (a) any agreement by the employer and the union (or unions) to end the bargaining arrangements;
- (b) any withdrawal of the application by the worker (or workers);
- (c) the CAC being informed of the result of a relevant ballot by the person conducting it;

and a relevant ballot is a ballot held by virtue of this Part of this Schedule.

(5) If this paragraph applies—
- (a) the CAC must give the worker (or workers), the employer and the union (or unions) notice that it is satisfied as mentioned in sub-paragraph (1)(c) or (3)(b), and
- (b) the application under paragraph 137 shall be treated as not having been made.

Ballot on derecognition

147.—(1) Paragraph 117 applies if—
- (a) the CAC accepts an application under paragraph 137, and
- (b) in the period mentioned in paragraph 142(1) or 145(3) there is no agreement or withdrawal as there described,

(as well as in the cases mentioned in paragraph 117(1) and (2)).

(2) Paragraphs 118 to 121 apply accordingly, but as if—
- (a) the reference in paragraph 119(3)(a) to paragraph 112 were to paragraph 112 or 137;
- (b) the reference in paragraph 121(4) to paragraph 106, 107 or 112 were to paragraph 106, 107, 112 or 137;
- (c) the reference in paragraph 119(4) to the CAC refusing an application under paragraph 119(2) included a reference to it being required to give notice under paragraph 146(5).

Derecognition: other cases

148.—(1) This paragraph applies if as a result of a declaration by the CAC another union is (or other unions are) recognised as entitled to conduct collective bargaining on behalf of a group of workers at least one of whom falls within the bargaining unit.

(2) The CAC must issue a declaration that the bargaining arrangements are to cease to have effect on a date specified by the CAC in the declaration.

(3) If a declaration is issued under sub-paragraph (2) the bargaining arrangements shall cease to have effect accordingly.

(4) It is for the CAC to decide whether sub-paragraph (1) is fulfilled, but in deciding the CAC may take account of the views of any person it believes has an interest in the matter.

Employment Relations Act 1999, Sch 1

Definitions In the Trade Union and Labour Relations (Consolidation) Act 1992, for "recognised", see s 178(3) thereof; for "Certification Officer", see s 254 thereof; for "worker", see ss 279, 280, 296(1) thereof; for "employer", see ss 279, 295, 296(2) thereof; for "the CAC", see Sch A1, Pt IX, para 172(1) thereof, as inserted by this Schedule; for "working day", see Sch A1, Pt IX, para 172(2) thereof, as so inserted.
References See para 2.29.

PART VII
LOSS OF INDEPENDENCE

Introduction

149.—(1) This Part of this Schedule applies if the CAC has issued a declaration that a union is (or unions are) recognised as entitled to conduct collective bargaining on behalf of a bargaining unit.

(2) In such a case references in this Part of this Schedule to the bargaining arrangements are to the declaration and to the provisions relating to the collective bargaining method.

(3) For this purpose the provisions relating to the collective bargaining method are—
- (a) the parties' agreement as to the method by which collective bargaining is to be conducted,
- (b) anything effective as, or as if contained in, a legally enforceable contract and relating to the method by which collective bargaining is to be conducted, or
- (c) any provision of Part III of this Schedule that a method of collective bargaining is to have effect.

150.—(1) This Part of this Schedule also applies if—
- (a) the parties have agreed that a union is (or unions are) recognised as entitled to conduct collective bargaining on behalf of a bargaining unit,
- (b) the CAC has specified to the parties under paragraph 63(2) the method by which they are to conduct collective bargaining, and
- (c) the parties have not agreed in writing to replace the method or that paragraph 63(3) shall not apply.

(2) In such a case references in this Part of this Schedule to the bargaining arrangements are to—
- (a) the parties' agreement mentioned in sub-paragraph (1)(a), and
- (b) anything effective as, or as if contained in, a legally enforceable contract by virtue of paragraph 63.

151. References in this Part of this Schedule to the parties are to the employer and the union (or unions) concerned.

Loss of certificate

152.—(1) This paragraph applies if—
- (a) only one union is a party, and
- (b) under section 7 the Certification Officer withdraws the union's certificate of independence.

(2) This paragraph also applies if—
- (a) more than one union is a party, and
- (b) under section 7 the Certification Officer withdraws the certificate of independence of each union (whether different certificates are withdrawn on the same or on different days).

(3) Sub-paragraph (4) shall apply on the day after—
- (a) the day on which the Certification Officer informs the union (or unions) of the withdrawal (or withdrawals), or
- (b) if there is more than one union, and he informs them on different days, the last of those days.

Employment Relations Act 1999, Sch 1

(4) The bargaining arrangements shall cease to have effect; and the parties shall be taken to agree that the union is (or unions are) recognised as entitled to conduct collective bargaining on behalf of the bargaining unit concerned.

Certificate re-issued

153.—(1) This paragraph applies if—
  (a) only one union is a party,
  (b) paragraph 152 applies, and
  (c) as a result of an appeal under section 9 against the decision to withdraw the certificate, the Certification Officer issues a certificate that the union is independent.

(2) This paragraph also applies if—
  (a) more than one union is a party,
  (b) paragraph 152 applies, and
  (c) as a result of an appeal under section 9 against a decision to withdraw a certificate, the Certification Officer issues a certificate that any of the unions concerned is independent.

(3) Sub-paragraph (4) shall apply, beginning with the day after—
  (a) the day on which the Certification Officer issues the certificate, or
  (b) if there is more than one union, the day on which he issues the first or only certificate.

(4) The bargaining arrangements shall have effect again; and paragraph 152 shall cease to apply.

Miscellaneous

154. Parts III to VI of this Schedule shall not apply in the case of the parties at any time when, by virtue of this Part of this Schedule, the bargaining arrangements do not have effect.

155. If—
  (a) by virtue of paragraph 153 the bargaining arrangements have effect again beginning with a particular day, and
  (b) in consequence section 70B applies in relation to the bargaining unit concerned,
for the purposes of section 70B(3) that day shall be taken to be the day on which section 70B first applies in relation to the unit.

Definitions In the Trade Union and Labour Relations (Consolidation) Act 1992, for "collective bargaining", see s 178(1), (2) thereof; for "recognised", see s 178(3) thereof; for "Certification Officer", see s 254 thereof; for "employer", see ss 279, 295, 296(2) thereof; for "the CAC", see Sch A1, Pt IX, para 172(1) thereof, as inserted by this Schedule.
References See para 2.29.

PART VIII
DETRIMENT

Detriment

156.—(1) A worker has a right not to be subjected to any detriment by any act, or any deliberate failure to act, by his employer if the act or failure takes place on any of the grounds set out in sub-paragraph (2).

(2) The grounds are that—
  (a) the worker acted with a view to obtaining or preventing recognition of a union (or unions) by the employer under this Schedule;
  (b) the worker indicated that he supported or did not support recognition of a union (or unions) by the employer under this Schedule;
  (c) the worker acted with a view to securing or preventing the ending under this Schedule of bargaining arrangements;
  (d) the worker indicated that he supported or did not support the ending under this Schedule of bargaining arrangements;

(e) the worker influenced or sought to influence the way in which votes were to be cast by other workers in a ballot arranged under this Schedule;
(f) the worker influenced or sought to influence other workers to vote or to abstain from voting in such a ballot;
(g) the worker voted in such a ballot;
(h) the worker proposed to do, failed to do, or proposed to decline to do, any of the things referred to in paragraphs (a) to (g).

(3) A ground does not fall within sub-paragraph (2) if it constitutes an unreasonable act or omission by the worker.

(4) This paragraph does not apply if the worker is an employee and the detriment amounts to dismissal within the meaning of the Employment Rights Act 1996.

(5) A worker may present a complaint to an employment tribunal on the ground that he has been subjected to a detriment in contravention of this paragraph.

(6) Apart from the remedy by way of complaint as mentioned in sub-paragraph (5), a worker has no remedy for infringement of the right conferred on him by this paragraph.

157.—(1) An employment tribunal shall not consider a complaint under paragraph 156 unless it is presented—
(a) before the end of the period of 3 months starting with the date of the act or failure to which the complaint relates or, if that act or failure is part of a series of similar acts or failures (or both), the last of them, or
(b) where the tribunal is satisfied that it was not reasonably practicable for the complaint to be presented before the end of that period, within such further period as it considers reasonable.

(2) For the purposes of sub-paragraph (1)—
(a) where an act extends over a period, the reference to the date of the act is a reference to the last day of that period;
(b) a failure to act shall be treated as done when it was decided on.

(3) For the purposes of sub-paragraph (2), in the absence of evidence establishing the contrary an employer must be taken to decide on a failure to act—
(a) when he does an act inconsistent with doing the failed act, or
(b) if he has done no such inconsistent act, when the period expires within which he might reasonably have been expected to do the failed act if it was to be done.

158. On a complaint under paragraph 156 it shall be for the employer to show the ground on which he acted or failed to act.

159.—(1) If the employment tribunal finds that a complaint under paragraph 156 is well-founded it shall make a declaration to that effect and may make an award of compensation to be paid by the employer to the complainant in respect of the act or failure complained of.

(2) The amount of the compensation awarded shall be such as the tribunal considers just and equitable in all the circumstances having regard to the infringement complained of and to any loss sustained by the complainant which is attributable to the act or failure which infringed his right.

(3) The loss shall be taken to include—
(a) any expenses reasonably incurred by the complainant in consequence of the act or failure complained of, and
(b) loss of any benefit which he might reasonably be expected to have had but for that act or failure.

(4) In ascertaining the loss, the tribunal shall apply the same rule concerning the duty of a person to mitigate his loss as applies to damages recoverable under the common law of England and Wales or Scotland.

(5) If the tribunal finds that the act or failure complained of was to any extent caused or contributed to by action of the complainant, it shall reduce the amount of the compensation by such proportion as it considers just and equitable having regard to that finding.

Employment Relations Act 1999, Sch 1

160.—(1) If the employment tribunal finds that a complaint under paragraph 156 is well-founded and—
- (a) the detriment of which the worker has complained is the termination of his worker's contract, but
- (b) that contract was not a contract of employment,

any compensation awarded under paragraph 159 must not exceed the limit specified in sub-paragraph (2).

(2) The limit is the total of—
- (a) the sum which would be the basic award for unfair dismissal, calculated in accordance with section 119 of the Employment Rights Act 1996, if the worker had been an employee and the contract terminated had been a contract of employment, and
- (b) the sum for the time being specified in section 124(1) of that Act which is the limit for a compensatory award to a person calculated in accordance with section 123 of that Act.

Dismissal

161.—(1) For the purposes of Part X of the Employment Rights Act 1996 (unfair dismissal) the dismissal of an employee shall be regarded as unfair if the dismissal was made—
- (a) for a reason set out in sub-paragraph (2), or
- (b) for reasons the main one of which is one of those set out in sub-paragraph (2).

(2) The reasons are that—
- (a) the employee acted with a view to obtaining or preventing recognition of a union (or unions) by the employer under this Schedule;
- (b) the employee indicated that he supported or did not support recognition of a union (or unions) by the employer under this Schedule;
- (c) the employee acted with a view to securing or preventing the ending under this Schedule of bargaining arrangements;
- (d) the employee indicated that he supported or did not support the ending under this Schedule of bargaining arrangements;
- (e) the employee influenced or sought to influence the way in which votes were to be cast by other workers in a ballot arranged under this Schedule;
- (f) the employee influenced or sought to influence other workers to vote or to abstain from voting in such a ballot;
- (g) the employee voted in such a ballot;
- (h) the employee proposed to do, failed to do, or proposed to decline to do, any of the things referred to in paragraphs (a) to (g).

(3) A reason does not fall within sub-paragraph (2) if it constitutes an unreasonable act or omission by the employee.

Selection for redundancy

162. For the purposes of Part X of the Employment Rights Act 1996 (unfair dismissal) the dismissal of an employee shall be regarded as unfair if the reason or principal reason for the dismissal was that he was redundant but it is shown—
- (a) that the circumstances constituting the redundancy applied equally to one or more other employees in the same undertaking who held positions similar to that held by him and who have not been dismissed by the employer, and
- (b) that the reason (or, if more than one, the principal reason) why he was selected for dismissal was one falling within paragraph 161(2).

Employees with fixed-term contracts

163. Section 197(1) of the Employment Rights Act 1996 (fixed-term contracts) does not prevent Part X of that Act from applying to a dismissal which is regarded as unfair by virtue of paragraph 161 or 162.

Exclusion of requirement as to qualifying period

164. Sections 108 and 109 of the Employment Rights Act 1996 (qualifying period and upper age limit for unfair dismissal protection) do not apply to a dismissal which by virtue of paragraph 161 or 162 is regarded as unfair for the purposes of Part X of that Act.

Employment Relations Act 1999, Sch 1

Meaning of worker's contract

165. References in this Part of this Schedule to a worker's contract are to the contract mentioned in paragraph (a) or (b) of section 296(1) or the arrangements for the employment mentioned in paragraph (c) of section 296(1).

Definitions   In the Trade Union and Labour Relations (Consolidation) Act 1992, for "recognition", see s 178(3) thereof; for "contract of employment", see ss 235, 273(4)(a), 278(4)(a), 295(1) thereof; for "undertaking", see ss 273(4)(e), 278(4)(c), (d) thereof; for "employee", see ss 273(4)(a), 278(4)(a), 280, 295(1) thereof; for "dismissal", see ss 273(4)(b), 278(4)(b), 298 thereof; for "worker", see ss 279, 280, 296(1) thereof; for "employer", see ss 279, 295, 296(2) thereof; for "act" and "contravention", see s 298 thereof; for "bargaining arrangements", see Sch A1, Pts III, IV, V, VI, paras 64(2)(b), 96(2), 122(2), 134(2) thereof, as inserted by this Schedule.
References   See para 2.30.

PART IX
GENERAL

Power to amend

166.—(1) If the CAC represents to the Secretary of State that paragraph 22 or 87 has an unsatisfactory effect and should be amended, he may by order amend it with a view to rectifying that effect.

(2) He may amend it in such way as he thinks fit, and not necessarily in a way proposed by the CAC (if it proposes one).

(3) An order under this paragraph shall be made by statutory instrument.

(4) No such order shall be made unless a draft of it has been laid before Parliament and approved by a resolution of each House of Parliament.

Guidance

167.—(1) The Secretary of State may issue guidance to the CAC on the way in which it is to exercise its functions under paragraph 22 or 87.

(2) The CAC must take into account any such guidance in exercising those functions.

(3) However, no guidance is to apply with regard to an application made to the CAC before the guidance in question was issued.

(4) The Secretary of State must—
 (a) lay before each House of Parliament any guidance issued under this paragraph, and
 (b) arrange for any such guidance to be published by such means as appear to him to be most appropriate for drawing it to the attention of persons likely to be affected by it.

Method of conducting collective bargaining

168.—(1) After consulting ACAS the Secretary of State may by order specify for the purposes of paragraphs 31(3) and 63(2) a method by which collective bargaining might be conducted.

(2) If such an order is made the CAC—
 (a) must take it into account under paragraphs 31(3) and 63(2), but
 (b) may depart from the method specified by the order to such extent as the CAC thinks it is appropriate to do so in the circumstances.

(3) An order under this paragraph shall be made by statutory instrument subject to annulment in pursuance of a resolution of either House of Parliament.

Directions about certain applications

169.—(1) The Secretary of State may make to the CAC directions as described in sub-paragraph (2) in relation to any case where—
 (a) two or more applications are made to the CAC,
 (b) each application is a relevant application,

Employment Relations Act 1999, Sch 2

(c) each application relates to the same bargaining unit, and
(d) the CAC has not accepted any of the applications.

(2) The directions are directions as to the order in which the CAC must consider the admissibility of the applications.

(3) The directions may include—
(a) provision to deal with a case where a relevant application is made while the CAC is still considering the admissibility of another one relating to the same bargaining unit;
(b) other incidental provisions.

(4) A relevant application is an application under paragraph 101, 106, 107, 112 or 128.

Notice of declarations

170.—(1) If the CAC issues a declaration under this Schedule it must notify the parties of the declaration and its contents.

(2) The reference here to the parties is to—
(a) the union (or unions) concerned and the employer concerned, and
(b) if the declaration is issued in consequence of an application by a worker or workers, the worker or workers making it.

CAC's general duty

171. In exercising functions under this Schedule in any particular case the CAC must have regard to the object of encouraging and promoting fair and efficient practices and arrangements in the workplace, so far as having regard to that object is consistent with applying other provisions of this Schedule in the case concerned.

General interpretation

172.—(1) References in this Schedule to the CAC are to the Central Arbitration Committee.

(2) For the purposes of this Schedule in its application to a part of Great Britain a working day is a day other than—
(a) a Saturday or a Sunday,
(b) Christmas day or Good Friday, or
a day which is a bank holiday under the Banking and Financial Dealings Act 1971 in that part of Great Britain."

Definitions In the Trade Union and Labour Relations (Consolidation) Act 1992, for "collective bargaining", see s 178(1), (2) thereof; for "ACAS", see s 247(1) thereof; for "worker", see ss 279, 280, 296(1) thereof; for "employer", see ss 279, 295, 296(2) thereof.

SCHEDULE 2

Section 2

UNION MEMBERSHIP: DETRIMENT

Introduction

1. The Trade Union and Labour Relations (Consolidation) Act 1992 shall be amended as provided in this Schedule.

Detriment

2.—(1) Section 146 (action short of dismissal on grounds related to union membership or activities) shall be amended as follows.

(2) In subsection (1) for "have action short of dismissal taken against him as an individual by his employer" substitute "be subjected to any detriment as an individual by any act, or any deliberate failure to act, by his employer if the act or failure takes place".

Employment Relations Act 1999, Sch 2

(3) In subsection (3) for "have action short of dismissal taken against him" substitute "be subjected to any detriment as an individual by any act, or any deliberate failure to act, by his employer if the act or failure takes place

(4) In subsection (4) for "action short of dismissal taken against him" substitute "a detriment to which he has been subjected as an individual by an act of his employer taking place".

(5) In subsection (5) for "action has been taken against him" substitute "he has been subjected to a detriment".

(6) After subsection (5) insert—

"(6) For the purposes of this section detriment is detriment short of dismissal."

Time limit for proceedings

3.—(1) Section 147 shall be amended as follows.

(2) Before "An" insert "(1)".

(3) In paragraph (a) of subsection (1) (as created by sub-paragraph (2) above) for the words from "action to which" to "those actions" substitute "act or failure to which the complaint relates or, where that act or failure is part of a series of similar acts or failures (or both) the last of them".

(4) After subsection (1) (as created by sub-paragraph (2) above) insert—

"(2) For the purposes of subsection (1)—
    (a) where an act extends over a period, the reference to the date of the act is a reference to the last day of that period;
    (b) a failure to act shall be treated as done when it was decided on.

(3) For the purposes of subsection (2), in the absence of evidence establishing the contrary an employer shall be taken to decide on a failure to act—
    (a) when he does an act inconsistent with doing the failed act, or
    (b) if he has done no such inconsistent act, when the period expires within which he might reasonably have been expected to do the failed act if it was to be done."

Consideration of complaint

4.—(1) Section 148 shall be amended as follows.

(2) In subsection (1) for "action was taken against the complainant" substitute "he acted or failed to act".

(3) In subsection (2) for "action was taken by the employer or the purpose for which it was taken" substitute "the employer acted or failed to act, or the purpose for which he did so".

(4) In subsection (3)—
    (a) for "action was taken by the employer against the complainant" substitute "the employer acted or failed to act";
    (b) for the words from "took the action" to "would take" substitute "acted or failed to act, unless it considers that no reasonable employer would act or fail to act in the way concerned".

(5) For subsection (4) substitute—

"(4) Where the tribunal determines that—
    (a) the complainant has been subjected to a detriment by an act or deliberate failure to act by his employer, and
    (b) the act or failure took place in consequence of a previous act or deliberate failure to act by the employer,
paragraph (a) of subsection (3) is satisfied if the purpose mentioned in that paragraph was the purpose of the previous act or failure."

Remedies

5. In section 149 for "action" there shall be substituted "act or failure"—
    (a) in subsections (1), (2) and (3)(a) and (b), and

(b) in subsection (6), in the first place where "action" occurs.

Awards against third parties

6. In section 150(1)—
   (a) in paragraph (a) for "action has been taken against the complainant by his employer" there shall be substituted "the complainant has been subjected to detriment by an act or failure by his employer taking place";
   (b) in paragraph (b) for "take the action" there shall be substituted "act or fail to act in the way".

Definitions   In the Trade Union and Labour Relations (Consolidation) Act 1992, for "dismissal", see ss 273(4)(b), 278(4)(b), 298 thereof; for "employer", see ss 279, 295, 296(2) thereof; for "act", see s 298 thereof.
References   See paras 4.4–4.9.

SCHEDULE 3

Section 4

BALLOTS AND NOTICES

Introduction

1. The Trade Union and Labour Relations (Consolidation) Act 1992 shall be amended as provided by this Schedule.

Support of ballot

2.—(1) Section 226 (requirement of ballot before action by trade union) shall be amended as follows.

(2) In subsection (2) (industrial action to be regarded as having support of ballot only if certain conditions are fulfilled) in paragraph (a)(ii) for "231A" substitute "231", omit the word "and" at the end of paragraph (b), and after paragraph (b) insert—

"(bb)   section 232A does not prevent the industrial action from being regarded as having the support of the ballot; and".

(3) After subsection (3) insert—

"(3A) If the requirements of section 231A fall to be satisfied in relation to an employer, as respects that employer industrial action shall not be regarded as having the support of a ballot unless those requirements are satisfied in relation to that employer."

Documents for employers

3.—(1) Section 226A (notice of ballot and sample voting paper for employers) shall be amended as follows.

(2) In subsection (2)(c) (notice of ballot must describe employees entitled to vote) for "describing (so that he can readily ascertain them) the employees of the employer" substitute "containing such information in the union's possession as would help the employer to make plans and bring information to the attention of those of his employees".

(3) After subsection (3) insert—

"(3A) These rules apply for the purposes of paragraph (c) of subsection (2)—
   (a) if the union possesses information as to the number, category or work-place of the employees concerned, a notice must contain that information (at least);
   (b) if a notice does not name any employees, that fact shall not be a ground for holding that it does not comply with paragraph (c) of subsection (2).

(3B) In subsection (3) references to employees are to employees of the employer concerned."

Entitlement to vote

4. In section 227 (entitlement to vote in ballot) subsection (2) (position where member is denied entitlement to vote) shall be omitted.

Employment Relations Act 1999, Sch 3

Separate workplace ballots

5. The following shall be substituted for section 228 (separate workplace ballots)—

"228 Separate workplace ballots

(1) Subject to subsection (2), this section applies if the members entitled to vote in a ballot by virtue of section 227 do not all have the same workplace.

(2) This section does not apply if the union reasonably believes that all those members have the same workplace.

(3) Subject to section 228A, a separate ballot shall be held for each workplace; and entitlement to vote in each ballot shall be accorded equally to, and restricted to, members of the union who—
   (a) are entitled to vote by virtue of section 227, and
   (b) have that workplace.

(4) In this section and section 228A "workplace" in relation to a person who is employed means—
   (a) if the person works at or from a single set of premises, those premises, and
   (b) in any other case, the premises with which the person's employment has the closest connection.

228A Separate workplaces: single and aggregate ballots

(1) Where section 228(3) would require separate ballots to be held for each workplace, a ballot may be held in place of some or all of the separate ballots if one of subsections (2) to (4) is satisfied in relation to it.

(2) This subsection is satisfied in relation to a ballot if the workplace of each member entitled to vote in the ballot is the workplace of at least one member of the union who is affected by the dispute.

(3) This subsection is satisfied in relation to a ballot if entitlement to vote is accorded to, and limited to, all the members of the union who—
   (a) according to the union's reasonable belief have an occupation of a particular kind or have any of a number of particular kinds of occupation, and
   (b) are employed by a particular employer, or by any of a number of particular employers, with whom the union is in dispute.

(4) This subsection is satisfied in relation to a ballot if entitlement to vote is accorded to, and limited to, all the members of the union who are employed by a particular employer, or by any of a number of particular employers, with whom the union is in dispute.

(5) For the purposes of subsection (2) the following are members of the union affected by a dispute—
   (a) if the dispute relates (wholly or partly) to a decision which the union reasonably believes the employer has made or will make concerning a matter specified in subsection (1)(a), (b) or (c) of section 244 (meaning of "trade dispute"), members whom the decision directly affects,
   (b) if the dispute relates (wholly or partly) to a matter specified in subsection (1)(d) of that section, members whom the matter directly affects,
   (c) if the dispute relates (wholly or partly) to a matter specified in subsection (1)(e) of that section, persons whose membership or non-membership is in dispute,
   (d) if the dispute relates (wholly or partly) to a matter specified in subsection (1)(f) of that section, officials of the union who have used or would use the facilities concerned in the dispute."

Voting paper

6.—(1) Section 229 (voting paper) shall be amended as follows.

(2) After subsection (2) (voting paper must ask whether voter is prepared to take part in a strike or industrial action short of a strike) insert—

"(2A) For the purposes of subsection (2) an overtime ban and a call-out ban constitute industrial action short of a strike."

(3) At the end of the statement in subsection (4) (statement that industrial action may be a breach of employment contract to be set out on every voting paper) insert—

"However, if you are dismissed for taking part in strike or other industrial action which is called officially and is otherwise lawful, the dismissal will be unfair if it takes place fewer than eight weeks after you started taking part in the action, and depending on the circumstances may be unfair if it takes place later."

(4) In the definition of "strike" in section 246 (interpretation) after "means" there shall be inserted "(except for the purposes of section 229(2))".

Conduct of ballot: merchant seamen

7. In section 230 (conduct of ballot) for subsections (2A) and (2B) there shall be substituted—

"(2A) Subsection (2B) applies to a merchant seaman if the trade union reasonably believes that—
  (a) he will be employed in a ship either at sea or at a place outside Great Britain at some time in the period during which votes may be cast, and
  (b) it will be convenient for him to receive a voting paper and to vote while on the ship or while at a place where the ship is rather than in accordance with subsection (2).

(2B) Where this subsection applies to a merchant seaman he shall, if it is reasonably practicable—
  (a) have a voting paper made available to him while on the ship or while at a place where the ship is, and
  (b) be given an opportunity to vote while on the ship or while at a place where the ship is."

Inducement

8. After section 232 insert—

"232A Inducement of member denied entitlement to vote

Industrial action shall not be regarded as having the support of a ballot if the following conditions apply in the case of any person—
  (a) he was a member of the trade union at the time when the ballot was held,
  (b) it was reasonable at that time for the trade union to believe he would be induced to take part or, as the case may be, to continue to take part in the industrial action,
  (c) he was not accorded entitlement to vote in the ballot, and
  (d) he was induced by the trade union to take part or, as the case may be, to continue to take part in the industrial action."

Disregard of certain failures

9. After section 232A there shall be inserted—

"232B Small accidental failures to be disregarded

(1) If—
  (a) in relation to a ballot there is a failure (or there are failures) to comply with a provision mentioned in subsection (2) or with more than one of those provisions, and
  (b) the failure is accidental and on a scale which is unlikely to affect the result of the ballot or, as the case may be, the failures are accidental and taken together are on a scale which is unlikely to affect the result of the ballot,
the failure (or failures) shall be disregarded.

(2) The provisions are section 227(1), section 230(2) and section 230(2A)."

Employment Relations Act 1999, Sch 3

Period of ballot's effectiveness

10. In section 234 (period after which ballot ceases to be effective) for subsection (1) there shall be substituted—

"(1) Subject to the following provisions, a ballot ceases to be effective for the purposes of section 233(3)(b) in relation to industrial action by members of a trade union at the end of the period, beginning with the date of the ballot—
  (a) of four weeks, or
  (b) of such longer duration not exceeding eight weeks as is agreed between the union and the members' employer."

Notice of industrial action

11.—(1) Section 234A (notice to employers of industrial action) shall be amended as follows.

(2) In subsection (3)(a) (notice relating to industrial action must describe employees intended to take part in industrial action) for "describes (so that he can readily ascertain them) the employees of the employer who" substitute "contains such information in the union's possession as would help the employer to make plans and bring information to the attention of those of his employees whom".

(3) After subsection (5) insert—

"(5A) These rules apply for the purposes of paragraph (a) of subsection (3)—
  (a) if the union possesses information as to the number, category or work-place of the employees concerned, a notice must contain that information (at least);
  (b) if a notice does not name any employees, that fact shall not be a ground for holding that it does not comply with paragraph (a) of subsection (3)."

(4) In subsection (7)—
  (a) insert at the beginning the words "Subject to subsections (7A) and (7B),", and
  (b) in paragraph (a) the words "otherwise than to enable the union to comply with a court order or an undertaking given to a court" shall cease to have effect.

(5) After subsection (7) insert—

"(7A) Subsection (7) shall not apply where industrial action ceases to be authorised or endorsed in order to enable the union to comply with a court order or an undertaking given to a court.

(7B) Subsection (7) shall not apply where—
  (a) a union agrees with an employer, before industrial action ceases to be authorised or endorsed, that it will cease to be authorised or endorsed with effect from a date specified in the agreement ("the suspension date") and that it may again be authorised or endorsed with effect from a date not earlier than a date specified in the agreement ("the resumption date"),
  (b) the action ceases to be authorised or endorsed with effect from the suspension date, and
  (c) the action is again authorised or endorsed with effect from a date which is not earlier than the resumption date or such later date as may be agreed between the union and the employer."

(6) In subsection (9) for "subsection (7)" substitute "subsections (7) to (7B)".

Definitions For "trade union", see Trade Union and Labour Relations (Consolidation) Act 1992, s 1; for "official", see s 119 of that Act; for "date of the ballot", see s 246 thereof; for "employee", see ss 235, 273(4)(a), 278(4)(a), 280, 295(1) thereof; for "dismissal", see ss 273(4)(b), 278(4)(b), 298 thereof; for "employer", see ss 235, 279, 295, 296(2) thereof, 453; for "action", see s 298 thereof.
References See paras 3.4–3.11.

SCHEDULE 4

Sections 7, 8 and 9

LEAVE FOR FAMILY REASONS ETC

PART I
MATERNITY LEAVE AND PARENTAL LEAVE

NEW PART VIII OF EMPLOYMENT RIGHTS ACT 1996

"PART VIII
CHAPTER I
MATERNITY LEAVE

71 Ordinary maternity leave

(1) An employee may, provided that she satisfies any conditions which may be prescribed, be absent from work at any time during an ordinary maternity leave period.

(2) An ordinary maternity leave period is a period calculated in accordance with regulations made by the Secretary of State.

(3) Regulations under subsection (2)—
  (a) shall secure that no ordinary maternity leave period is less than 18 weeks;
  (b) may allow an employee to choose, subject to any prescribed restrictions, the date on which an ordinary maternity leave period starts.

(4) Subject to section 74, an employee who exercises her right under subsection (1)—
  (a) is entitled to the benefit of the terms and conditions of employment which would have applied if she had not been absent,
  (b) is bound by any obligations arising under those terms and conditions (except in so far as they are inconsistent with subsection (1)), and
  (c) is entitled to return from leave to the job in which she was employed before her absence.

(5) In subsection (4)(a) "terms and conditions of employment"—
  (a) includes matters connected with an employee's employment whether or not they arise under her contract of employment, but
  (b) does not include terms and conditions about remuneration.

(6) The Secretary of State may make regulations specifying matters which are, or are not, to be treated as remuneration for the purposes of this section.

(7) An employee's right to return under subsection (4)(c) is a right to return—
  (a) with her seniority, pension rights and similar rights as they would have been if she had not been absent (subject to paragraph 5 of Schedule 5 to the Social Security Act 1989 (equal treatment under pension schemes: maternity)), and
  (b) on terms and conditions not less favourable than those which would have applied if she had not been absent.

72 Compulsory maternity leave

(1) An employer shall not permit an employee who satisfies prescribed conditions to work during a compulsory maternity leave period.

(2) A compulsory maternity leave period is a period calculated in accordance with regulations made by the Secretary of State.

(3) Regulations under subsection (2) shall secure—
  (a) that no compulsory leave period is less than two weeks, and
  (b) that every compulsory maternity leave period falls within an ordinary maternity leave period.

(4) Subject to subsection (5), any provision of or made under the Health and Safety at Work etc Act 1974 shall apply in relation to the prohibition under subsection (1) as if it were imposed by regulations under section 15 of that Act.

Employment Relations Act 1999, Sch 4

(5) Section 33(1)(c) of the 1974 Act shall not apply in relation to the prohibition under subsection (1); and an employer who contravenes that subsection shall be—
  (a) guilty of an offence, and
  (b) liable on summary conviction to a fine not exceeding level 2 on the standard scale.

73 Additional maternity leave

(1) An employee who satisfies prescribed conditions may be absent from work at any time during an additional maternity leave period.

(2) An additional maternity leave period is a period calculated in accordance with regulations made by the Secretary of State.

(3) Regulations under subsection (2) may allow an employee to choose, subject to prescribed restrictions, the date on which an additional maternity leave period ends.

(4) Subject to section 74, an employee who exercises her right under subsection (1)—
  (a) is entitled, for such purposes and to such extent as may be prescribed, to the benefit of the terms and conditions of employment which would have applied if she had not been absent,
  (b) is bound, for such purposes and to such extent as may be prescribed, by obligations arising under those terms and conditions (except in so far as they are inconsistent with subsection (1)), and
  (c) is entitled to return from leave to a job of a prescribed kind.

(5) In subsection (4)(a) "terms and conditions of employment"—
  (a) includes matters connected with an employee's employment whether or not they arise under her contract of employment, but
  (b) does not include terms and conditions about remuneration.

(6) The Secretary of State may make regulations specifying matters which are, or are not, to be treated as remuneration for the purposes of this section.

(7) The Secretary of State may make regulations making provision, in relation to the right to return under subsection (4)(c), about—
  (a) seniority, pension rights and similar rights;
  (b) terms and conditions of employment on return.

74 Redundancy and dismissal

(1) Regulations under section 71 or 73 may make provision about redundancy during an ordinary or additional maternity leave period.

(2) Regulations under section 71 or 73 may make provision about dismissal (other than by reason of redundancy) during an ordinary or additional maternity leave period.

(3) Regulations made by virtue of subsection (1) or (2) may include—
  (a) provision requiring an employer to offer alternative employment;
  (b) provision for the consequences of failure to comply with the regulations (which may include provision for a dismissal to be treated as unfair for the purposes of Part X).

(4) Regulations under section 73 may make provision—
  (a) for section 73(4)(c) not to apply in specified cases, and
  (b) about dismissal at the conclusion of an additional maternity leave period.

75 Sections 71 to 73: supplemental

(1) Regulations under section 71, 72 or 73 may—
  (a) make provision about notices to be given, evidence to be produced and other procedures to be followed by employees and employers;
  (b) make provision for the consequences of failure to give notices, to produce evidence or to comply with other procedural requirements;
  (c) make provision for the consequences of failure to act in accordance with a notice given by virtue of paragraph (a);
  (d) make special provision for cases where an employee has a right which corresponds to a right under this Chapter and which arises under her contract of employment or otherwise;

(e) make provision modifying the effect of Chapter II of Part XIV (calculation of a week's pay) in relation to an employee who is or has been absent from work on ordinary or additional maternity leave;
(f) make provision applying, modifying or excluding an enactment, in such circumstances as may be specified and subject to any conditions specified, in relation to a person entitled to ordinary, compulsory or additional maternity leave;
(g) make different provision for different cases or circumstances.

(2) In sections 71 to 73 "prescribed" means prescribed by regulations made by the Secretary of State.

CHAPTER II
PARENTAL LEAVE

76 Entitlement to parental leave

(1) The Secretary of State shall make regulations entitling an employee who satisfies specified conditions—
(a) as to duration of employment, and
(b) as to having, or expecting to have, responsibility for a child,
to be absent from work on parental leave for the purpose of caring for a child.

(2) The regulations shall include provision for determining—
(a) the extent of an employee's entitlement to parental leave in respect of a child;
(b) when parental leave may be taken.

(3) Provision under subsection (2)(a) shall secure that where an employee is entitled to parental leave in respect of a child he is entitled to a period or total period of leave of at least three months; but this subsection is without prejudice to any provision which may be made by the regulations for cases in which—
(a) a person ceases to satisfy conditions under subsection (1);
(b) an entitlement to parental leave is transferred.

(4) Provision under subsection (2)(b) may, in particular, refer to—
(a) a child's age, or
(b) a specified period of time starting from a specified event.

(5) Regulations under subsection (1) may—
(a) specify things which are, or are not, to be taken as done for the purpose of caring for a child;
(b) require parental leave to be taken as a single period of absence in all cases or in specified cases;
(c) require parental leave to be taken as a series of periods of absence in all cases or in specified cases;
(d) require all or specified parts of a period of parental leave to be taken at or by specified times;
(e) make provision about the postponement by an employer of a period of parental leave which an employee wishes to take;
(f) specify a minimum or maximum period of absence which may be taken as part of a period of parental leave.
(g) specify a maximum aggregate of periods of parental leave which may be taken during a specified period of time.

77 Rights during and after parental leave

(1) Regulations under section 76 shall provide—
(a) that an employee who is absent on parental leave is entitled, for such purposes and to such extent as may be prescribed, to the benefit of the terms and conditions of employment which would have applied if he had not been absent,
(b) that an employee who is absent on parental leave is bound, for such purposes and to such extent as may be prescribed, by any obligations arising under those terms and conditions (except in so far as they are inconsistent with section 76(1)), and

Employment Relations Act 1999, Sch 4

        (c)   that an employee who is absent on parental leave is entitled, subject to section 78(1), to return from leave to a job of such kind as the regulations may specify.

    (2)   In subsection (1)(a) "terms and conditions of employment"—
        (a)   includes matters connected with an employee's employment whether or not they arise under a contract of employment, but
        (b)   does not include terms and conditions about remuneration.

    (3)   Regulations under section 76 may specify matters which are, or are not, to be treated as remuneration for the purposes of subsection (2)(b) above.

    (4)   The regulations may make provision, in relation to the right to return mentioned in subsection (1)(c), about—
        (a)   seniority, pension rights and similar rights;
        (b)   terms and conditions of employment on return.

78 Special cases

    (1)   Regulations under section 76 may make provision—
        (a)   about redundancy during a period of parental leave;
        (b)   about dismissal (other than by reason of redundancy) during a period of parental leave.

    (2)   Provision by virtue of subsection (1) may include—
        (a)   provision requiring an employer to offer alternative employment;
        (b)   provision for the consequences of failure to comply with the regulations (which may include provision for a dismissal to be treated as unfair for the purposes of Part X).

    (3)   Regulations under section 76 may provide for an employee to be entitled to choose to exercise all or part of his entitlement to parental leave—
        (a)   by varying the terms of his contract of employment as to hours of work, or
        (b)   by varying his normal working practice as to hours of work,
in a way specified in or permitted by the regulations for a period specified in the regulations.

    (4)   Provision by virtue of subsection (3)—
        (a)   may restrict an entitlement to specified circumstances;
        (b)   may make an entitlement subject to specified conditions (which may include conditions relating to obtaining the employer's consent);
        (c)   may include consequential and incidental provision.

    (5)   Regulations under section 76 may make provision permitting all or part of an employee's entitlement to parental leave in respect of a child to be transferred to another employee in specified circumstances.

    (6)   The reference in section 77(1)(c) to absence on parental leave includes, where appropriate, a reference to a continuous period of absence attributable partly to maternity leave and partly to parental leave.

    (7)   Regulations under section 76 may provide for specified provisions of the regulations not to apply in relation to an employee if any provision of his contract of employment—
        (a)   confers an entitlement to absence from work for the purpose of caring for a child, and
        (b)   incorporates or operates by reference to all or part of a collective agreement, or workforce agreement, of a kind specified in the regulations.

79 Supplemental

    (1)   Regulations under section 76 may, in particular—
        (a)   make provision about notices to be given and evidence to be produced by employees to employers, by employers to employees, and by employers to other employers;
        (b)   make provision requiring employers or employees to keep records;

(c) make provision about other procedures to be followed by employees and employers;
(d) make provision (including provision creating criminal offences) specifying the consequences of failure to give notices, to produce evidence, to keep records or to comply with other procedural requirements;
(e) make provision specifying the consequences of failure to act in accordance with a notice given by virtue of paragraph (a);
(f) make special provision for cases where an employee has a right which corresponds to a right conferred by the regulations and which arises under his contract of employment or otherwise;
(g) make provision applying, modifying or excluding an enactment, in such circumstances as may be specified and subject to any conditions specified, in relation to a person entitled to parental leave;
(h) make different provision for different cases or circumstances.

(2) The regulations may make provision modifying the effect of Chapter II of Part XIV (calculation of a week's pay) in relation to an employee who is or has been absent from work on parental leave.

(3) Without prejudice to the generality of section 76, the regulations may make any provision which appears to the Secretary of State to be necessary or expedient—
(a) for the purpose of implementing Council Directive 96/34/EC on the framework agreement on parental leave, or
(b) for the purpose of dealing with any matter arising out of or related to the United Kingdom's obligations under that Directive.

80 Complaint to employment tribunal

(1) An employee may present a complaint to an employment tribunal that his employer—
(a) has unreasonably postponed a period of parental leave requested by the employee, or
(b) has prevented or attempted to prevent the employee from taking parental leave.

(2) An employment tribunal shall not consider a complaint under this section unless it is presented—
(a) before the end of the period of three months beginning with the date (or last date) of the matters complained of, or
(b) within such further period as the tribunal considers reasonable in a case where it is satisfied that it was not reasonably practicable for the complaint to be presented before the end of that period of three months.

(3) Where an employment tribunal finds a complaint under this section well-founded it—
(a) shall make a declaration to that effect, and
(b) may make an award of compensation to be paid by the employer to the employee.

(4) The amount of compensation shall be such as the tribunal considers just and equitable in all the circumstances having regard to—
(a) the employer's behaviour, and
(b) any loss sustained by the employee which is attributable to the matters complained of."

Definitions In the Employment Rights Act 1996, for "prescribed", see s 75(2) thereof, as substituted by this Part of this Schedule; for "employee", see s 230(1) thereof; for "contract of employment", see s 230(2) thereof; for "employment" and "employed", see s 230(5) thereof; for "job" and "week", see s 235(1) thereof; for "ordinary maternity leave period", see s 71(2) thereof, as substituted by this Part of this Schedule; for "employer", see s 230(4) thereof; for "week", see s 235(1) thereof; for "additional maternity leave period", see s 73(2) thereof, as substituted by this Part of this Schedule; for "redundancy", see s 139 thereof;
References See paras 6.4–6.7, 6.17, 6.18.

PART II
TIME OFF FOR DEPENDANTS

PROVISIONS TO BE INSERTED AFTER SECTION 57 OF THE EMPLOYMENT RIGHTS ACT 1996

"Dependants

57A Time off for dependants

(1) An employee is entitled to be permitted by his employer to take a reasonable amount of time off during the employee's working hours in order to take action which is necessary—
- (a) to provide assistance on an occasion when a dependant falls ill, gives birth or is injured or assaulted,
- (b) to make arrangements for the provision of care for a dependant who is ill or injured,
- (c) in consequence of the death of a dependant,
- (d) because of the unexpected disruption or termination of arrangements for the care of a dependant, or
- (e) to deal with an incident which involves a child of the employee and which occurs unexpectedly in a period during which an educational establishment which the child attends is responsible for him.

(2) Subsection (1) does not apply unless the employee—
- (a) tells his employer the reason for his absence as soon as reasonably practicable, and
- (b) except where paragraph (a) cannot be complied with until after the employee has returned to work, tells his employer for how long he expects to be absent.

(3) Subject to subsections (4) and (5), for the purposes of this section "dependant" means, in relation to an employee—
- (a) a spouse,
- (b) a child,
- (c) a parent,
- (d) a person who lives in the same household as the employee, otherwise than by reason of being his employee, tenant, lodger or boarder.

(4) For the purposes of subsection (1)(a) or (b) "dependant" includes, in addition to the persons mentioned in subsection (3), any person who reasonably relies on the employee—
- (a) for assistance on an occasion when the person falls ill or is injured or assaulted, or
- (b) to make arrangements for the provision of care in the event of illness or injury.

(5) For the purposes of subsection (1)(d) "dependant" includes, in addition to the persons mentioned in subsection (3), any person who reasonably relies on the employee to make arrangements for the provision of care.

(6) A reference in this section to illness or injury includes a reference to mental illness or injury.

57B Complaint to employment tribunal

(1) An employee may present a complaint to an employment tribunal that his employer has unreasonably refused to permit him to take time off as required by section 57A.

(2) An employment tribunal shall not consider a complaint under this section unless it is presented—
- (a) before the end of the period of three months beginning with the date when the refusal occurred, or
- (b) within such further period as the tribunal considers reasonable in a case where it is satisfied that it was not reasonably practicable for the complaint to be presented before the end of that period of three months.

Employment Relations Act 1999, Sch 4

(3) Where an employment tribunal finds a complaint under subsection (1) well-founded, it—
 (a) shall make a declaration to that effect, and
 (b) may make an award of compensation to be paid by the employer to the employee.

(4) The amount of compensation shall be such as the tribunal considers just and equitable in all the circumstances having regard to—
 (a) the employer's default in refusing to permit time off to be taken by the employee, and
 (b) any loss sustained by the employee which is attributable to the matters complained of."

Definitions In the Employment Rights Act 1996, for "employee", see s 230(1) thereof; for "employer", see s 230(4) thereof.
References See paras 6.23–6.24.

PART III
CONSEQUENTIAL AMENDMENTS

Trade Union and Labour Relations (Consolidation) Act 1992 (c 52)

1. The Trade Union and Labour Relations (Consolidation) Act 1992 shall be amended as follows.

2. In section 237(1A) (dismissal of those taking part in unofficial industrial action)—
 (a) for the words from "section 99(1) to (3)" to the end substitute

"or under—
 (a) section 99, 100, 101A(d), 103 or 103A of the Employment Rights Act 1996 (dismissal in family, health and safety, working time, employee representative and protected disclosure cases),
 (b) section 104 of that Act in its application in relation to time off under section 57A of that Act (dependants);" and

 (b) at the end insert "; and a reference to a specified reason for dismissal includes a reference to specified circumstances of dismissal".

3. In section 238(2A) (dismissal in connection with other industrial action)—
 (a) for the words from "section 99(1) to (3)" to the end substitute

"or under—
 (a) section 99, 100, 101A(d) or 103 of the Employment Rights Act 1996 (dismissal in family, health and safety, working time and employee representative cases),
 (b) section 104 of that Act in its application in relation to time off under section 57A of that Act (dependants);" and

 (b) at the end insert "; and a reference to a specified reason for dismissal includes a reference to specified circumstances of dismissal".

Employment Tribunals Act 1996 (c 17)

4. In section 13(2) of the Employment Tribunals Act 1996 (costs and expenses) the following shall cease to have effect—
 (a) the word "or" after paragraph (a),
 (b) paragraph (b), and
 (c) the words ", or which she held before her absence,".

Employment Rights Act 1996 (c 18)

5. The Employment Rights Act 1996 shall be amended as follows.

6. In section 37 (contractual requirements for Sunday work: protected workers) omit the following—
 (a) subsection (4),
 (b) the word "and" after subsection (5)(a), and
 (c) subsection (5)(b).

Employment Relations Act 1999, Sch 4

7. In section 43 (contractual requirements relating to Sunday work: opting out) omit the following—
    (a) subsection (4),
    (b) the word "and" after subsection (5)(a), and
    (c) subsection (5)(b).

8. After section 47B (protection from detriment: disclosures) insert—

"47C Leave for family and domestic reasons

(1) An employee has the right not to be subjected to any detriment by any act, or any deliberate failure to act, by his employer done for a prescribed reason.

(2) A prescribed reason is one which is prescribed by regulations made by the Secretary of State and which relates to—
    (a) pregnancy, childbirth or maternity,
    (b) ordinary, compulsory or additional maternity leave,
    (c) parental leave, or
    (d) time off under section 57A.

(3) A reason prescribed under this section in relation to parental leave may relate to action which an employee takes, agrees to take or refuses to take under or in respect of a collective or workforce agreement.

(4) Regulations under this section may make different provision for different cases or circumstances."

9. In section 48(1) (detriment: complaints to employment tribunals) for "or 47A" substitute ", 47A or 47C".

10. In section 88(1)(c) (notice period: employment with normal working hours) after "childbirth" insert "or on parental leave".

11. In section 89(3)(b) (notice period: employment without normal working hours) after "childbirth" insert "or on parental leave".

12. In section 92(4)(b) (right to written statement of reasons for dismissal) for "maternity leave period" substitute "ordinary or additional maternity leave period".

13. Omit section 96 (failure to permit return after childbirth treated as dismissal).

14. Omit section 97(6) (effective date of termination: section 96).

15. In section 98 (fairness of dismissal)—
    (a) omit subsection (5), and
    (b) in subsection (6) for "subsections (4) and (5)" substitute "subsection (4)".

16. For section 99 (unfair dismissal: pregnancy and childbirth) substitute—

"99 Leave for family reasons

(1) An employee who is dismissed shall be regarded for the purposes of this Part as unfairly dismissed if—
    (a) the reason or principal reason for the dismissal is of a prescribed kind, or
    (b) the dismissal takes place in prescribed circumstances.

(2) In this section "prescribed" means prescribed by regulations made by the Secretary of State.

(3) A reason or set of circumstances prescribed under this section must relate to—
    (a) pregnancy, childbirth or maternity,
    (b) ordinary, compulsory or additional maternity leave,
    (c) parental leave, or
    (d) time off under section 57A;
and it may also relate to redundancy or other factors.

(4) A reason or set of circumstances prescribed under subsection (1) satisfies subsection (3)(c) or (d) if it relates to action which an employee—
    (a) takes,
    (b) agrees to take, or

(c) refuses to take,
under or in respect of a collective or workforce agreement which deals with parental leave.

(5) Regulations under this section may—
 (a) make different provision for different cases or circumstances
 (b) apply any enactment, in such circumstances as may be specified and subject to any conditions specified, in relation to persons regarded as unfairly dismissed by reason of this section."

17. In section 105 (unfair dismissal: redundancy) omit subsection (2).

18. In section 108 (qualifying period of employment) omit subsection (3)(a).

19. In section 109 (upper age limit) omit subsection (2)(a).

20. In section 114 (order for reinstatement) omit subsection (5).

21. In section 115 (order for re-engagement) omit subsection (4).

22. In section 118(1)(b) (compensation: general) omit ", 127".

23. In section 119 (compensation: basic award) omit subsection (6).

24. Omit section 127 (dismissal at or after end of maternity leave period).

25. Omit section 137 (failure to permit return after childbirth treated as dismissal).

26. In section 145 (redundancy payments: relevant date) omit subsection (7).

27. In section 146 (supplemental provisions) omit subsection (3).

28. In section 156 (upper age limit) omit subsection (2).

29. In section 157 (exemption orders) omit subsection (6).

30. In section 162 (amount of redundancy payment) omit subsection (7).

31. In section 192(2) (armed forces)—
 (a) after paragraph (aa) insert—
  "(ab) section 47C,", and
 (b) in paragraph (b) for "55 to 57" substitute "55 to 57B".

32. In section 194(2)(c) (House of Lords staff) for "and 47" substitute ", 47 and 47C".

33. In section 195(2)(c) (House of Commons staff) for "and 47" substitute ", 47 and 47C".

34. In section 199 (mariners)—
 (a) in subsection (2) for "50 to 57" substitute "47C, 50 to 57B".
 (b) in subsection (2) omit the words "(subject to subsection (3))", and
 (c) omit subsection (3).

35. In section 200(1) (police officers)—
 (a) after "47B," insert "47C,",
 (b) for "to 57" substitute "to 57B",
 (c) after "93" insert "and", and
 (d) omit "and section 137".

36. In section 202(2) (national security)—
 (a) in paragraph (b) for "and 47" substitute ", 47 and 47C",
 (b) in paragraph (c) for "55 to 57" substitute "55 to 57B", and
 (c) in paragraph (g) for sub-paragraph (i) substitute—
  "(i) by section 99, 100, 101A(d) or 103, or by section 104 in its application in relation to time off under section 57A,".

37. In section 209 (power to amend Act) omit subsection (6).

38.—(1) Section 212 (weeks counted in computing period of employment) is amended as follows.

(2) Omit subsection (2).

Employment Relations Act 1999, Sch 4

(3) In subsection (3)—
  (a) insert "or" after paragraph (b),
  (b) omit "or" after paragraph (c), and
  (c) omit paragraph (d).

(4) In subsection (4) omit "or (subject to subsection (2)) subsection (3)(d)".

39. In section 225(5)(b) (calculation date: rights during employment) for sub-paragraph (i) substitute—

"(i) where the day before that on which the suspension begins falls during a period of ordinary or additional maternity leave, the day before the beginning of that period,".

40. In section 226 (rights on termination) omit subsections (3)(a) and (5)(a).

41. In section 235(1) (interpretation: other definitions) omit the definitions of "maternity leave period" and "notified day of return".

42.—(1) Section 236 (orders and regulations) shall be amended as follows.

(2) In subsection (2)(a) after "order" insert "or regulations".

(3) In subsection (3)—
  (a) after "and no order" insert "or regulations",
  (b) for "72(3), 73(5), 79(3)," substitute "47C, 71, 72, 73, 76, 99,", and
  (c) for "or order" substitute ", order or regulations".

Definitions   In the Trade Union and Labour Relations (Consolidation) Act 1992, for "dismissal", see ss 273(4)(b), 278(4)(b), 298 thereof.
In the Employment Rights Act 1996, for "ordinary maternity leave period", see s 71(2) thereof, as substituted by Pt I of this Schedule; for "additional maternity leave period", see s 73(2) thereof, as so substituted; for "redundancy", see s 139 thereof; for "employee", see s 230(1) thereof; for "employer", see s 230(4) thereof; for "act", "action", "childbirth" and "collective agreement", see s 235(1) thereof.
References   See para 6.25.

SCHEDULE 5

Section 16

UNFAIR DISMISSAL OF STRIKING WORKERS

Trade Union and Labour Relations (Consolidation) Act 1992 (c 52)

1. The Trade Union and Labour Relations (Consolidation) Act 1992 shall be amended as follows.

2. In section 238 (dismissals in connection with industrial action) after subsection (2A) there shall be inserted—

"(2B) Subsection (2) does not apply in relation to an employee who is regarded as unfairly dismissed by virtue of section 238A below."

3. The following shall be inserted after section 238—

"238A   Participation in official industrial action

(1)   For the purposes of this section an employee takes protected industrial action if he commits an act which, or a series of acts each of which, he is induced to commit by an act which by virtue of section 219 is not actionable in tort.

(2)   An employee who is dismissed shall be regarded for the purposes of Part X of the Employment Rights Act 1996 (unfair dismissal) as unfairly dismissed if—
  (a) the reason (or, if more than one, the principal reason) for the dismissal is that the employee took protected industrial action, and
  (b) subsection (3), (4) or (5) applies to the dismissal.

(3)   This subsection applies to a dismissal if it takes place within the period of eight weeks beginning with the day on which the employee started to take protected industrial action.

(4) This subsection applies to a dismissal if—
  (a) it takes place after the end of that period, and
  (b) the employee had stopped taking protected industrial action before the end of that period.

(5) This subsection applies to a dismissal if—
  (a) it takes place after the end of that period,
  (b) the employee had not stopped taking protected industrial action before the end of that period, and
  (c) the employer had not taken such procedural steps as would have been reasonable for the purposes of resolving the dispute to which the protected industrial action relates.

(6) In determining whether an employer has taken those steps regard shall be had, in particular, to—
  (a) whether the employer or a union had complied with procedures established by any applicable collective or other agreement;
  (b) whether the employer or a union offered or agreed to commence or resume negotiations after the start of the protected industrial action;
  (c) whether the employer or a union unreasonably refused, after the start of the protected industrial action, a request that conciliation services be used;
  (d) whether the employer or a union unreasonably refused, after the start of the protected industrial action, a request that mediation services be used in relation to procedures to be adopted for the purposes of resolving the dispute.

(7) In determining whether an employer has taken those steps no regard shall be had to the merits of the dispute.

(8) For the purposes of this section no account shall be taken of the repudiation of any act by a trade union as mentioned in section 21 in relation to anything which occurs before the end of the next working day (within the meaning of section 237) after the day on which the repudiation takes place."

4.—(1) Section 239 (supplementary provisions relating to unfair dismissal) shall be amended as follows.

(2) In subsection (1) for "Sections 237 and 238" there shall be substituted "Sections 237 to 238A".

(3) At the end of subsection (1) there shall be added "; but sections 108 and 109 of that Act (qualifying period and age limit) shall not apply in relation to section 238A of this Act."

(4) In subsection (2) after "section 238" there shall be inserted "or 238A".

(5) At the end there shall be added—

"(4) In relation to a complaint under section 111 of the 1996 Act (unfair dismissal: complaint to employment tribunal) that a dismissal was unfair by virtue of section 238A of this Act—
  (a) no order shall be made under section 113 of the 1996 Act (reinstatement or re-engagement) until after the conclusion of protected industrial action by any employee in relation to the relevant dispute,
  (b) regulations under section 7 of the Employment Tribunals Act 1996 may make provision about the adjournment and renewal of applications (including provision requiring adjournment in specified circumstances), and
  (c) regulations under section 9 of that Act may require a pre-hearing review to be carried out in specified circumstances."

Employment Rights Act 1996 (c 18)

5.—(1) Section 105 of the Employment Rights Act 1996 (redundancy) shall be amended as follows.

(2) In subsection (1)(c) for "subsections (2) to (7)" there shall be substituted "subsections (2) to (7C).".

Employment Relations Act 1999, Sch 5

(3) After subsection (7B) (inserted by Schedule 3 to the Tax Credits Act 1999) there shall be inserted—

"(7C) This subsection applies if—
  (a) the reason (or, if more than one, the principal reason) for which the employee was selected for dismissal was the reason mentioned in section 238A(2) of the Trade Union and Labour Relations (Consolidation) Act 1992 (participation in official industrial action), and
  (b) subsection (3), (4) or (5) of that section applies to the dismissal."

Definitions   In the Trade Union and Labour Relations (Consolidation) Act 1992, s 239, for "employee", see ss 273(4)(a), 278(4)(a), 280, 295(1) thereof, for "dismissal", see ss 273(4)(b), 278(4)(b), 298 thereof, for "employer", see ss 279, 295, 296(2) thereof, and for "act", see s 298 thereof.
In the Employment Rights Act 1996, for "employee", see s 230(1) thereof.
References   See paras 5.22–5.26.

SCHEDULE 6

Section 29

THE CERTIFICATION OFFICER

Introduction

1. The Trade Union and Labour Relations (Consolidation) Act 1992 shall be amended as provided by this Schedule.

Register of members

2. In section 24 (duty to maintain register of members' names and addresses) the second sentence of subsection (6) (application to Certification Officer does not prevent application to court) shall be omitted.

3. In section 24A (securing confidentiality of register during ballots) the second sentence of subsection (6) (application to Certification Officer does not prevent application to court) shall be omitted.

4.—(1) Section 25 (application to Certification Officer for declaration of breach of duty regarding register of members' names and addresses) shall be amended as follows.

(2) In subsection (2)(b) (duty to give opportunity to be heard where Certification Officer considers it appropriate) omit "where he considers it appropriate,".

(3) After subsection (5) insert—

"(5A) Where the Certification Officer makes a declaration he shall also, unless he considers that to do so would be inappropriate, make an enforcement order, that is, an order imposing on the union one or both of the following requirements—
  (a) to take such steps to remedy the declared failure, within such period, as may be specified in the order;
  (b) to abstain from such acts as may be so specified with a view to securing that a failure of the same or a similar kind does not occur in future.

(5B) Where an enforcement order has been made, any person who is a member of the union and was a member at the time it was made is entitled to enforce obedience to the order as if he had made the application on which the order was made."

(4) After subsection (8) insert—

"(9)   A declaration made by the Certification Officer under this section may be relied on as if it were a declaration made by the court.

(10)   An enforcement order made by the Certification Officer under this section may be enforced in the same way as an order of the court.

(11)   The following paragraphs have effect if a person applies under section 26 in relation to an alleged failure—
  (a) that person may not apply under this section in relation to that failure;

(b) on an application by a different person under this section in relation to that failure, the Certification Officer shall have due regard to any declaration, order, observations or reasons made or given by the court regarding that failure and brought to the Certification Officer's notice."

5.—(1) Section 26 (application to court for declaration of breach of duty regarding register of members' names and addresses) shall be amended as follows.

(2) Omit subsection (2) (position where application in respect of the same matter has been made to Certification Officer).

(3) After subsection (7) insert—

"(8) The following paragraphs have effect if a person applies under section 25 in relation to an alleged failure—
(a) that person may not apply under this section in relation to that failure;
(b) on an application by a different person under this section in relation to that failure, the court shall have due regard to any declaration, order, observations or reasons made or given by the Certification Officer regarding that failure and brought to the court's notice."

Accounting records

6.—(1) Section 31 (remedy for failure to comply with request for access to accounting records) shall be amended as follows.

(2) In subsection (1) after "the court" insert "or to the Certification Officer".

(3) In subsection (2) (court to make order if claim well-founded) after "Where" insert "on an application to it" and for "that person" substitute "the applicant".

(4) After subsection (2) insert—

"(2A) On an application to him the Certification Officer shall—
(a) make such enquiries as he thinks fit, and
(b) give the applicant and the trade union an opportunity to be heard.

(2B) Where the Certification Officer is satisfied that the claim is well-founded he shall make such order as he considers appropriate for ensuring that the applicant—
(a) is allowed to inspect the records requested,
(b) is allowed to be accompanied by an accountant when making the inspection of those records, and
(c) is allowed to take, or is supplied with, such copies of, or of extracts from, the records as he may require.

(2C) In exercising his functions under this section the Certification Officer shall ensure that, so far as is reasonably practicable, an application made to him is determined within six months of being made."

(5) In subsection (3) (court's power to grant interlocutory relief) after "an application" insert "to it".

(6) After subsection (3) insert—

"(4) Where the Certification Officer requests a person to furnish information to him in connection with enquiries made by him under this section, he shall specify the date by which that information is to be furnished and, unless he considers that it would be inappropriate to do so, shall proceed with his determination of the application notwithstanding that the information has not been furnished to him by the specified date.

(5) An order made by the Certification Officer under this section may be enforced in the same way as an order of the court.

(6) If a person applies to the court under this section in relation to an alleged failure he may not apply to the Certification Officer under this section in relation to that failure.

(7) If a person applies to the Certification Officer under this section in relation to an alleged failure he may not apply to the court under this section in relation to that failure."

Employment Relations Act 1999, Sch 6

Offenders

7.—(1) Section 45C (application to Certification Officer or court for declaration of breach of duty to secure positions not held by certain offenders) shall be amended as follows.

(2) In subsection (2) (Certification Officer's powers and duties) insert before paragraph (a)—

"(aa) shall make such enquiries as he thinks fit,"

(3) In subsection (2)(a) (duty to give opportunity to be heard where Certification Officer considers it appropriate) omit ", where he considers it appropriate,".

(4) Omit subsections (3) and (4) (different applications in respect of the same matter).

(5) After subsection (5) insert—

"(5A) Where the Certification Officer makes a declaration he shall also, unless he considers that it would be inappropriate, make an order imposing on the trade union a requirement to take within such period as may be specified in the order such steps to remedy the declared failure as may be so specified.

(5B) The following paragraphs have effect if a person applies to the Certification Officer under this section in relation to an alleged failure—
  (a) that person may not apply to the court under this section in relation to that failure;
  (b) on an application by a different person to the court under this section in relation to that failure, the court shall have due regard to any declaration, order, observations or reasons made or given by the Certification Officer regarding that failure and brought to the court's notice.

(5C) The following paragraphs have effect if a person applies to the court under this section in relation to an alleged failure—
  (a) that person may not apply to the Certification Officer under this section in relation to that failure;
  (b) on an application by a different person to the Certification Officer under this section in relation to that failure, the Certification Officer shall have regard to any declaration, order, observations or reasons made or given by the court regarding that failure and brought to the Certification Officer's notice."

(6) In subsection (6) (entitlement to enforce order) after "been made" insert "under subsection (5) or (5A)".

(7) After subsection (6) insert—

"(7) Where the Certification Officer requests a person to furnish information to him in connection with enquiries made by him under this section, he shall specify the date by which that information is to be furnished and, unless he considers that it would be inappropriate to do so, shall proceed with his determination of the application notwithstanding that the information has not been furnished to him by the specified date.

(8) A declaration made by the Certification Officer under this section may be relied on as if it were a declaration made by the court.

(9) An order made by the Certification Officer under this section may be enforced in the same way as an order of the court."

Trade union administration: appeals

8. After section 45C there shall be inserted—

"45D Appeals from Certification Officer

An appeal lies to the Employment Appeal Tribunal on any question of law arising in proceedings before or arising from any decision of the Certification Officer under section 25, 31 or 45C."

Elections

9. In section 54 (remedy for failure to comply with the duty regarding elections) the second sentence of subsection (1) (application to Certification Officer does not prevent application to court) shall be omitted.

10.—(1) Section 55 (application to Certification Officer for declaration of breach of duty regarding elections) shall be amended as follows.

(2) In subsection (2)(b) (duty to give opportunity to be heard where Certification Officer considers it appropriate) omit "where he considers it appropriate,".

(3) After subsection (5) insert—

"(5A) Where the Certification Officer makes a declaration he shall also, unless he considers that to do so would be inappropriate, make an enforcement order, that is, an order imposing on the union one or more of the following requirements—
  (a) to secure the holding of an election in accordance with the order;
  (b) to take such other steps to remedy the declared failure as may be specified in the order;
  (c) to abstain from such acts as may be so specified with a view to securing that a failure of the same or a similar kind does not occur in future.

The Certification Officer shall in an order imposing any such requirement as is mentioned in paragraph (a) or (b) specify the period within which the union is to comply with the requirements of the order.

(5B) Where the Certification Officer makes an order requiring the union to hold a fresh election, he shall (unless he considers that it would be inappropriate to do so in the particular circumstances of the case) require the election to be conducted in accordance with the requirements of this Chapter and such other provisions as may be made by the order.

(5C) Where an enforcement order has been made—
  (a) any person who is a member of the union and was a member at the time the order was made, or
  (b) any person who is or was a candidate in the election in question, is entitled to enforce obedience to the order as if he had made the application on which the order was made."

(4) After subsection (7) insert—

"(8) A declaration made by the Certification Officer under this section may be relied on as if it were a declaration made by the court.

(9) An enforcement order made by the Certification Officer under this section may be enforced in the same way as an order of the court.

(10) The following paragraphs have effect if a person applies under section 56 in relation to an alleged failure—
  (a) that person may not apply under this section in relation to that failure;
  (b) on an application by a different person under this section in relation to that failure, the Certification Officer shall have due regard to any declaration, order, observations or reasons made or given by the court regarding that failure and brought to the Certification Officer's notice."

11.—(1) Section 56 (application to court for declaration of failure to comply with requirements regarding elections) shall be amended as follows.

(2) Omit subsection (2) (position where application in respect of the same matter has been made to the Certification Officer).

(3) After subsection (7) insert—

"(8) The following paragraphs have effect if a person applies under section 55 in relation to an alleged failure—
  (a) that person may not apply under this section in relation to that failure;
  (b) on an application by a different person under this section in relation to that failure, the court shall have due regard to any declaration, order, observations or reasons made or given by the Certification Officer regarding that failure and brought to the court's notice."

12. After section 56 there shall be inserted—

"56A Appeals from Certification Officer

An appeal lies to the Employment Appeal Tribunal on any question of law arising in proceedings before or arising from any decision of the Certification Officer under section 55."

Application of funds for political objects

13. After section 72 there shall be inserted—

"72A Application of funds in breach of section 71

(1) A person who is a member of a trade union and who claims that it has applied its funds in breach of section 71 may apply to the Certification Officer for a declaration that it has done so.

(2) On an application under this section the Certification Officer—
   (a) shall make such enquiries as he thinks fit,
   (b) shall give the applicant and the union an opportunity to be heard,
   (c) shall ensure that, so far as is reasonably practicable, the application is determined within six months of being made,
   (d) may make or refuse the declaration asked for,
   (e) shall, whether he makes or refuses the declaration, give reasons for his decision in writing, and
   (f) may make written observations on any matter arising from, or connected with, the proceedings.

(3) If he makes a declaration he shall specify in it—
   (a) the provisions of section 71 breached, and
   (b) the amount of the funds applied in breach.

(4) If he makes a declaration and is satisfied that the union has taken or agreed to take steps with a view to—
   (a) remedying the declared breach, or
   (b) securing that a breach of the same or any similar kind does not occur in future,
he shall specify those steps in making the declaration.

(5) If he makes a declaration he may make such order for remedying the breach as he thinks just under the circumstances.

(6) Where the Certification Officer requests a person to furnish information to him in connection with enquiries made by him under this section, he shall specify the date by which that information is to be furnished and, unless he considers that it would be inappropriate to do so, shall proceed with his determination of the application notwithstanding that the information has not been furnished to him by the specified date.

(7) A declaration made by the Certification Officer under this section may be relied on as if it were a declaration made by the court.

(8) Where an order has been made under this section, any person who is a member of the union and was a member at the time it was made is entitled to enforce obedience to the order as if he had made the application on which the order was made.

(9) An order made by the Certification Officer under this section may be enforced in the same way as an order of the court.

(10) If a person applies to the Certification Officer under this section in relation to an alleged breach he may not apply to the court in relation to the breach; but nothing in this subsection shall prevent such a person from exercising any right to appeal against or challenge the Certification Officer's decision on the application to him.

(11) If—
   (a) a person applies to the court in relation to an alleged breach, and
   (b) the breach is one in relation to which he could have made an application to the Certification Officer under this section,
he may not apply to the Certification Officer under this section in relation to the breach."

Political ballot rules

14. In section 79 (remedy for failure to comply with political ballot rules) the second sentence of subsection (1) (application to Certification Officer does not prevent application to court) shall be omitted.

15.—(1) Section 80 (application to Certification Officer for declaration of failure to comply with political ballot rules) shall be amended as follows.

(2) In subsection (2)(b) (duty to give opportunity to be heard where Certification Officer considers it appropriate) omit "where he considers it appropriate,".

(3) After subsection (5) insert—

"(5A) Where the Certification Officer makes a declaration he shall also, unless he considers that to do so would be inappropriate, make an enforcement order, that is, an order imposing on the union one or more of the following requirements—
  (a) to secure the holding of a ballot in accordance with the order;
  (b) to take such other steps to remedy the declared failure as may be specified in the order;
  (c) to abstain from such acts as may be so specified with a view to securing that a failure of the same or a similar kind does not occur in future.

The Certification Officer shall in an order imposing any such requirement as is mentioned in paragraph (a) or (b) specify the period within which the union must comply with the requirements of the order.

(5B) Where the Certification Officer makes an order requiring the union to hold a fresh ballot, he shall (unless he considers that it would be inappropriate to do so in the particular circumstances of the case) require the ballot to be conducted in accordance with the union's political ballot rules and such other provisions as may be made by the order.

(5C) Where an enforcement order has been made, any person who is a member of the union and was a member at the time the order was made is entitled to enforce obedience to the order as if he had made the application on which the order was made."

(4) After subsection (7) insert—

"(8) A declaration made by the Certification Officer under this section may be relied on as if it were a declaration made by the court.

(9) An enforcement order made by the Certification Officer under this section may be enforced in the same way as an order of the court.

(10) The following paragraphs have effect if a person applies under section 81 in relation to a matter—
  (a) that person may not apply under this section in relation to that matter;
  (b) on an application by a different person under this section in relation to that matter, the Certification Officer shall have due regard to any declaration, order, observations, or reasons made or given by the court regarding that matter and brought to the Certification Officer's notice."

16.—(1) Section 81 (application to court for declaration of failure to comply with political ballot rules) shall be amended as follows.

(2) Omit subsection (2) (position where application in respect of the same matter has been made to Certification Officer).

(3) After subsection (7) insert—

"(8) The following paragraphs have effect if a person applies under section 80 in relation to a matter—
  (a) that person may not apply under this section in relation to that matter;
  (b) on an application by a different person under this section in relation to that matter, the court shall have due regard to any declaration, order, observations or reasons made or given by the Certification Officer regarding that matter and brought to the court's notice."

Political fund

17.—(1) Section 82 (rules as to political fund) shall be amended as follows.

(2) After subsection (2) insert—

"(2A) On a complaint being made to him the Certification Officer shall make such enquiries as he thinks fit."

(3) After subsection (3) insert—

"(3A) Where the Certification Officer requests a person to furnish information to him in connection with enquiries made by him under this section, he shall specify the date by which that information is to be furnished and, unless he considers that it would be inappropriate to do so, shall proceed with his determination of the application notwithstanding that the information has not been furnished to him by the specified date."

Amalgamation or transfer of engagements

18.—(1) Section 103 (complaints about procedure relating to amalgamation or transfer of engagements) shall be amended as follows.

(2) After subsection (2) insert—

"(2A) On a complaint being made to him the Certification Officer shall make such enquiries as he thinks fit."

(3) After subsection (5) insert—

"(6) Where the Certification Officer requests a person to furnish information to him in connection with enquiries made by him under this section, he shall specify the date by which that information is to be furnished and, unless he considers that it would be inappropriate to do so, shall proceed with his determination of the application notwithstanding that the information has not been furnished to him by the specified date.

(7) A declaration made by the Certification Officer under this section may be relied on as if it were a declaration made by the court.

(8) Where an order has been made under this section, any person who is a member of the union and was a member at the time it was made is entitled to enforce obedience to the order as if he had made the application on which the order was made.

(9) An order made by the Certification Officer under this section may be enforced in the same way as an order of the court."

Breach of union rules

19. In Part I, after Chapter VII there shall be inserted—

"CHAPTER VIIA
BREACH OF RULES

108A Right to apply to Certification Officer

(1) A person who claims that there has been a breach or threatened breach of the rules of a trade union relating to any of the matters mentioned in subsection (2) may apply to the Certification Officer for a declaration to that effect, subject to subsections (3) to (7).

(2) The matters are—
  (a) the appointment or election of a person to, or the removal of a person from, any office;
  (b) disciplinary proceedings by the union (including expulsion);
  (c) the balloting of members on any issue other than industrial action;
  (d) the constitution or proceedings of any executive committee or of any decision-making meeting;
  (e) such other matters as may be specified in an order made by the Secretary of State.

(3) The applicant must be a member of the union, or have been one at the time of the alleged breach or threatened breach.

(4) A person may not apply under subsection (1) in relation to a claim if he is entitled to apply under section 80 in relation to the claim.

(5) No application may be made regarding—
 (a) the dismissal of an employee of the union;
 (b) disciplinary proceedings against an employee of the union.

(6) An application must be made—
 (a) within the period of six months starting with the day on which the breach or threatened breach is alleged to have taken place, or
 (b) if within that period any internal complaints procedure of the union is invoked to resolve the claim, within the period of six months starting with the earlier of the days specified in subsection (7).

(7) Those days are—
 (a) the day on which the procedure is concluded, and
 (b) the last day of the period of one year beginning with the day on which the procedure is invoked.

(8) The reference in subsection (1) to the rules of a union includes references to the rules of any branch or section of the union.

(9) In subsection (2)(c) "industrial action" means a strike or other industrial action by persons employed under contracts of employment.

(10) For the purposes of subsection (2)(d) a committee is an executive committee if—
 (a) it is a committee of the union concerned and has power to make executive decisions on behalf of the union or on behalf of a constituent body,
 (b) it is a committee of a major constituent body and has power to make executive decisions on behalf of that body, or
 (c) it is a sub-committee of a committee falling within paragraph (a) or (b).

(11) For the purposes of subsection (2)(d) a decision-making meeting is—
 (a) a meeting of members of the union concerned (or the representatives of such members) which has power to make a decision on any matter which, under the rules of the union, is final as regards the union or which, under the rules of the union or a constituent body, is final as regards that body, or
 (b) a meeting of members of a major constituent body (or the representatives of such members) which has power to make a decision on any matter which, under the rules of the union or the body, is final as regards that body.

(12) For the purposes of subsections (10) and (11), in relation to the trade union concerned—
 (a) a constituent body is any body which forms part of the union, including a branch, group, section or region;
 (b) a major constituent body is such a body which has more than 1,000 members.

(13) Any order under subsection (2)(e) shall be made by statutory instrument; and no such order shall be made unless a draft of it has been laid before and approved by resolution of each House of Parliament.

(14) If a person applies to the Certification Officer under this section in relation to an alleged breach or threatened breach he may not apply to the court in relation to the breach or threatened breach; but nothing in this subsection shall prevent such a person from exercising any right to appeal against or challenge the Certification Officer's decision on the application to him.

(15) If—
 (a) a person applies to the court in relation to an alleged breach or threatened breach, and
 (b) the breach or threatened breach is one in relation to which he could have made an application to the Certification Officer under this section,
he may not apply to the Certification Officer under this section in relation to the breach or threatened breach.

108B Declarations and orders

(1) The Certification Officer may refuse to accept an application under section 108A unless he is satisfied that the applicant has taken all reasonable steps to resolve the claim by the use of any internal complaints procedure of the union.

(2) If he accepts an application under section 108A the Certification Officer—
   (a) shall make such enquiries as he thinks fit,
   (b) shall give the applicant and the union an opportunity to be heard,
   (c) shall ensure that, so far as is reasonably practicable, the application is determined within six months of being made,
   (d) may make or refuse the declaration asked for, and
   (e) shall, whether he makes or refuses the declaration, give reasons for his decision in writing.

(3) Where the Certification Officer makes a declaration he shall also, unless he considers that to do so would be inappropriate, make an enforcement order, that is, an order imposing on the union one or both of the following requirements—
   (a) to take such steps to remedy the breach, or withdraw the threat of a breach, as may be specified in the order;
   (b) to abstain from such acts as may be so specified with a view to securing that a breach or threat of the same or a similar kind does not occur in future.

(4) The Certification Officer shall in an order imposing any such requirement as is mentioned in subsection (3)(a) specify the period within which the union is to comply with the requirement.

(5) Where the Certification Officer requests a person to furnish information to him in connection with enquiries made by him under this section, he shall specify the date by which that information is to be furnished and, unless he considers that it would be inappropriate to do so, shall proceed with his determination of the application notwithstanding that the information has not been furnished to him by the specified date.

(6) A declaration made by the Certification Officer under this section may be relied on as if it were a declaration made by the court.

(7) Where an enforcement order has been made, any person who is a member of the union and was a member at the time it was made is entitled to enforce obedience to the order as if he had made the application on which the order was made.

(8) An enforcement order made by the Certification Officer under this section may be enforced in the same way as an order of the court.

(9) An order under section 108A(2)(e) may provide that, in relation to an application under section 108A with regard to a prescribed matter, the preceding provisions of this section shall apply with such omissions or modifications as may be specified in the order; and a prescribed matter is such matter specified under section 108A(2)(e) as is prescribed under this subsection.

108C Appeals from Certification Officer

An appeal lies to the Employment Appeal Tribunal on any question of law arising in proceedings before or arising from any decision of the Certification Officer under this Chapter."

Employers' associations

20.—(1) Section 132 (provisions about application of funds for political objects to apply to unincorporated employers' associations) shall be amended as follows.

(2) For "The" substitute "(1) Subject to subsections (2) to (5), the".

(3) After subsection (1) (as created by sub-paragraph (2)) insert—

"(2) Subsection (1) does not apply to these provisions—
   (a) section 72A;
   (b) in section 80, subsections (5A) to (5C) and (8) to (10);
   (c) in section 81, subsection (8).

(3) In its application to an unincorporated employers' association, section 79 shall have effect as if at the end of subsection (1) there were inserted—

"The making of an application to the Certification Officer does not prevent the applicant, or any other person, from making an application to the court in respect of the same matter."

(4) In its application to an unincorporated employers' association, section 80(2)(b) shall have effect as if the words "where he considers it appropriate," were inserted at the beginning.

(5) In its application to an unincorporated employers' association, section 81 shall have effect as if after subsection (1) there were inserted—

"(2) If an application in respect of the same matter has been made to the Certification Officer, the court shall have due regard to any declaration, reasons or observations of his which are brought to its notice."

21. In section 133 (provisions about amalgamations and similar matters to apply to unincorporated employers' associations) in subsection (2)(c) after "101(3)" there shall be inserted ", 103(2A) and (6) to (9)".

Procedure before Certification Officer

22. In section 256 (procedure before Certification Officer) for subsection (2) (provision for restricting disclosure of individual's identity) there shall be substituted—

"(2) He shall in particular make provision about the disclosure, and restriction of the disclosure, of the identity of an individual who has made or is proposing to make any such application or complaint.

(2A) Provision under subsection (2) shall be such that if the application or complaint relates to a trade union—
(a) the individual's identity is disclosed to the union unless the Certification Officer thinks the circumstances are such that it should not be so disclosed;
(b) the individual's identity is disclosed to such other persons (if any) as the Certification Officer thinks fit."

23. After section 256 there shall be inserted—

"256A Vexatious litigants

(1) The Certification Officer may refuse to entertain any application or complaint made to him under a provision of Chapters III to VIIA of Part I by a vexatious litigant.

(2) The Certification Officer must give reasons for such a refusal.

(3) Subsection (1) does not apply to a complaint under section 37E(1)(b) or to an application under section 41.

(4) For the purposes of subsection (1) a vexatious litigant is a person who is the subject of—
(a) an order which is made under section 33(1) of the Employment Tribunals Act 1996 and which remains in force,
(b) a civil proceedings order or an all proceedings order which is made under section 42(1) of the Supreme Court Act 1981 and which remains in force,
(c) an order which is made under section 1 of the Vexatious Actions (Scotland) Act 1898, or
(d) an order which is made under section 32 of the Judicature (Northern Ireland) Act 1978.

256B Vexatious litigants: applications disregarded

(1) For the purposes of a relevant enactment an application to the Certification Officer shall be disregarded if—
(a) it was made under a provision mentioned in the relevant enactment, and
(b) it was refused by the Certification Officer under section 256A(1).

(2) The relevant enactments are sections 26(8), 31(7), 45C(5B), 56(8), 72A(10), 81(8) and 108A(13)."

Annual report by Certification Officer

24. In section 258(1) (Certification Officer: annual report) for "calendar year" there shall be substituted "financial year".

Employment Relations Act 1999, Sch 6

Definitions For "trade union", see the Trade Union and Labour Relations (Consolidation) Act 1992, s 1; for "accountant", see s 30(4) thereof; for "the court", see s 121 thereof; for "Certification Officer", see s 254 thereof; for "act", see s 298 thereof; for "branch or section" and "rules", see s 119 thereof; for "contract of employment", see ss 235, 273(4)(a), 278(4)(a), 295(1) thereof, 439, 442, 452; for "employee", see ss 273(4)(a), 278(4)(a), 280, 295(1) thereof; for "dismissal", see ss 273(4)(b), 278(4)(b), 298 thereof; for "prescribed", see s 293(1) of that Act; for "action", see s 298 thereof; for "employers' association", see s 122 thereof; for "financial year", see s 272 thereof.
References See paras 9.8–9.14.

SCHEDULE 7

Section 31

EMPLOYMENT AGENCIES

Introduction

1. The Employment Agencies Act 1973 shall be amended as provided in this Schedule.

General regulations

2.—(1) Section 5 (power to make general regulations) shall be amended as follows.

(2) In subsection (1) there shall be substituted for paragraphs (f) and (g) and the proviso following paragraph (g)—

"(ea) restricting the services which may be provided by persons carrying on such agencies and businesses;
(eb) regulating the way in which and the terms on which services may be provided by persons carrying on such agencies and businesses;
(ec) restricting or regulating the charging of fees by persons carrying on such agencies and businesses."

(3) After subsection (1) there shall be inserted—

"(1A) A reference in subsection (1)(ea) to (ec) of this section to services includes a reference to services in respect of—
(a) persons seeking employment outside the United Kingdom;
(b) persons normally resident outside the United Kingdom seeking employment in the United Kingdom."

Charges

3. For section 6(1) (restriction on demand or receipt of fee for finding or seeking to find employment) there shall be substituted—

"(1) Except in such cases or classes of case as the Secretary of State may prescribe—
(a) a person carrying on an employment agency shall not request or directly or indirectly receive any fee from any person for providing services (whether by the provision of information or otherwise) for the purpose of finding him employment or seeking to find him employment;
(b) a person carrying on an employment business shall not request or directly or indirectly receive any fee from an employee for providing services (whether by the provision of information or otherwise) for the purpose of finding or seeking to find another person, with a view to the employee acting for and under the control of that other person;
(c) a person carrying on an employment business shall not request or directly or indirectly receive any fee from a second person for providing services (whether by the provision of information or otherwise) for the purpose of finding or seeking to find a third person, with a view to the second person becoming employed by the first person and acting for and under the control of the third person."

Inspection

4.—(1) Section 9 (inspection) shall be amended as follows.

(2) In subsection (1) (power to inspect)—
(a) for paragraph (a) there shall be substituted—

"(a) enter any relevant business premises;", and
(b) after paragraph (c) there shall be inserted—
"; and
(d) take copies of records and other documents inspected under paragraph (b).".

(3) After subsection (1) there shall be inserted—

"(1A) If an officer seeks to inspect or acquire, in accordance with subsection (1)(b) or (c), a record or other document or information which is not kept at the premises being inspected, he may require any person on the premises—
(a) to inform him where and by whom the record, other document or information is kept, and
(b) to make arrangements, if it is reasonably practicable for the person to do so, for the record, other document or information to be inspected by or furnished to the officer at the premises at a time specified by the officer.

(1B) In subsection (1) "relevant business premises" means premises—
(a) which are used, have been used or are to be used for or in connection with the carrying on of an employment agency or employment business,
(b) which the officer has reasonable cause to believe are used or have been used for or in connection with the carrying on of an employment agency or employment business, or
(c) which the officer has reasonable cause to believe are used for the carrying on of a business by a person who also carries on or has carried on an employment agency or employment business, if the officer also has reasonable cause to believe that records or other documents which relate to the employment agency or employment business are kept there.

(1C) For the purposes of subsection (1)—
(a) "document" includes information recorded in any form, and
(b) information is kept at premises if it is accessible from them."

(4) For subsection (2) (self-incrimination) there shall be substituted—

"(2) Nothing in this section shall require a person to produce, provide access to or make arrangements for the production of anything which he could not be compelled to produce in civil proceedings before the High Court or (in Scotland) the Court of Session.

(2A) Subject to subsection (2B), a statement made by a person in compliance with a requirement under this section may be used in evidence against him in criminal proceedings.

(2B) Except in proceedings for an offence under section 5 of the Perjury Act 1911 (false statements made otherwise than on oath), no evidence relating to the statement may be adduced, and no question relating to it may be asked, by or on behalf of the prosecution unless—
(a) evidence relating to it is adduced, or
(b) a question relating to it is asked,
by or on behalf of the person who made the statement."

(5) In subsection (3) (offence)—
(a) for "or (b)" there shall be substituted ", (b) or (d)", and
(b) after the words "paragraph (c) of that subsection" there shall be inserted "or under subsection (1A)".

(6) In subsection (4)(a) (restriction on disclosure of information) in sub-paragraph (iv) (exception for criminal proceedings pursuant to or arising out of the Act) the words "pursuant to or arising out of this Act" shall be omitted.

Offences

5. After section 11 there shall be inserted—

Employment Relations Act 1999, Sch 7

"11A Offences: extension of time limit

(1) For the purposes of subsection (2) of this section a relevant offence is an offence under section 3B, 5(2), 6(2), 9(4)(b) or 10(2) of this Act for which proceedings are instituted by the Secretary of State.

(2) Notwithstanding section 127(1) of the Magistrates' Courts Act 1980 (information to be laid within 6 months of offence) an information relating to a relevant offence which is triable by a magistrates' court in England and Wales may be so tried if it is laid at any time—
    (a) within 3 years after the date of the commission of the offence, and
    (b) within 6 months after the date on which evidence sufficient in the opinion of the Secretary of State to justify the proceedings came to his knowledge.

(3) Notwithstanding section 136 of the Criminal Procedure (Scotland) Act 1995 (time limit for prosecuting certain statutory offences) in Scotland proceedings in respect of an offence under section 3B, 5(2), 6(2), 9(4)(b) or 10(2) of this Act may be commenced at any time—
    (a) within 3 years after the date of the commission of the offence, and
    (b) within 6 months after the date on which evidence sufficient in the opinion of the Lord Advocate to justify the proceedings came to his knowledge.

(4) For the purposes of this section a certificate of the Secretary of State or Lord Advocate (as the case may be) as to the date on which evidence came to his knowledge is conclusive evidence.

11B Offences: cost of investigation

The court in which a person is convicted of an offence under this Act may order him to pay to the Secretary of State a sum which appears to the court not to exceed the costs of the investigation which resulted in the conviction."

Regulations and orders

6. For section 12(5) (regulations and orders: procedure) there shall be substituted—

"(5) Regulations under section 5(1) or 6(1) of this Act shall not be made unless a draft has been laid before, and approved by resolution of, each House of Parliament.

(6) Regulations under section 13(7)(i) of this Act or an order under section 14(3) shall be subject to annulment in pursuance of a resolution of either House of Parliament."

Interpretation

7. In section 13(2) (definition of employment agency) for "workers" (in each place) there shall be substituted "persons".

Exemptions

8. For section 13(7)(i) there shall be substituted—

    "(i) any prescribed business or service, or prescribed class of business or service or business or service carried on or provided by prescribed persons or classes of person."

Definitions For "employment", "fee" and "prescribed", see the Employment Agencies Act 1973, s 13(1); for "employment agency", see s 13(1), (2), (4), (7) thereof, as amended (s 13(2)) by para 7 above; for "employment business", see s 13(1), (3), (7) thereof, as amended (s 13(7)) by para 8 above.
References See paras 10.2, 10.3.

SCHEDULE 8

Section 41

NATIONAL SECURITY

1. The following shall be substituted for section 193 of the Employment Rights Act 1996 (national security)—

Employment Relations Act 1999, Sch 8

"**193. National security**

Part IVA and section 47B of this Act do not apply in relation to employment for the purposes of—
- (a) the Security Service,
- (b) the Secret Intelligence Service, or
- (c) the Government Communications Headquarters."

2. Section 4(7) of the Employment Tribunals Act 1996 (composition of tribunal: national security) shall cease to have effect.

3. The following shall be substituted for section 10 of that Act (national security, &c)—

"**10 National security**

(1) If on a complaint under—
- (a) section 146 of the Trade Union and Labour Relations (Consolidation) Act 1992 (detriment: trade union membership), or
- (b) section 111 of the Employment Rights Act 1996 (unfair dismissal),

it is shown that the action complained of was taken for the purpose of safeguarding national security, the employment tribunal shall dismiss the complaint.

(2) Employment tribunal procedure regulations may make provision about the composition of the tribunal (including provision disapplying or modifying section 4) for the purposes of proceedings in relation to which—
- (a) a direction is given under subsection (3), or
- (b) an order is made under subsection (4).

(3) A direction may be given under this subsection by a Minister of the Crown if—
- (a) it relates to particular Crown employment proceedings, and
- (b) the Minister considers it expedient in the interests of national security.

(4) An order may be made under this subsection by the President or a Regional Chairman in relation to particular proceedings if he considers it expedient in the interests of national security.

(5) Employment tribunal procedure regulations may make provision enabling a Minister of the Crown, if he considers it expedient in the interests of national security—
- (a) to direct a tribunal to sit in private for all or part of particular Crown employment proceedings;
- (b) to direct a tribunal to exclude the applicant from all or part of particular Crown employment proceedings;
- (c) to direct a tribunal to exclude the applicant's representatives from all or part of particular Crown employment proceedings;
- (d) to direct a tribunal to take steps to conceal the identity of a particular witness in particular Crown employment proceedings;
- (e) to direct a tribunal to take steps to keep secret all or part of the reasons for its decision in particular Crown employment proceedings.

(6) Employment tribunal procedure regulations may enable a tribunal, if it considers it expedient in the interests of national security, to do anything of a kind which a tribunal can be required to do by direction under subsection (5)(a) to (e).

(7) In relation to cases where a person has been excluded by virtue of subsection (5)(b) or (c) or (6), employment tribunal procedure regulations may make provision—
- (a) for the appointment by the Attorney General, or by the Advocate General for Scotland, of a person to represent the interests of the applicant;
- (b) about the publication and registration of reasons for the tribunal's decision;
- (c) permitting an excluded person to make a statement to the tribunal before the commencement of the proceedings, or the part of the proceedings, from which he is excluded.

(8) Proceedings are Crown employment proceedings for the purposes of this section if the employment to which the complaint relates—
- (a) is Crown employment, or
- (b) is connected with the performance of functions on behalf of the Crown.

(9) The reference in subsection (4) to the President or a Regional Chairman is to a person appointed in accordance with regulations under section 1(1) as—
    (a) a Regional Chairman,
    (b) President of the Employment Tribunals (England and Wales), or
    (c) President of the Employment Tribunals (Scotland).

10A Confidential information

(1) Employment tribunal procedure regulations may enable an employment tribunal to sit in private for the purpose of hearing evidence from any person which in the opinion of the tribunal is likely to consist of—
    (a) information which he could not disclose without contravening a prohibition imposed by or by virtue of any enactment,
    (b) information which has been communicated to him in confidence or which he has otherwise obtained in consequence of the confidence reposed in him by another person, or
    (c) information the disclosure of which would, for reasons other than its effect on negotiations with respect to any of the matters mentioned in section 178(2) of the Trade Union and Labour Relations (Consolidation) Act 1992, cause substantial injury to any undertaking of his or in which he works.

(2) The reference in subsection (1)(c) to any undertaking of a person or in which he works shall be construed—
    (a) in relation to a person in Crown employment, as a reference to the national interest,
    (b) in relation to a person who is a relevant member of the House of Lords staff, as a reference to the national interest or (if the case so requires) the interests of the House of Lords, and
    (c) in relation to a person who is a relevant member of the House of Commons staff, as a reference to the national interest or (if the case so requires) the interests of the House of Commons.

10B Restriction of publicity in cases involving national security

(1) This section applies where a tribunal has been directed under section 10(5) or has determined under section 10(6)—
    (a) to take steps to conceal the identity of a particular witness, or
    (b) to take steps to keep secret all or part of the reasons for its decision.

(2) It is an offence to publish—
    (a) anything likely to lead to the identification of the witness, or
    (b) the reasons for the tribunal's decision or the part of its reasons which it is directed or has determined to keep secret.

(3) A person guilty of an offence under this section is liable on summary conviction to a fine not exceeding level 5 on the standard scale.

(4) Where a person is charged with an offence under this section it is a defence to prove that at the time of the alleged offence he was not aware, and neither suspected nor had reason to suspect, that the publication in question was of, or included, the matter in question.

(5) Where an offence under this section committed by a body corporate is proved to have been committed with the consent or connivance of, or to be attributable to any neglect on the part of—
    (a) a director, manager, secretary or other similar officer of the body corporate, or
    (b) a person purporting to act in any such capacity,
he as well as the body corporate is guilty of the offence and liable to be proceeded against and punished accordingly.

(6) A reference in this section to publication includes a reference to inclusion in a programme which is included in a programme service, within the meaning of the Broadcasting Act 1990."

4. Section 28(5) of the Employment Tribunals Act 1996 (composition of Appeal Tribunal: national security) shall cease to have effect.

5.—(1) Section 30 of that Act (Appeal Tribunal Procedure rules) shall be amended as follows.

(2) In subsection (2)(d) for "section 10" substitute "section 10A".

(3) After subsection (2) insert—

"(2A) Appeal Tribunal procedure rules may make provision of a kind which may be made by employment tribunal procedure regulations under section 10(2), (5), (6) or (7).

(2B) For the purposes of subsection (2A)—
- (a) the reference in section 10(2) to section 4 shall be treated as a reference to section 28, and
- (b) the reference in section 10(4) to the President or a Regional Chairman shall be treated as a reference to a judge of the Appeal Tribunal.

(2C) Section 10B shall have effect in relation to a direction to or determination of the Appeal Tribunal as it has effect in relation to a direction to or determination of an employment tribunal."

6. After section 69(2) of the Race Relations Act 1976 (evidence: Minister's certificate as to national security, &c) there shall be inserted—

"(2A) Subsection (2)(b) shall not have effect for the purposes of proceedings on a complaint under section 54."

7. Paragraph 4(1)(b) of Schedule 3 to the Disability Discrimination Act 1995 (evidence: Minister's certificate as to national security, &c) shall cease to have effect.

Definitions   In the Employment Tribunals Act 1996, for "employment tribunal procedure regulations", see s 7(1) thereof; for "Crown employment", see s 38(2) thereof; for "relevant member of the House of Lords staff", see s 39(4) thereof; for "relevant member of the House of Commons staff", see s 39(5) thereof.
References   See para 10.4.

SCHEDULE 9

Section 44

REPEALS

1. BALLOTS AND NOTICES

Chapter	Short title	Extent of repeal
1992 c 52	Trade Union and Labour Relations (Consolidation) Act 1992.	In section 226(2) the word "and" at the end of paragraph (b).
		Section 227(2).
		In section 234A(7)(a) the words "otherwise than to enable the union to comply with a court order or an undertaking given to a court".

2. LEAVE FOR FAMILY REASONS ETC

Chapter	Short title	Extent of repeal
1996 c 17	Employment Tribunals Act 1996.	In section 13(2)— the word "or" after paragraph (a), paragraph (b), and the words ", or which she held before her absence,".

Employment Relations Act 1999, Sch 9

Chapter	Short title	Extent of repeal
1996 c 18	Employment Rights Act 1996	In section 37, subsection (4), the word "and" after subsection (5)(a), and subsection (5)(b).
		In section 43, subsection (4), the word "and" after subsection (5)(a), and subsection (5)(b).
		Section 96.
		Section 97(6).
		Section 98(5).
		Section 105(2).
		Section 108(3)(a).
		Section 109(2)(a).
		Section 114(5).
		Section 115(4).
		In section 118(1)(b), the word ", 127".
		Section 119(6).
		Section 127.
		Section 137.
		Section 145(7).
		Section 146(3).
		Section 156(2).
		Section 157(6).
		Section 162(7).
		In section 199, the words "(subject to subsection (3)" in subsection (2), and subsection (3).
		In section 200(1), the words "and section 137".
		Section 209(6).
		In section 212— subsection (2), in subsection (3), the word "or" after paragraph (c), and paragraph (d), in subsection (4) the words "or (subject to subsection (2)) subsection (3)(d)".
		Section 226(3)(a) and (5)(a).
		In section 235(1), the definitions of "maternity leave period" and "notified day of return".
SI 1994/2479	Maternity (Compulsory Leave) Regulations 1994.	The whole instrument.

3. AGREEMENT TO EXCLUDE DISMISSAL RIGHTS

Chapter	Short title	Extent of repeal
1992 c 52	Trade Union and Labour Relations (Consolidation) Act 1992.	In Schedule A1, Paragraph 163.
1996 c 18	Employment Rights Act 1996.	In section 44(4) the words from the beginning to "the dismissal,".
		In section 45A(4) the words from ", unless" to the end.
		In section 46(2) the words from the beginning to "the dismissal,".
		In section 47(2) the words from the beginning to "the dismissal,".
		In section 47A(2) the words from the beginning to "the dismissal,".
		In section 47B(2) the words from the beginning to "the dismissal,".
		Section 197(1) and (2). In section 197(4) the words "(1) or".
		In section 203(2)(d) the words "(1) or".
		In section 209(2)(g) the words "and 197(1)".
1999 c 26	Employment Relations Act 1999.	Section 18(6)

4. POWER TO CONFER RIGHTS ON INDIVIDUALS

Chapter	Short title	Extent of repeal
1996 c 18	Employment Rights Act 1996.	Section 209(7).

5. ACAS: GENERAL DUTY

Chapter	Short title	Extent of repeal
1992 c 52	Trade Union and Labour Relations (Consolidation) Act 1992.	In section 209 the words from ", in particular" to the end.
1993 c 19	Trade Union Reform and Employment Rights Act 1993.	Section 43(1).

6. COMMISSIONERS

Chapter	Short title	Extent of repeal
1967 c 13	Parliamentary Commissioner Act 1967.	In Schedule 2, the entries relating to—
		the Office of the Commissioner for Protection Against Unlawful Industrial Action, and
		the Office of the Commissioner for the Rights of Trade Union Members.
1975 c 24	House of Commons Disqualification Act 1975.	In Part III of Schedule 1, the entries relating to—
		the Commissioner for Protection Against Unlawful Industrial Action, and
		The Commissioner for the Rights of Trade Union Members.
1975 c 25	Northern Ireland Assembly Disqualification Act 1975.	In Part III of Schedule 1, the entries relating to—
		The Commissioner for Protection Against Unlawful Industrial Action, and
		The Commissioner for the Rights of Trade Union Members.
1992 c 52	Trade Union and Labour Relations (Consolidation) Act 1992.	In section 65(3) the words "the Commissioner for the Rights of Trade Union Members or".
		In Part I, Chapter VIII.
		Sections 235B and 235C.
		Section 266 (and the heading immediately preceding it) and sections 267 to 271.
		In Schedule 7, paragraph 20.
		In Schedule 8, paragraphs 2, 6, 7, 58 to 60 and 79 to 84.
1993 c 19	Trade Union Reform and Employment Rights Act 1993.	In Schedule 7, paragraph 20. In Schedule 8, paragraphs 2, 6, 7, 58 to 60 and 79 to 84.

7. THE CERTIFICATION OFFICER

Chapter	Short title	Extent of repeal
1992 c 52	Trade Union and Labour Relations (Consolidation) Act 1992.	In section 24(6), the second sentence.
		In section 24A(6), the second sentence.
		In section 25(2)(b) the words "where he considers it appropriate,".
		Section 26(2).
		In section 45C(2)(a) the words ", where he considers it appropriate," and section 45C(3) and (4).
		In section 54(1), the second sentence.
		In section 55(2)(b) the words "where he considers it appropriate,".
		Section 56(2).
		In section 79(1), the second sentence.
		In section 80(2)(b) the words "where he considers it appropriate,".
		Section 81(2).

8. EMPLOYMENT AGENCIES

Chapter	Short title	Extent of repeal
1973 c 35	Employment Agencies Act 1973.	In section 9(4)(a)(iv) the words "pursuant to or arising out of this Act".

9. EMPLOYMENT RIGHTS: EMPLOYMENT OUTSIDE GREAT BRITAIN

Chapter	Short title	Extent of repeal
1996 c 18	Employment Rights Act 1996.	Section 196.
		In section 199(6), the words "Section 196(6) does not apply to an employee, and".
		In section 201(3)(g), the word "196,".
		Section 204(2).
		In section 209(2)(g), the words "196(1) and".
		In section 209(5), the words ", 196(2), (3) and (5)".

10. SECTIONS 33 TO 36

Chapter	Short title	Extent of repeal
1992 c 52	Trade Union and Labour Relations (Consolidation) Act 1992.	Section 157.
		Section 158.
		Section 159.
		Section 176(7) and (8).
1996 c 18	Employment Rights Act 1996.	In section 117, subsection (4)(b) and the word "or" before it, and subsections (5) and (6).
		Section 118(2) and (3).
		Section 120(2).
		Section 124(2).
		Section 125.
		Section 186(2).
		Section 208.
		Section 227(2) to (4).
		Section 236(2)(c).
		In section 236(3) the words "120(2), 124(2)".
		In Schedule 1, paragraph 56(10) and (11).
1998 c 8	Employment Rights (Dispute Resolution) Act 1998.	Section 14(1).

11. COMPENSATORY AWARD: REMOVAL OF LIMIT IN CERTAIN CASES

Chapter	Short title	Extent of repeal
1996 c 18	Employment Rights Act 1996.	In section 112(4), the words "or in accordance with regulations under section 127B".
		In section 117(2) and (3), the words "and to regulations under section 127B".
		In section 118(1), the words "Subject to regulations under section 127B,".
		Section 127B.
1998 c 23	Public Interest Disclosure Act 1998.	Section 8. Section 18(4)(b).

12. NATIONAL SECURITY

Chapter	Short title	Extent of repeal
1995 c 50	Disability Discrimination Act 1995.	Paragraph 4(1)(b) of Schedule 3, and the word "or" Immediately before it.
1996 c 17	Employment Tribunals Act 1996.	Section 4(7)
		Section 28(5).
1998 c 23	Public Interest Disclosure Act 1998.	Section 11

Index

Advisory, Conciliation and Arbitration Service, 9.4–9.6
functions, 9.4
Age discrimination, 1.8

Blacklists, 4.12–4.14

Central Arbitration Committee, 9.1–9.3
changes to composition, 9.2
changes to proceedings, 9.3
Certification Officer, 9.8–9.14
adding to jurisdiction, 9.10
appeal to EAT, 9.12
changes to statutory jurisdiction, 9.9–9.12
increasing powers in existing jurisdictions, 9.11
jurisdiction over breaches of union rules, 9.13
procedure before, 9.14
Collective agreements
detriment, and, 4.10, 4.11
dismissal, and, 4.10, 4.11
Commencement, 1.9
Commissioner for the Rights of Trade Union Members, 9.7

Dependants, time off for, 6.21–6.24
domestic emergencies, 6.21–6.24
Detriment
collective agreements, and, 4.10, 4.11
disciplinary matters, and, 7.14
trade union membership, related to, 4.2, 4.3
Disciplinary matters, 7.1–7.15
ACAS Code of Practice, 7.1, 7.9
common law developments, 7.2
detriment, and, 7.14
dismissal, and, 7.14
national security, and, 7.15
nature of right, 7.7–7.14
no obligation to accompany, 7.12
provisions of 1999 Act, 7.6
refusal to permit worker to be accompanied, 7.13
time for preparation, 7.10
time off to accompany worker, 7.11
White Paper, 7.4, 7.5
Dismissal
collective agreements, and, 4.10, 4.11
disciplinary matters, and, 7.14
Domestic emergencies, 6.21–6.24

Employment
meaning, 8.13–8.16
Employment agencies, 10.2
Employment Relations Act
main element, 1.6–1.8

Employment Relations Bill
introduction, 1.1
passage of, 1.4
Extension of employment status, 8.13–8.17
Act of 1999, 8.17
definition of employment, 8.13–8.16

Fixed term contracts
unfair dismissal, and, 5.12

Industrial action, 3.1–3.11
accidental failures, 3.4
ballot, effectiveness of, 3.7
inducement, 3.11
information to employer, 3.5, 3.6
Labour Party manifesto, and, 3.1
notification, 3.5, 3.6
technical amendments, 3.10
voting papers, 3.8, 3.9
'government health warning', 3.8
White Paper, 3.2
Industrial relations settlement, 1.1–1.3
fundamental strands, 1.3

Maternity leave, 6.2–6.15
additional, 6.6
background, 6.2
compulsory, 6.5
consultation document, 6.8–6.15
contract of employment, 6.14
early return, 6.11
maternity leave plan, 6.15
penalty for failure to comply with notice requirements, 6.13
postponement of return, 6.12
remuneration, 6.14
returning to work, 6.10
starting ordinary and additional maternity leave, 6.9
contract of employment, 6.3
dismissal, and, 6.7
employment protection, 6.25
ordinary, 6.4
redundancy, and, 6.7

National minimum wage, 10.5
National Minimum Wage Act
amendment, 8.18
National security
disciplinary matters, and, 7.15
National security employees, 10.4

Parental leave, 6.16–6.20
consultation document, 6.19
Directive, 6.16
employment protection, 6.25
entitlement, 6.17
rights concerning, 6.17

173

Index

Parental leave—*contd*
scheme, 6.20
special cases, 6.18
Part-time worker protection, 8.1–8.12
Code of Practice, 8.11
discrimination against part–time workers, 8.2–8.12
Part-time Work Directive, 8.3–8.12
non–discrimination, 8.4
opportunities for part–time work, 8.5–8.12
requests by workers for transfer, 8.6–8.8
steps to implement, 8.10
Partnerships at work, 10.8

School staff, 10.6
Sexual orientation, 1.8
Statutory bodies
reforms to, 9.1–9.14
Strikes
unfair dismissals, and, 5.16–5.21
Subordinate legislation, 1.5

Trade union membership
detriment related to, 4.2, 4.3
Transfer of undertakings, 10.7

Unfair dismissal, 5.1–5.27
additional awards, 5.8
agreements to exclude rights, 5.10–5.12
compensation cap, 5.6
special cases, 5.7
fixed term contracts, and, 5.12
indexation, 5.9
industrial disputes, and, 5.22–5.26
jurisdiction, 5.13–5.15
employment outside Great Britain, 5.13–5.15
protected industrial action, and, 5.23
protection for striking workers, 5.16–5.21
reduction of qualifying period, 5.4
qualifying period order, 5.5
special awards, 5.8
White Paper, 5.2, 5.3

Victimisation, 4.1–4.15
blacklists, 4.12–4.14
collective agreements, 4.10, 4.11
criminal sanctions, 4.15
debate in Parliament, 4.6–4.9
detriment related to trade union membership, 4.2, 4.3
provisions of Act, 4.4–4.15
White Paper, 4.3